D0947170

BILL LAVARACK   WAYNE HARRIS   GEOFF STOCKER

DENDROBIUM
AND ITS RELATIVES

Timber Press
Portland, Oregon

Mt Kinabalu in Sabah.
Reaching 4101 m in
altitude, Mt Kinabalu is
an example of high
altitude habitats. It is
home to about 80 species
of the Dendrobiinae.

Contents

Acknowledgments

The authors are indebted to many people for assistance in compiling this book. Len Lawler is owed a special vote of thanks for providing Chapter 4 on traditional uses of dendrobiums. Dr Phillip Cribb of the Royal Botanic Gardens, Kew, wrote the Foreword and supplied many photographs, and also helped with discussions on many aspects of the Dendrobiinae. Jeffery Woods, also of Kew, assisted in the identification of some species. Will Smith of the Queensland Herbarium provided some important technical help with the text figures. Jim Comber and Peter O'Byrne both supplied several photographs and also took part in some useful discussions on *Dendrobium* in Malesia. Paul Ormerod assisted with identifications and comments on several species. Ray Robinson provided many interesting species from his collection, photographs of which appear in Part II.

Photos
The following people, in addition to those listed above, provided photographs to supplement our own: David Banks, David Titmuss, Nev Howcroft, Gerald McCraith, Mary Maclennan, Bruce Gray, G. Fuller, Howard Gunn, J.R. Oddy, Lex Barton, S. Sprunger, Royal Botanic Gardens, Kew.

Foreword

In 1978, the International Orchid Registrar asked the International Orchid Commission (IOC) if they could recommend anyone to revise two sections of the genus *Dendrobium* which were causing him immense problems because orchid hybridisers were trying to register new hybrids using suspect parental names. The IOC asked the Royal Botanic Gardens, Kew, for help and thus began my interest in the genus, an interest that has taken me to New Guinea, Australia, the south-west Pacific islands and latterly to China, the Himalayas and Indochina.

The dendrobiums have not disappointed. In New Guinea I have been fortunate enough to study two of the most spectacular sections of the genus, namely *Latouria* and *Spatulata*, the former best represented in the highlands of New Guinea and the latter, the spectacular antelope dendrobiums, on the coast. Several trips to the Solomon Islands, Vanuatu, and New Caledonia also gave me an introduction to the strange floras of these islands and to the wealth of orchids that they possess. My memories of gliding across a mirror-calm blue lagoon in the Solomons to see the blue form of the antelope-petalled *Dendrobium gouldii* will remain with me forever. Finding *Dendrobium finisterrae*, which has the hairiest flowers of all orchids, and brilliant coloured oxyglossums, calyptrochilus and pedilonums on the slopes of the Baliem Valley is another moment to treasure.

For the past fifteen years I have explored the orchid-rich lands of the Malay Archipelago and tropical mainland Asia. Dendrobiums abound, especially on the mountains such as Mt Kinabalu in Sabah where we have documented over 60 species to date. In Bhutan I had the pleasure of walking down a mountainside through oak – magnolia forest dripping with flowering *Dendrobium falconeri* and *D. nobile* and then lunching under a grand oak with a branch laden with flowering *D. devonianum* – what a day! Southern China has also produced many memorable meetings with dendrobiums, which suffer the fate of being collected for Chinese medicine, apparently to cure bronchial problems. *Dendrobium thyrsiflorum* was found on a barren hot hillside on a rock under the only surviving tree on the mountain. *Dendrobium fimbriatum* and *D. loddigesii* are other favourites that grow on the sharp karst limestone of southern China. The former has metre-long canes bearing bunches of golden flowers marked with deep maroon on the lip; the latter grows in tight colonies and can be covered with its cheerful pink flowers with a white and gold lip tipped with pink.

One cannot but sit back and admire the work of Rudolf Schlechter in the early years of the century. He knew the genus at first hand from his own collecting activities in New Guinea, Sulawesi and Sumatra, and in the herbarium, where his productivity was legendary. He not only described hundreds of species from New Guinea and the Malay Archipelago but also published an infrageneric treatment of *Dendrobium* that is still used today.

Dendrobium is a large and complex genus, comprising over 1000 species in over 40 sections. Recent research has emphasised that a thorough understanding of the evolutionary relationships of species and genera is fundamental to the production of robust classifications. A few of the more distinctive of Schlechter's sections, such as *Diplocaulobium, Cadetia* and *Flickingeria*, have been raised to generic rank by subsequent authors and are widely accepted. Recent work utilising embryological and molecular data suggests strongly that these genera nest within a broader *Dendrobium* – in other words, that in an evolutionary sense they are part of *Dendrobium* as it is currently understood. The move to recognise more sections at generic level to allow the retention of *Diplocaulobium* and its like has already begun and has caused great controversy, mainly because the rationale for doing so has been poorly explained by some authors. Others have suggested that it might be better to subsume these genera into a more widely circumscribed *Dendrobium*. The arguments continue and have yet to be resolved, which makes it all the more significant that the current authors have tackled *Dendrobium*, in the sense used by Schlechter, at this stage.

Such an account is sorely needed, especially to enable readers to identify and name the species. Apart from revisions of a few sections, such as *Oxyglossum, Formosae, Latourea* and *Spatulata*, and the incomparable floristic treatments of Thai and Indochinese species by Gunnar Seidenfaden, little of significance has appeared in recent years. Specific delimitation is still unclear in many sections and naming plants to the level of species can be difficult. Indeed the whole notion of what is a species is currently being debated with some passion. This is particularly true in Australia where well known but variable species such as *Dendrobium speciosum, D. bigibbum* and *D. canaliculatum* have each recently been split into several species. The authors' vast knowledge of these orchids in nature allows them to present opinions on the practicality of these controversial taxonomic decisions. Hybrids, both natural and artificial, further complicate matters and are dealt with in detail here by the authors. Certainly, this book will help growers name their plants, currently a difficult task even for the taxonomist with a herbarium and library at his disposal. An account of all of the dendrobiums is therefore timely, and may help readers make up their own minds as to whether the genus should be split up or not.

The authors have a wealth of experience of *Dendrobium*, both in the cultivation of the genus and of the plants in the field, particularly in Australia, New Guinea and adjacent islands. I had the pleasure of accompanying Bill Lavarack on an expedition to the north end of Cape York in 1983. One of the highlights of that tour was seeing *Dendrobium carronii*, which Bill and I had recently described, in the wild in the Iron Range.

Knowledge of how plants grow in nature (their ecology) is an immense help to scientists, conservationists and to those attempting to grow their plants optimally. Having said that, well-grown plants in cultivation are seldom matched in the field, especially today when habitats are disappearing at a rate faster than ever before. It may already be too late to see some of the showier species in nature; others are sure to follow as their habitats are destroyed. I have just returned, as I write, from Vietnam, where the rich forests on karst limestone in the north have shrunk to a mere fraction of their previous extent in a matter of ten years or so. Over-collection of orchids for horticulture and traditional medicine contributes to the rapid decline of many species, including some that have yet to be described by science. Orchid growers bemoan the fate of their favourite plants but many fail to realise that they can make a difference by growing their species plants to the best of their ability, pollinating flowers, raising seedlings and offering them to others, and by spurning those nurseries that still offer wild-collected materials.

Dendrobiums are among the most spectacular and variable of all orchids – long may they remain so to enchant us all as we enter the new millennium!

Phillip Cribb
The Herbarium
Royal Botanic Gardens, Kew

Preface

The usually compact size, the immense variety of colourful flowers and the relative ease of cultivation have resulted in *Dendrobiums* becoming one of the great horticultural genera of the world. The range of habitats and altitudes at which the species grow, means that there is usually a group of species suited to cultivation in any particular climate.

Members of this genus are a common and sometimes spectacular feature of the forests of southern Asia, the Malesian Islands including New Guinea, the Pacific Islands and Australia. Many are familiar to travellers in this region, often festooning wayside trees and forming a major feature of many tropical gardens. In less commonly visited areas such as the foothills of the Himalayas or the highlands of Papua New Guinea, visitors with an interest in the rural environment, are often rewarded with colourful displays adorning roadside cuttings or along walking trails in mountain forests. Since these species make up a large and diverse group, numbering well upwards of one thousand species, their characteristics are difficult to satisfactorily summarise in a single volume. Indeed a book describing and illustrating all species would be extremely large and expensive and would inevitably be outdated even before it was published as new species are being discovered at a surprising rate. In this volume the authors have attempted to introduce all the subdivisions of the subtribe Dendrobiinae with at least one illustration of each and, in addition, to present some ideas on the biology, classification, conservation and cultivation of the group.

The authors are very conscious of the many attempts over the last 150 years to classify the group in a way that reflects its ancestry. Until the last decade this has been attempted using morphological characters almost exclusively. But in recent times new techniques such as molecular biology have caused a revolution in botanists' thinking. We are in a time of change in the science of classification and new relationships, new genera and new species are constantly being proposed. This has caused many a fierce debate among scientists and poses major problems to hobbyists, most of whom dislike seeing well-established, familiar names being replaced with new ones. Readers will discover examples of such changes throughout this book and it is often not possible to be sure which name is currently 'correct'. Other than documenting the reasons for this debate, this book this book does not seek to take sides – all it seeks to do is discuss and illustrate this fascinating group.

PART ONE

Threatened species

Dendrobium antennatum is an abundant species in New Guinea, but in Australia is restricted to a small area and is in demand by collectors. The Australian population is therefore considered endangered, but on a world distribution it is not under threat. BILL LAVARACK

Opposite page: *Dendrobium parishii*.
BILL LAVARACK

CHAPTER ONE

Introduction

Fig. 1 Range of the Dendrobiinae.

The Dendrobiinae – an introduction

Dendrobium and its relatives occur from India and Sri Lanka in the west to Tahiti in the east, and from Japan and Korea in the north to Stewart Island, just south of the South Island of New Zealand, in the south. They grow in habitats ranging from semi-desert to rainforest, from the hot steamy lowlands of Borneo to the cooler seasonal climates of the Himalayan foothills and the year-round cool moist conditions in the Central Ranges of New Guinea, where they have been reported at altitudes up to 3800 m. They are also present in the hot seasonal climate of northern Australia and in the cool temperate rainforests of Tasmania and New Zealand, and in Korea and Japan. They are found fringing coral beaches, in tall rainforest, in mangrove swamps, in coconut and rubber plantations, on rock faces, on roadside cuttings, in freshwater swamps, on misty mountain ridges, on stunted shrubs in heathland, beside waterfalls, on paperbark trees in tropical savannas, in gallery forest lining streams, and on street trees in towns and cities. They are equally at home as epiphytes or lithophytes. A few grow as terrestrials, including some terrestrial species from New Caledonia, which can grow to five metres tall.

TABLE 1 THE DENDROBIINAE

Group	Current status	Estimated no. of species	Range	Centre of distribution
Amblyanthus	Section	14	Peninsular Malaysia to the Solomons	New Guinea
Aporum	Section	45	India to New Guinea	Thailand to Borneo
Australorchis	Section	3	Australia	NE Australia
Bolbidium	Section	6	India to Borneo	Peninsular Malaysia
Breviflores	Section	12	India to Java	SE Asian mainland
Cadetia	Genus	50	New Guinea, Australia to the Solomons	New Guinea
Calcarifera	Section	50	India to New Guinea	Borneo
Callista	Section	10	India to Peninsular Malaysia	Burma, Thailand, Indochina
Calyptrochilus	Section	40	Peninsular Malaysia to Samoa	New Guinea
Cannaeorchis	Genus*	11	New Caledonia	New Caledonia
Conostalix	Section	10	Burma to New Guinea and Australia	Borneo
Cuthbertsonia	Section	3	New Guinea to Fiji	New Guinea to Fiji
Dendrobium	Section	60	India to Australia	Burma to Indochina
Dendrocoryne	Section	15	Australia to Fiji	Australia
Dichopus	Section**	1	New Guinea	New Guinea
Diplocaulobium	Genus	100	Peninsular Malaysia to Samoa	New Guinea
Distichophyllum	Section	35	Burma to New Caledonia	Borneo
Dockrillia	Genus*	39	New Guinea, Australia, Fiji	NE Australia
Dolichocentrum	Section	1	Sulawesi	Sulawesi
Eleutheroglossum	Section	4	New Caledonia, NE Australia	New Caledonia
Epigeneium	Genus	35	India to Java and Borneo	Borneo
Eriopexis	Genus*	6	New Guinea	New Guinea
Euphlebium	Section	4	Peninsular Malaysia to New Guinea	New Guinea
Flickingeria	Genus	65	India to Samoa	Borneo
Formosae	Section	30	India to Philippines and Borneo	India to Thailand, Indochina
Fytchianthe	Section	3	India and Burma	India and Burma
Grastidium	Genus*	190	Burma to Fiji	New Guinea
Herpethophytum	Section	14	New Guinea	New Guinea
Inobulbum	Genus	2	New Caledonia	New Caledonia
Kinetochilus	Section	4	New Caledonia	New Caledonia
Latouria	Section	50	Philippines to Samoa	New Guinea
Liohenastrum	Section	3	Australia	NE Australia
Microphylanthe	Section	3	New Guinea	New Guinea
Monanthos	Section	25	Sulawesi to the Solomons and Australia	New Guinea
Oxyglossum	Section	30	Sulawesi to Fiji	New Guinea
Oxystophyllum	Section	15	India to New Guinea	New Guinea – Borneo
Pedilonum	Section	60	India to Tahiti	New Guinea
Phalaenanthe	Section	4	Tanimbar Islands, New Guinea, Northern Australia,	Northern Australia Southern New Guinea
Platycaulon	Section	3	Burma to Fiji	SE Asia to Fiji
Pleianthe	Section	1	New Guinea	New Guinea
Pseuderia	Genus	18	Moluccas to Samoa	New Guinea
Rhopalanthe	Section	45	India to New Guinea and Samoa	Borneo
Spatulata	Section	50	Philippines to Samoa	New Guinea
Stachyobium	Section	35	India to Java	Thailand
Strongyle	Section	20	India to New Guinea	SE Asian mainland, Indonesian islands
Tetrodon	Genus*	2	New Caledonia	New Caledonia
Trachyrhizum	Section	8	New Guinea, Australia, New Caledonia	New Guinea
Winika	Genus*	1	New Zealand	New Zealand

Section = a section of the genus Dendrobium. Genus = a well-established genus
* = a recently proposed genus. ** = the status of this group is uncertain

Following the classification proposed by Dressler in 1993, they are part of the tribe Dendrobieae, which comprises the subtribes Dendrobiinae and Bulbophyllinae. *Dendrobium*, with about 1000 species, is one of the largest of the genera in the Orchidaceae. In the Old World, only *Bulbophyllum*, with around 1000 species, is of comparable size, while the New World genera *Pleurothallis* and *Epidendrum* have a similar number. Comparisons are difficult because botanists are constantly revising all these groups. For example, *Bulbophyllum* becomes considerably smaller if *Cirrhopetalum*, with 150 to 200 species, is removed, as has recently been proposed.

Lowland vegetation in New Guinea. This area supports many species in groups such as *Pedilonum*, *Spatulata*, *Grastidium* and *Diplocaulobium*.
BILL LAVARACK

The number of species in the subtribe is not clear, but estimates range from as high as 1700, with *Dendrobium* (prior to the separation of the latest genera) providing between 1000 and 1400 species. Table 1 indicates a figure of around 1200 to 1300 may be close to the mark for the subtribe, with 900 to 1000 in *Dendrobium* (in the broader sense). Baker and Baker (1996) found 2425 names for *Dendrobium* alone, of which they state that 1230 appear to be currently valid. The word 'currently' is important here as the position changes almost daily. The uncertainty in numbers arises largely from the situation in New Guinea where some groups, such as *Grastidium, Monanthos, Calyptrochilus, Cadetia* and *Diplocaulobium*, are poorly known. In genera and sections such as these there are undoubtedly many undescribed species, but there are also likely to be many cases where names will be reduced to synonymy by further study. Similar problems are present in most other areas, but not usually to the extent that they occur in New Guinea.

Being such a large group of species, it is hardly surprising that there is much variation in *Dendrobium* and its relatives. Stems or pseudobulbs up to five metres long have been reported for terrestrial species such as *Cannaeorchis deplanchei* and *C. sarcochilus* from New Caledonia. Several species from the section *Spatulata* reach three metres in length and *D. discolor* has been recorded at up to five metres long and five centimetres in diameter near the base. Other species can grow into very large clumps. Good examples of such plants include *D. speciosum* from eastern Australia and *D. macrophyllum* from New Guinea, both of which can be enormous. Captain Bartle Grant in his book *The Orchids of Burma* reports a plant of *D. hilderbrandii* (synonym of *D. signatum*) with upwards of 1500 blooms. At the other extreme there are some extremely small plants, such as *D. toressae* from north-eastern Australia, which forms dense mats comprising short rhizomes which give rise to small succulent leaves four to eight millimetres long and two to four millimetres wide, about the size and shape of a grain of wheat. *D. margaretae* from New Guinea has pseudobulbs that are three to seven millimetres long and three to five millimetres wide with a single leaf about six to 16 millimetres long. A few species, particularly in sections *Oxyglossum* and *Cuthbertsonia*, have large flowers on very small plants. *D. cuthbertsonii* produces flowers up to five centimetres across on pseudobulbs only one or two centimetres long.

There is much variation in plant form. *Dockrillia* (previously known as section *Rhizobium*) has long slender cylindrical leaves and wiry stems, while section *Dendrobium* has thin, flattened deciduous leaves and stems which are swollen into pseudobulbs. *D. canaliculatum* has almost globose pseudobulbs while other species such as those in *Grastidium* have slender stems with no swelling. Several groups including *Grastidium*, *Diplocaulobium* and *Bolbidium* have ephemeral flowers that last only a day or less, while some species in *Latouria*, *Oxyglossum* and *Spatulata* have flowers that last for several months.

The strategies used by different plants to survive in similar conditions vary. For example, many species of the section *Dendrobium* grow in strongly seasonal climates in the foothills of the Himalayas. Here most of the rain falls in summer, with cool dry winters. Most species have deciduous leaves that grow quickly in the wet season, then are shed in the winter, with the flowers being produced on the leafless stems in spring. In northern Australia, species from *Spatulata* (such as *D. canaliculatum*) have faced a similar problem of a long dry season in winter and spring, although with much warmer temperatures in winter. They have dealt with these conditions by means of fleshy persistent terete leaves in which the leaf surface is reduced to restrict water loss. The swollen stems

Montane grassland, forest and tree ferns at about 3000 m altitude in New Guinea. An area rich in many brightly coloured species in sections *Oxyglossum* and *Calyptrochilus*. GEOFF STOCKER

conserve water, and flowering is in spring shortly before the onset of the wet season. Another notable adaptation in many species in the highlands of New Guinea is the development of brightly coloured tubular flowers that are presumably adapted to pollination by birds. The variations are almost endless, as the illustrations and descriptions later in this book demonstrate.

The variety of brightly coloured flowers, many on relatively small plants that are easy to cultivate, has made *Dendrobium* and its allies one of the most popular groups among orchid growers and other gardeners. Many hybrids have been registered in groups such as the 'soft cane' group (section *Dendrobium*) and the 'hard cane' group (sections *Phalaenanthe* and *Spatulata*). New avenues are opening in sections such as *Latouria* and *Dendrocoryne*, while sections *Oxyglossum*, *Cuthbertsonia*, *Calyptrochilus* and *Pedilonum* have almost unlimited potential, but are largely untouched to date.

This popularity has inevitably lead to heavy collecting pressure on some species. This started in the early part of the nineteenth century and continues to this day. Recent trends towards growing hybrids, and line-breeding of superior forms of species, have resulted in some decrease in demand for plants from the wild. However, as this threat subsides, another more damaging threat has arisen in the form of land-clearing in South-East Asia, Malesia and the Pacific, which may well see the rainforests of the region reduced to 10 per cent of the original cover within a few years. Already much of the forest cover in many regions is gone, with the position particularly bad in the Philippines, Vietnam and China. The threat from land-clearing is far more dangerous than the threat from collecting, as it concerns all the species of an area, not just those that happen to have attractive flowers. The future seems almost certain to see many species become extinct or be represented only in cultivation.

An introduction to this book

Each chapter has been the prime responsibility of one of the authors as set out below, but all three authors have edited, added to and made suggestions on all chapters. Bill Lavarack was primarily responsible for Chapter 1, Introduction, Chapter 3, Distribution and Origins, and Chapter 5, Conservation; Wayne Harris for Chapter 2, Classification and Nomenclature, and Geoff Stocker for Chapter 6, Biology and Ecology, Chapter 7, Cultivation, and Chapter 8, Artificial Hybrids.

Coastal scenery on Bougainville Island, typical habitat of *Dendrobium gouldii*. BILL LAVARACK

All authors contributed to Part II, The Dendrobiinae. Len Lawler kindly provided Chapter 4 on Traditional Uses.

The authors were not always able to agree on controversial topics such as the origins of the Dendrobiinae and which names to use. Democratic practices prevailed and a vote was taken where there was a lack of agreement, although in such cases care has been taken to try to present all sides of the debate. This highlights the fact that taxonomy and the study of evolution are very inexact sciences and there is always room for debate and discussion. Such discussion is extremely healthy and beneficial to both the science and to those involved, as it requires much research on a range of topics and a consequent expansion of one's horizons.

As this book is intended to appeal to a wide non-scientific audience, references have not been cited in the text. Numerous references can destroy the flow of the text and make for annoying reading. At the same time it was felt that it would help to present the references with as much relation to the appropriate text as possible and they have been presented in Further Reading on a chapter by chapter basis. Not all the references consulted in the preparation of this book are present; to include them would require many more pages. Instead a selection of the more important is presented.

CHAPTER 2

Classification and Nomenclature

Ever since the first humans walked on the earth they have tried to classify both inanimate and biological objects in their environment to allow communication on a wide basis. A natural outcome of this was the desire to order the categories in an hierarchical system. The system that we now use is based on that created by Linnaeus in 1735 to provide principally for the ordering and cataloguing of all the biological material that was flowing into Europe from all over the world at that time. These first efforts were pre-Darwinian and therefore evolutionary processes were not a consideration. Following the publication of Darwin's theory of evolution by natural selection in 1859 there existed a rationale for the development of a system of classification that reflected evolutionary change. Thus was born the evolutionary approach to classification that we use today.

This is based on the Linnaean system and has the following features:

- it provides one standard hierarchy for purposes of efficient and exact communication on a world-wide basis;
- the species is the fundamental category and all other categories in the hierarchy relate directly or indirectly to this level; and
- it is assumed that all life has originated in the same general way through evolution by natural selection.

Why do names change?

Probably the most controversial aspect confronting orchid growers is deciding which name they should put on the tags to identify their plants. Nothing seems to upset growers more than the ever-present problem of name changes in orchids – not that it is confined to that group of plants. There are two common reasons why plant names change. First there is the application of the International Code of Botanical Nomenclature. This is a legalistic approach under which many name changes are the result of the application of the rules of priority as stipulated by the Code. The Code states that the earliest name always has priority, so that when a previously neglected earlier name is discovered, a commonly used name may have to change. An example of this was the golden orchid of north-east Australia and southern Papua New Guinea. This species was known from 1810 to 1963 by the apt name of *Dendrobium undulatum*. This was replaced in 1963 by the less attractive name *D. discolor*, when it was shown that the name *Dendrobium discolor* had been previously used in 1807 for a totally different species now considered to belong to the American genus *Xylobium*. Other examples of the application of the rules include the replacing of *Dendrobium pierardii* with *D. aphyllum*, and *D. aggregatum* with *D. lindleyi*. Such name changes can be infuriating to all orchid lovers, but the chaos which would result from not having a strict set of rules, or from not following the rules, would be far worse than the problems which arise from their application. All botanists are obliged to adhere to the Code and indeed any reputable journal will insist that the taxonomist follows such rules in publishing new names.

The second reason for name changes involves new interpretations of the identity of species. This can arise from traditional taxonomic studies which compare specimens from a range of localities, or it can arise from new scientific research. New techniques that allow the scientist to consider more than just the outward appearance of the plants are constantly being developed. It is now possible to consider a range of characters such as the DNA, the enzymes and other constituents of the plants. There are now computers readily available that can analyse large arrays of characters and tell us in the blink of an eye what is the overall level of similarity between many different plants. Based on this type of data, many 'old' species are being split into new species and new genera are being created.

This is where controversy rages among botanists and orchid hobbyists. Do we accept these changes in classification along with the ensuing new nomenclature, or should we reject them? The answer to this question is not clear-cut and each individual must make up his or her mind on the evidence presented. Even when writing this book there was no unanimity among the authors on which names to use, either at the level of the genus or the species in some of the more controversial groups. The authors have had a difficult task in deciding whether to adopt a conservative approach or to incorporate some major changes in nomenclature and taxonomic thinking that are impacting markedly on *Dendrobium* in particular. The authors make no apology for this situation and would remind readers that much of this apparent confusion can be resolved only when more in-depth studies are completed. We realise that this book may be out of date, as far as nomenclature is concerned, even before it is published! Future editions will certainly see changes.

The species concept

Central to all of these problems is the question of what constitutes a species. As previously discussed, the species is the fundamental category of the taxonomic hierarchy. It is the building block of biological classification and this immediately raises the question: 'What is a species?' Enormous amounts of paper have been generated in debating the concept of species and we can only touch on a fraction of the debate in this book. Over the years since the development of the Linnaean classification system many species concepts have been proposed, but there are perhaps only three that are relevant today – the morphological species concept, the biological species concept, and the phylogenetic species concept.

The morphological species approach This the basis of classical taxonomy. It is still widely used

Opposite: In common with many other species in the highlands of New Guinea, *Dendrobium cuthbertsonii* has several colour forms. Some of these have been described as separate species in the past. WAYNE HARRIS GEOFF STOCKER

and, as the name suggests, it is based wholly on the morphological similarities and differences between the structure of the plants as measured by a set of characters.

The biological species approach The second concept relies on the recognition either that there is a group of interbreeding populations or that one group is reproductively isolated from other such groups. A species is seen as being a group of individuals genetically separated from other related groups. However, while the basic principle of this concept is recognised as theoretically valid, it is rare for a taxonomist to be able to observe in detail the interactions of populations in the field. In most cases they are forced to use more observable morphological characters in recognising separate species. Biological characters, which may indicate possible genetic isolation, can be useful as indicators, but until a much better understanding of the biology is gained, they may be better treated with caution. For example, variations in flower colour could indicate different pollinators and therefore genetic isolation, but in most cases we have no idea if this is a real situation or not. (See the illustrations of *Dendrobium cuthbertsonii* on page 19, in which the different colours often grow intermingled.) Even if there is an isolation caused by pollinators, it can readily be broken down by dispersal of seeds which are designed for travelling long distances on the wind.

Phylogenetic species concept The third concept, also known as the cladistic approach, states that a species is a single lineage derived from a common ancestor shared with other closely related species. A cladistic study produces cladograms (which are similar to a family tree) and the terminal groups of these can be of any rank. Several characters based on data from morphology, biochemistry and genetics (e.g. DNA sequences), are analysed by computer programs to derive the cladogram, which indicates relationships between groups, not only at the species rank but also at other levels. While biochemistry and DNA can be useful characters, obtaining the data is an expensive operation and may be of only limited use. The cladogram illustrates the relationships between the plants included in the study – it does not state whether the different levels of the cladogram are varieties, species, genera or some other rank. This remains for the taxonomist to interpret.

What approach is the modern taxonomist to take in defining a species? This is probably one of the most difficult, but one of the most important, activities of the taxonomist. The definition of species in complex groups has always been difficult, regardless of what species concept is used. We have to rely on the experience of the taxonomist working on the particular group. He or she must have an intimate knowledge of all species described in the particular group and must know which characters are useful in species definition and which are not. As becomes clear from the preceding three paragraphs, the morphology remains the key to defining species, no matter which concept a taxonomist embraces.

An illustration from *Dendrobium* will emphasise this point. J.J. Wood in the *Kew Bulletin* in 1986 synonymised no less than 12 previously described species, placing them in one variable species, *D. subclausum*. He did this on the basis of observation by himself and others, concluding that characters such as the degree of wartiness on the leaf sheaths, floral bracts and petals, and flower colour, which had in the past been used to distinguish species, were unreliable when the total range of variation was taken into account. He had observed many gradations from one extreme to another and went on to say that the number of synonyms could more than double when a thorough revision of section *Calyptochilus* was completed. A possible explanation of the problems with *D. subclausum* is that it is a species in the process of evolving into several separate species, but that the process at this point has not reached the stage where different species should be recognised. It is largely up to the judgment of the taxonomist to determine whether *D. subclausum* is one variable species or several closely related species.

At this point it is relevant to make some remarks about 'splitters' and 'lumpers'. The example outlined above might be seen as 'lumping', i.e. many previously validly described species being brought together under one name, creating a much broader concept. The 'splitters', on the other hand, have a more typological approach. This means that they allow only small variations away from the type specimen. (The type specimen is the specimen designated as typical or representative of the species.) Ideally we should tread the midline, recognising that the type specimen should be representative of the species, but at the same time recognising that populations have variations that must also be included.

Another example which illustrates the argument is *Homo sapiens*, our species, which shows an enormous variation in colour, height, hairiness, etc. An observer from another planet might be tempted to recognise some of these groupings as separate species, but as we know, each and every group is able to interbreed with each other and thus neatly fits the biological species concept. However, human mobility, and hence the ability to interbreed, is very different from a species of orchid evolving on a rapidly rising mountain chain in Papua New Guinea. The degree of isolation necessary for species recognition must be judged in each case on all of the available evidence – morphological, genetic, ecological.

To complicate matters further, it would seem that not all species are equivalent. While it suits the ordered mind of human beings to place all plants and animals in neat, uniform boxes labelled 'species', that is not necessarily the situation in nature. Some groups of species have recently diverged from a common ancestor, while others have been separated for a much longer period. Some are extremely variable, some are not. A scientist working with mammals may have a quite different concept of a species to that held by one working on orchids. The situation may also be quite different for orchid species using different methods of pollination.

There are those who put their faith in computer programs to settle these questions, but there are no easy answers and only time, increased knowledge and usage will produce a final result. It is largely up to the individual to make a decision based on the available evidence, and it is the combined weight of these separate decisions that will eventually settle the matter. All this means that taxonomy is not an exact science and the differences necessary to separate species cannot be fully or precisely defined. The taxonomist must therefore make a somewhat subjective decision based on knowledge, experience and sound judgment. The more knowledge and the more meaningful experience the taxonomist has, the sounder will be the judgment. Perhaps no one should be allowed to revise a group of plants until they have a few battle scars and grey hairs!

The genus

The genus is even more difficult to define than the species. A vague definition would read like this: 'A genus is a group of species which through their likeness are more nearly related to each other than they are to other species'. Thus a genus is a group of species held together by a few to many characters and distinct from other such groups. Genera should be easily recognisable groups. Once a number of species are united under a genus, further newly described species should be readily recognisable as members of that genus. Difficulties arise when we try to draw limits between closely related genera, where decisions have to be made whether to recognise a group as an independent genus, or to include it in an existing genus.

We can illustrate this with an example from *Dendrobium*. Brieger separated *Dockrillia* from *Dendrobium* on the basis of its vegetative distinctiveness. Members of *Dockrillia* were formerly included in section *Rhizobium* of *Dendrobium*. The question, then, is do we afford this group generic status or do we recognise it at a sub-generic level (i.e. as a section) under *Dendrobium*? One line of reasoning would be that *Dockrillia* species, as we know them at present, form a group that is readily recognised as such and, in one sense, are probably monophyletic (have come ultimately from one original ancestor), although this has not been documented. On the other hand, while they obviously have many similarities, what about the dis-similarities – how distinct are they from other related groups? Are they distinct enough to be placed in a separate genus?

Recently Australian botanists elevated several sections of *Dendrobium* to the status of genera. This has been controversial and has not been accepted by a number of botanists inside and outside Australia. However, modern trends in botany suggest that it is likely that these genera, or some similar to them, will eventually be accepted, and in this book the new names are used with the old names in brackets. The new genera are *Grastidium* (section *Grastidium*), *Eriopexis* (section *Eriopexis*), *Dockrillia* (section *Rhizobium*), *Inobulbum* (section *Inobulbum*), *Tetrodon* (section *Tetrodon*), *Cannaeorchis* (section *Macrocladium*) and *Winika* (formerly *Dendrobium cunninghamii*). This process is ongoing, and by the time this book is printed it is possible that more such changes may have been proposed.

What then can the orchid hobby-grower make of this? Such people should make an effort to be knowledgeable about their favourite groups and to read about the different classifications and the different interpretations and to make up their own minds. There are no prison sentences or fines for using the 'wrong' name. If, after digesting all the arguments, you prefer the name '*Dendrobium teretifolium* var. *aureum*' to '*Dockrillia dolichophylla*', and put it on your labels, that is your decision and you have committed no crime – at worst you are simply old-fashioned, at best you are leading the way.

The section

Many large genera in the plant kingdom have been subdivided into sections to make them easier to deal with. *Dendrobium* is a good example. There have been varying numbers of sections within *Dendrobium* recognised over the years, with some groups being regarded as sections or as genera on several different occasions. Much less effort has been expended on defining a section than has gone into the definition of species and genera. Sections have been regarded as categories of convenience in which groups of generally similar species have been loosely placed. In most cases they have worked well, but questions arise in large, closely related groups such as the group of sections related to *Pedilonum*. For example, should *Calcarifera* and *Platycaulon* be separated from *Pedilonum*, and should *Cuthbertsonia* be separated from *Oxyglossum*?

Sections generally are separated from each other on only one or two characters, which are mostly quite clear-cut and obvious. For example, the section *Platycaulon* is separated from *Calcarifera* solely by its conspicuous flat stems. While the Code applies equally to sections, there has been much less debate over their delineation than there has for genera and species, and one gets the impression that they are often designated by a 'gentleman's agreement' rather than by legalistic processes. Despite this – or perhaps because of it – the section has proved a most useful tool in breaking the huge genus *Dendrobium* down into bite-sized pieces.

Classification of the Dendrobiinae

Olaf Swartz established the genus *Dendrobium* in 1799. It is a conserved name as there are two earlier names – *Ceraia* Lour. and *Callista* Lour. The type species is *Dendrobium moniliforme* (L.) Sw. from Japan, Korea, the Ryukyu Islands, China and Taiwan, which was originally described by Linnaeus in 1753 as '*Epidendrum moniliforme*' and transferred to *Dendrobium* by Swartz in 1799.

The plants in this book fall within the subtribe Dendrobiinae of the family Orchidaceae. The full classification of members of the subtribe can be arranged in the hierarchical system as follows:

Family *Orchidaceae*
  Subfamily *Epidendroideae*
    Tribe *Dendrobieae*
      Subtribe *Dendrobiinae*

As well as the genus *Dendrobium*, the Dendrobiinae includes the following well-established genera: *Cadetia, Pseuderia, Diplocaulobium, Flickingeria* and *Epigeneium*, as well as the recently proposed *Dockrillia, Grastidium, Eriopexis, Cannaeorchis, Tetrodon, Inobulbum* and *Winika*.

Recent evidence from chloroplast DNA might result in further changes, in that *Pseuderia* does not appear to be as closely related to the other genera as previously thought and would be better placed in another subtribe related to *Eria* or *Podochilus*. If *Pseuderia* is excluded, the Dendrobiinae is one of the most distinctive and natural orchid subtribes. While they differ widely in their vegetative characters, there are features of the flowers that unite the genera. The column has a prominent foot and the flowers usually have a spur formed from the column foot or by the lip and column foot; the anther is terminal with two cells and four naked pollinia in two pairs without caudicles or viscidia. The genus *Dendrobium* itself is readily recognised on floral character by the mentum that is formed by the fusion of the column foot with the bases of the lateral sepals. The lip is divided into a claw and lamina, with the claw fused to the base of the column foot.

However, there is a very wide variation in vegetative characters and this, along with the sheer size of the genus *Dendrobium*, has led botanists to subdivide it into several sections. In this book 36 sections within *Dendrobium* are used to classify most of the 400 species described. The rest are in the 12 separate genera mentioned previously. Sections have also been described in *Diplocaulobium, Cadetia* and *Flickingeria*, but these have not been as widely used as have those in

Dendrobium. While it is recognised that these sections are valid, to avoid confusion the species have been grouped under the name of the genus in this book. Many of the sections and genera used in the following pages have gone by other names at different times and the most commonly encountered of these are presented in Table 2.

John Lindley provided the first classification of *Dendrobium* in 1844, recognising four sections. In 1851 he increased this to ten. Other classifications by Reichenbach, Bentham and Hooker, and Pfitzer followed. In 1910 Kraenzlin recognised 32 sections in a system considered aberrant by many modern botanists. The landmark classification of *Dendrobium* is that of Rudolf Schlechter, published in 1912 in his *Die Orchidaceen von Deutsch Neu Guinea*. Unlike most of his predecessors and successors, Schlechter was familiar with many of the species in the field and this probably accounts in large measure for the success of his system.

Schlechter divided *Dendrobium* into four subgenera (*Athecebium, Eu-Dendrobium, Rhopalobium* and *Xerobium*) and 41 sections. A few of his sections came to be accepted as genera over the years. These include *Desmotrichum* (*Flickingeria*), *Diplocaulobium, Sarcopodium* (*Epigeneium*), *Goniobulbon* (*Diplocaulobium* in part). Several other changes to Schlechter's classification have become accepted (e.g. the recognition of *Calcarifera* as a section). A few sections have recently been elevated to generic status (*Grastidium, Eriopexis, Rhizobium, Macrocladium, Inobulbum, Tetrodon*).

TABLE 2
SCHLECHTER'S CLASSIFICATION

Athecebium	Eu-Dendrobium	Rhopalobium	Xerobium
Leaves without sheaths	Leaves with sheaths, stems fleshy for the whole length	Leaves with sheaths, stems thickened on 1 to 3 internodes only	Leaves with sheaths, stems wiry, always very slender
Desmotrichum	Eugenanthe	Rhopalanthe	Aporum
Microphytanthe	Platycaulon		Oxystophyllum
Goniobulbon	Pedilonum		Grastidium
Diplocaulobium	Calyptrochilus		Dichopus
Bolbidium	Cuthbertsonia		Eriopexis
Euphlebium	Oxyglossum		Pleianthe
Rhizobium	Brachyanthe		Macrocladium
Sarcopodium	Stachyobium		Dolichocentrum
Dendrocoryne	Fytchianthe		Conostalix
Latourea	Phalaenanthe		Monanthos
Inobulbon	Eleutheroglossum		Herpethophytum
Callista	Ceratobium		
	Trachyrhizum		
	Distichophyllum		
	Oxygenianthe		
	Amblyanthus		
	Kinetochilus		

TABLE 3

SUMMARY OF THE NAMES OF GROUPS USED IN THIS BOOK

Group	Current status	Other names and notes
Amblyanthus	Section	—
Aporum	Section	Sometimes Oxystophyllum is included in this section
Australorchis	Section	Also known as section Monophyllaea
Bolbidium	Section	—
Breviflores	Section	The name Goldschmidtia has also been used for this section
Cadetia	Genus	Regarded by some earlier writers as a section of Dendrobium
Calcarifera	Section	Originally regarded as part of section Pedilonum
Callista	Section	Also known as section Chrysotoxa
Calyptrochilus	Section	Previously known, in part, as section Glomerata
Cannaeorchis	Genus	Recently raised to genus, previously section Macrocladium of Dendrobium
Conostalix	Section	—
Cuthbertsonia	Section	Often regarded as part of section Oxyglossum
Dendrobium	Section	Also known as Eu-Dendrobium and Eugenanthe
Dendrocoryne	Section	Also known as section Speciosa in part
Dichopus	Section	Very close to Grastidium, sometimes regarded as part of it
Diplocaulobium	Genus	Regarded by Schlechter as a section of Dendrobium
Distichophyllum	Section	Kraenzlin created a section named Revoluta for this group
Dockrillia	Genus	Recently raised to genus, previously section Rhizobium of Dendrobium
Dolichocentrum	Section	A monotypic section related to Conostalix
Eleutheroglossum	Section	—
Epigeneium	Genus	Previously known as section Sarcopodium of Dendrobium
Eriopexis	Genus	Recently raised to genus, previously section Eriopexis of Dendrobium
Euphleblum	Section	—
Flickingeria	Genus	Regarded as section Desmotrichum within Dendrobium by Schlechter. Also known as Ephemeranthera
Formosae	Section	Also known as section Nigrohirsutae and Oxygenianthe (in part)
Fytchianthe	Section	—
Grastidium	Genus	Recently raised to genus, previously regarded as section of Dendrobium. Also known as section Bambusifoliae
Herpethophytum	Section	—
Inobulbum	Genus	Recently raised to genus, previously regarded as section Inobulbum of Dendrobium.
Kinetochilus	Section	—
Latouria	Section	Named (erroneously) section Athecebium by van Royen
Lichenastrum	Section	Regarded by some authorities as part of the section Rhizobium (genus Dockrillia)
Microphytanthe	Section	—
Monanthos	Section	Also known as section Bilobum
Oxyglossum	Section	Some authors include Cuthbertsonia, some exclude it
Oxystophyllum	Section	Sometime included within Aporum
Pedilonum	Section	Very close to Calcarifera, Calyptrochilus, Oxyglossum, Platycaulon, Cuthbertsonia
Phalaenanthe	Section	Also known as section Superbientia in part
Platycaulon	Section	Regarded as part of section Calcarifera or Pedilonum by some
Pleianthe	Section	—
Pseuderia	Genus	May not belong in Dendrobiinae
Rhopalanthe	Section	Also known as section Crumenata and (in part) as section Virgatae
Spatulata	Section	Also known as section Ceratobium
Stachyobium	Section	—
Strongyle	Section	Similar to Aporum and Rhopalanthe, but with terete leaves
Tetrodon	Genus	Recently raised to genus, previously regarded as section of Dendrobium
Trachyrhizum	Section	—
Winika	Genus	Recently raised to genus, previously placed in section Macrocladium of Dendrobium

Lowland rainforest fringing a stream. Several epiphytes including *Grastidium cancroides* and *Dendrobium nindii* occur here. BILL LAVARACK

F.G. Brieger proposed a major new classification in 1981. Brieger's classification is revolutionary, proposing many radical changes. He subdivides the subtribe Dendrobiinae into 44 genera that are grouped into six series. Several species, considered by virtually all other botanists to be in the subtribe Eriinae, are included in the Dendrobiinae. The Brieger classification has not been accepted by botanists, who cite his lack of familiarity with the full range of variation in the subtribe. However, many of his names will have priority if more genera are recognised within the Dendrobiinae in the future.

Revisions of all or part of the subtribe are currently under way at Kew and Canberra, and it seems almost certain that the next few years will see significant changes in a system of classification that has lasted largely intact for almost 90 years. These investigations are based on a wide range of data from biochemistry, genetics and embryology, as well as more traditional characters. It appears possible that many of the sections will be elevated to the status of genera. Past experience is that new classifications proposing major changes will gain acceptance from the scientific community and recreational growers only if they are backed up with detailed evidence and produced by botanists with a wide experience of the variation present in the plants in their habitats.

CHAPTER 3

Distribution and Origins

Distribution

The subtribe Dendrobiinae today occurs from India and Sri Lanka in the west to Tahiti in the east, and from Japan and Korea in the north to New Zealand in the south. No members are recorded from the Americas or Africa. A few species are very widely distributed. The prize for most cosmopolitan goes to *Dendrobium anosmum*, which occurs from India to South-East Asia, Malesia and New Guinea, or perhaps to *D. erosum*, which occurs from southern Thailand through Indochina, Peninsular Malaysia, Malesia and New Guinea to Vanuatu. *D. crumenatum* occurs from Myanmar (Burma) to Ambon and *D. lobbii* is found from Thailand to the Solomons and Australia. Other widespread species include *D. stuartii*, *D. secundum*, *D. macrophyllum* and *Flickingeria comata*. It is worth noting that all these are lowland species. Those from the highlands are almost all localised, which is hardly surprising given the isolated nature of upland areas.

The geographical range of the Dendrobiinae can be conveniently split into five major regions, as shown in Figure 2. These are:

Mainland Asian flora

This extends from Sri Lanka and India through Myanmar (Burma), Thailand, Laos, Cambodia, Vietnam and southern China, including Hainan and Taiwan. Research on the flora of Malesia (i.e. the islands to the east of South-East Asia) some years ago revealed two distinct lines of demarcation between different floras ('demarcation knots'), the first being on the Isthmus of Kra, which links Peninsular Malaysia with Thailand, the second being between the Philippines and Taiwan.

Malesian flora

More correctly this should be labelled as 'western and central Malesia'. This comprises Peninsular Malaysia, Sumatra, Java, Borneo, the Philippines, Sulawesi, the Moluccas and the Lesser Sunda Islands. The western and northern boundaries of this flora meet the southern and eastern boundaries of the mainland Asian flora. The eastern boundary is the edge of the Sahul Shelf, which means that New Guinea and the Aru Islands are excluded. From the orchid point of view, this is a real boundary although, like other such boundaries, there is considerable leakage across it.

Papuasian flora

This is the well-known New Guinea orchid flora. There is a recognised demarcation knot in Torres

Widespread species

This Page: *Dendrobium crumenatum*
occurs from Myanmar (Burma) to Ambon.
BILL LAVARACK

Opposite: *Dendrobium anosmum* occurs
from India to New Guinea.
WAYNE HARRIS

Widespread species

Above: *Flickingeria comata* occurs from
Peninsular Malaysia to Samoa.
BRUCE GRAY

Right: *Dendrobium lobbii* occurs from
Thailand to Australia and the Solomons.
BILL LAVARACK

Strait separating New Guinea from Australia, although its distinctness is sometimes challenged by various workers in specialised animal or plant groups. New Guinea and the Aru Islands lie on the Sahul Shelf and this corresponds with a floristic boundary which separates New Guinea ('Papuasia') from the western parts of Malesia. The eastern boundary of Papuasia is harder to define, with several alternatives being suggested over the years, but the consensus of botanists dealing with a range of plant groups is that it lies between the Solomon Islands and Vanuatu.

Australian flora

The Australian orchid flora is distinct, although with some intermingling with New Guinea and Malesia to the north and to a small extent with Pacific islands, in particular New Caledonia, to the east. To the north, Torres Strait, northern Cape York Peninsula and southern New Guinea represent an overlap area and the actual boundary is not clear.

Pacific flora

This includes all the Pacific Islands south and east of the Solomon Islands. Most islands are too small and too recent to have had a major impact on orchid evolution. New Caledonia is a major exception to this and has a high percentage of endemic species and higher groups, but also many species with a recent Papuasian origin. The Micronesian islands to the north and north-west of New Guinea could be placed with Papuasia, but appear best considered part of the Pacific

From Tables 4 and 5 it is clear that the island of New Guinea, even allowing for its larger size, has both the most species and the largest number of higher groups. In other words, New Guinea is richer than any other area, both in numbers and in diversity per unit area. Between 450 and

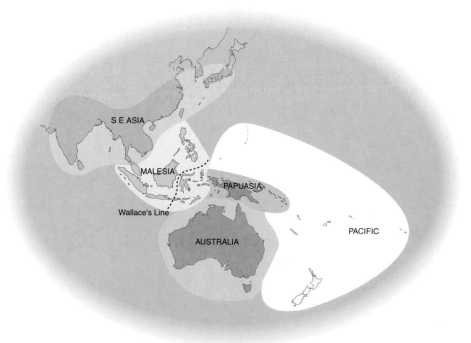

Fig. 2 The five natural regions of the Dendrobiinae.

500 species occur there, around 33 per cent of the total number of species for the subtribe. Thirty-two higher groups out of a total of 48 for the subtribe occur in New Guinea. Based on these figures, New Guinea would appear to be the centre of distribution of the group and some might argue that this is an indication that the subtribe originated there.

There are two problems with these figures. First, the subdivisions of the subtribe Dendrobiinae probably are not entirely natural. Largely devised by Rudolf Schlechter in 1914, they have proved extremely useful for classifying the large number of species that make up the group. However, modern techniques are tending to show problems with some parts of Schlechter's classification and it would seem that there is still some way to travel before a totally acceptable natural classification is reached. Recent proposals have not met with universal approval – for example, the splitting of *Pedilonum/Calcarifera*, *Grastidium/Dichopus* and *Oxyglossum/Cuthbertsonia* remains controversial, as does the elevation to generic status of groups such as *Dockrillia* and *Grastidium*.

More importantly New Guinea is a new land, having arisen from the sea only in the last 16 million years, and is unlikely to have been the area in which the group originated. The same could be said for the second most diverse area on the list above – Borneo – which is also a young land. If these areas are excluded, whence did *Dendrobium* and its relatives come? Next on the list is the India–Thailand or the Asian area, which is reasonably diverse and is much older. Could this be their origin? Or should we be looking at other ancient areas such as Australia and New Caledonia?

Unfortunately few, if any, fossils of the orchids have been found, so our ideas must be formulated with a great deal of guesswork, but based firmly on the now well-accepted theories on plate tectonics and drifting continents. Some other relevant aspects will now be considered.

Fig. 3 Distribution of the Dendrobiinae: the upper figure of each pair indicates the number of species known in the area, the lower figure the number of sections or genera represented.

Plant geography

Drifting continents

To understand the origin of *Dendrobium*, a brief summary of the effects of continental drift on the southern continents is required. In the nineteenth century and the first half of the twentieth century, scientists were at a loss to explain the obvious, yet sometimes surprising, similarities and differences between the plants and animals of many different parts of the world. Land bridges, long ago lost beneath the ocean, long-distance dispersal and mass extinctions, were used in an attempt to explain these anomalies. The concept of moving continents had been proposed previously, but there was no mechanism to explain how it could have occurred and it was generally discounted until the theory of plate tectonics burst upon the scientific community in the early 1960s. Now accepted as fact, plate tectonics explains how the continents have drifted, and continue to drift, extremely slowly over the surface of the earth, sometimes colliding and forming the large mountain ranges of the world. This in turn explains many of the previously puzzling plant and animal distributions (see Table 6).

TABLE 4

Number of higher groups (genera and sections of *Dendrobium*) in each region

Region	Number of higher groups
SE Asian mainland	19
Malesia	29
Papuasia	32
Australia	16
Pacific	25

TABLE 5
NUMBER OF SPECIES AND HIGHER GROUPS IN VARIOUS AREAS

Area	Region (see text)	Number of higher groups	Number of species
Sri Lanka	Asian mainland	5	9
India	Asian mainland	9	80
Thailand	Asian mainland	18	150
Indochina (Laos, Cambodia, Vietnam)	Asian mainland	17	120
China	Asian mainland	12	80
Taiwan	Asian mainland	6	15
Japan	Asian mainland	1	3
Peninsular Malaysia	Malesia	19	100
Sumatra	Malesia	20	150
Java	Malesia	22	70
Borneo	Malesia	19	170
Philippines	Malesia	18	100
Sulawesi	Malesia	17	60+
New Guinea (Irian Jaya, PNG)	Papuasia	32	450+
Bougainville and the Solomon Islands	Papuasia	23	70
Micronesia	Pacific	8	14
Vanuatu	Pacific	18	30
New Caledonia	Pacific	15	40
Fiji	Pacific	16	25
Samoa	Pacific	10	17
New Zealand	Pacific	1	1
Tahiti	Pacific	3	4
Australian mainland	Australia	16	60
Tasmania	Australia	1	1

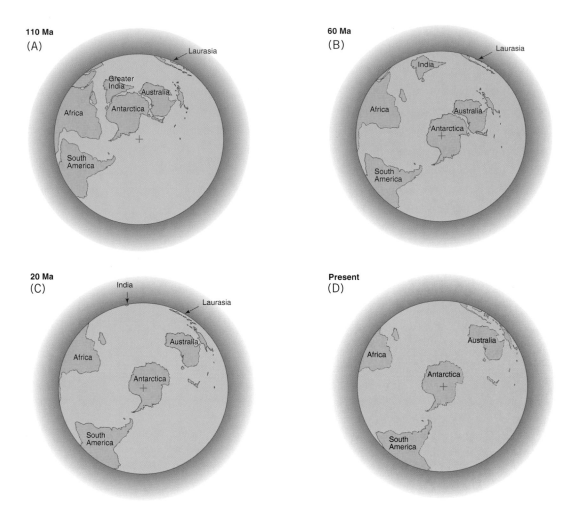

110 Ma
(A)

60 Ma
(B)

20 Ma
(C)

Present
(D)

Fig 4 Drifting continents. These maps show the modern continents. The margins of the continental shelves in past eras may be more important in showing joined land masses. For example in (A) the land areas of South America and Antarctica would have been much closer or touching than is shown here.

At its peak some 140 million years ago, the supercontinent of Gondwana comprised Antarctica, Australia, New Zealand, New Caledonia, Africa, Madagascar, India, Sri Lanka and South America. Slowly, over millions of years, Gondwana started to break up, a process that is still taking place. Early to break away and move north was India, which moved more rapidly than other land masses and eventually collided with the southern part of Laurasia some 40 million years ago. The impact caused the Himalayas to rise, much as by pushing on one end of a rug wrinkles are forced upwards. Next to break away was Africa, with South America and another smaller mass including Australia, New Caledonia and New Zealand following later. This Australasian plate along with South America remained connected through Antarctica until 50 million years ago. As the Australasian plate pushed north, it eventually collided with the Laurasian plate, causing the New Guinea and Indonesian mountains to rise. This elevation is still actively occurring, in fact parts of the Huon Peninsula of the north-east coast of Papua New

Guinea are the most active in the world, rising at the phenomenal rate of 300 metres in 10 000 years. Before this, New Guinea, if it existed at all, was a low-lying area to the north of Australia.

As a result of these events, Australia was isolated for 25 to 30 million years as it drifted slowly into lower latitudes. At the time that Australia broke away from Antarctica and South America, all these land masses probably shared a moist temperate climate with an extensive temperate rainforest, somewhat similar to that existing in Tasmania today. Clear evidence of this remains in the conifers of the southern continents, in particular the genus *Araucaria*, which occurs in South America, eastern Australia, New Caledonia and New Guinea. Antarctic beech (*Nothofagus*) has a similar distribution and fossils have been found in Antarctica.

Among the orchids, the terrestrial tribe Diurideae has a similar distribution, occurring in South America, Australia, New Caledonia, New Zealand and New Guinea, with a few species occurring to the west of New Guinea as far as the Asian mainland and Japan. It seems likely that the Diurideae were originally part of a Gondwana orchid flora, which was presumably terrestrial. Early in the history of the break-up of Gondwana, parts of this flora were in Africa, eventually giving rise to the Orchidoideae in Africa, and other groups in Asia and North America. Another part on the Indian plate possibly developed into the diverse orchid flora of South-East Asia. Yet another part was confined to Antarctica, Australasia (Australia, New Caledonia, New Zealand, New Guinea) and South America. Through later isolation, the components in Australasia and South America evolved separately to the point where they are now placed in separate subtribes.

Wallace's Line and the origin of the Dendrobiinae

Wallace's Line was proposed by Alfred Russel Wallace, one of the great biological thinkers of the nineteenth century, as a demarcation line between the Australian and Asian animals. The line, as he defined it, passed between Bali and Lombok and between Borneo and Sulawesi, with groups such as the marsupials to the east and placentals to the west. Since that time there have been numerous modifications of the line, some made by Wallace himself.

The demarcation is blurred. Many groups, such as birds, are able to cross areas of water. Many plants also have crossed the line as their seeds were dispersed by birds and wind. Therefore Wallace's Line, and other similar proposals, have less on-ground meaning for plants than they have for many animals. Although Wallace was unaware of it, his line represents, in general terms, the place where the Laurasian and Australian plates meet, and this could explain much of the present-day distributions. However, the lowering of sea levels with the emergence of land bridges and changed climates may well be of at least equal significance. While orchid seeds are light and able to be transported great distances by wind, they are not necessarily great colonisers of new habitats. They require a specific mycorrhizal fungus to survive and, as they lack stored food reserves, they must land in an extremely favourable environment. With this in mind, what significance does Wallace's Line hold for *Dendrobium* and its relatives? Are the higher groups restricted to one side or the other, possibly as a result of origins to the east or west of the line?

The classification of *Dendrobium* used most widely in the twentieth century has been that devised by Rudolf Schlechter in 1914 (see Table 3), which split *Dendrobium* into the four subgenera *Xerobium*, *Athecebium*, *Dendrobium* and *Rhopalobium*. Subgenus *Xerobium* includes sections such as *Aporum*, *Oxystophyllum*, *Grastidium* and *Cannaeorchis* (section *Macrocladium*).

Among these are groups from both east and west of Wallace's Line. If the Dendrobiinae includes two groups, each originating from a different plate, and if Schlechter's classification has defined naturally related groups, we should expect the classification to separate groups wholly, or at least largely, on the basis of an eastern or western origin. When analysed, this is found not to be the case. *Rhopalobium* consists of the section *Rhopalanthe* only and is equally spread east and west of Wallace's Line. The large subgenus *Dendrobium* includes sections such as *Dendrobium*, *Calcarifera*, *Formosae*, *Pedilonum*, *Spatulata* and *Phalaenanthe* – equally split between east and west. *Athecebium* includes sections such as *Bolbidium*, *Callista*, *Latouria* and *Dockrillia*, again distributed both east and west of the line. In summary, while certain genera, subgenera and sections are distributed on one side or the other (e.g. *Callista* to the west, *Latouria* to the east), the distribution of many others seems totally unrelated to the line.

However, there is a gradually increasing body of evidence which suggests that the familiar classification of Schlechter is perhaps not as natural as it might be. For example, the obviously closely related sections *Aporum* and *Rhopalanthe* are placed in different subgenera. Alternative classifications based on DNA, while still very incomplete, tend to place taxa distributed on one side of the line in one group and those from the other side in another. A great deal more data is required before this evidence could be considered totally reliable.

New Caledonia and its strange orchids

The evidence of attenuation into the Pacific and down the east Australian coast points to New Guinea as the point of origin of the South Pacific and Australian Dendrobiinae except, some might argue, for New Caledonia. The island of New Caledonia has long been recognised as a key area in the study of southern plants and animals. The tectonic history suggests that an area of the Pacific including New Zealand, New Caledonia, Lord Howe Island and Norfolk Island broke away from Antarctica and Australia as long as 80 million years ago. This area would have supported varying amounts of dry land over the years, but it seems likely that at least part of New Caledonia has always been above sea level over this period. Thus it is likely that New Caledonia has had an even longer period of isolation than Australia, although there may well have been island chains providing some linkage to the north. In addition, at times of lower sea levels the distance between Australia and New Caledonia would have been considerably shorter than it is today, so perhaps New Caledonia's isolation was far from complete. Pairs of very similar species are present in New Caledonia and north-east Australia, indicating relatively recent exchange of species.

New Caledonia is larger than other land masses between New Guinea and New Zealand, and has a mountainous backbone which provides numerous ecological niches. In the southern part of the island there is a rare and interesting vegetation type known as the *maquis*, which is developed on ancient rocks, originally part of the earth's crust below the ocean, rocks which are extremely rich in nickel, magnesium, chromium and manganese. The unique soil conditions give rise to the stunted, heath-like *maquis* vegetation in which many of New Caledonia's orchids grow. While many trees and shrubs become virtual bonsais in these conditions, some of the orchids, particularly in the genus *Cannaeorchis* (section *Macrocladium*) have become huge, with specimens up to five metres tall being reported.

The flora contains many non-orchid species that are interpreted as relics of Gondwana, including many primitive genera and a suite of gymnosperms with links to South America. The orchids are most interesting. *Megastylis*, a terrestrial genus, is closely related to species in South America, but the prevailing winds make long-distance dispersal most unlikely. This genus is almost universally taken as evidence of a common ancestry in Gondwana. There are several endemic groups in the Dendrobiinae that could similarly be interpreted as being relics of the Gondwana ancestors. These include *Dendrobium* section *Kinetochilus* and the genus *Cannaeorchis* (section *Macrocladium*), although they are clearly related to *Grastidium* and other typically New Guinean groups.

Why are New Guinea Dendrobiinae so diverse?

A problem with our theories is the huge diversity of the New Guinea Dendrobiinae. Surely, one could argue, New Guinea must be the 'home' of the Dendrobiinae as it has far more species and more higher groups than any other area? This diversity may be more apparent than real, as the classification of the Dendrobiinae probably has a large number of anomalies and may not be a very natural system. The other consideration is that New Guinea is a recent land mass. It probably has not been a factor in orchid evolution for more than 15 or 20 million years. It simply was not there when *Dendrobium* and its relatives were developing.

It seems certain that New Guinea received an influx of animals and plants in relatively recent times (i.e. about 15 to 20 million years ago). Whence did these come? From Asia or from Australia? The birds and mammals, there is no doubt, came from Australia (except for a few recent mobile interlopers such as some birds, rats, bats and *Homo sapiens*, along with his offsiders the dog and the pig). The plants came from both directions but perhaps predominantly from Australia. The orchids, most likely, also came from both directions, with terrestrial groups such as *Corybas*, *Acianthus*, *Thelymitra* and *Pterostylis* from Australia and *Habenaria*, *Goodyera*, *Malaxis* and *Phaius* from Asia. Where the Dendrobiinae came from depends on which of three theories is favoured. Perhaps they came from Australia, perhaps from Laurasia to the west, perhaps from both sources. Whatever their origin, they arrived in a land that was rapidly developing high mountains, year-round reliable rainfall in most areas and where there was little competition for niches. The resultant evolutionary explosion is still occurring. It is a spurt of evolutionary expansion in which species are continually developing and changing in a way that makes those attempting to classify them tear their hair out.

Many complex factors are no doubt affecting this process, not the least being relationships with pollinators. Many of the highland Dendrobiinae have brightly coloured tubular flowers adapted to bird pollination, a feature much less common in Asia. This adaptation may have opened the way to new ecological niches. Many species are extremely variable in colour, again in particular in the highlands, so much so that each ridgeline or peak seems to have its own colour form of some species in sections *Oxyglossum* and *Calyptrochilus*. An example of the confusion this creates lies in the classification of the section *Oxyglossum*. Van Royen, in his account of the section in *The Orchids of the High Mountains of New Guinea* in 1980, described 15 new species in this section, but Reeve and Woods, in their *A Revision of* Dendrobium *section* Oxyglossum (*Orchidaceae*) in 1989, reduced 13 of these to synonymy and one to varietal status. The archipelagos off New Guinea's east coast also offer spectacular examples of evolution in progress in the section *Spatulata*. Many island groups seem to have their own separate species, closely related to others nearby, but different enough to be a regarded as good species. In addition many individual islands have a distinctive colour form of species such as *D. gouldii*.

This ever-changing diversity of ecological niches, separated by flimsy, often ephemeral barriers to cross-pollination, is what accounts for the present-day diversity in New Guinea, not the possibility that it is an ancestral home.

Theories on the origin of the Dendrobiinae

There is now general agreement that the process described previously, that is, some from the south, some from the north, was how the terrestrial genera evolved, so would it not seem logical to suppose a similar scenario for the epiphytic groups, including *Dendrobium* and its relatives? Taking all this into account, there are three theories on the origin of the Dendrobiinae.

1. An origin on the Australian plate, whence they spread to Asia and the Pacific;
2. A dual origin with part coming from the Australian plate and part from Laurasia, ending with the two groups merging in Malesia; and
3. An origin in Laurasia (now Asia) with the progenitors arising on the Indian plate or perhaps from Africa, then spreading out to New Guinea and later to Australia and the Pacific.

While there are few, if any, hard facts to prove or disprove any of these theories, the following discussion presents arguments for and against each theory.

Origin on the Australian plate

This theory is strongly supported by the diversity of higher groups in regions originating from the Australian or Pacific plates, i.e. Australia, New Guinea and New Caledonia (see Table 5, page 33). New Guinea has 32 out of 48 higher groups, Bougainville and the Solomons have 23, and both Australia (16) and New Caledonia (15) are very well represented, considering their small size (Australia is large, but the area of suitable habitats is small). Mainland Asia has fewer higher groups and therefore appears less likely as a source of origin. The Malesian islands are reasonably diverse, but are probably of recent origin. To some extent they share some groups from the east and some from the west and may represent an overlap area, but several groups are clearly centred in the

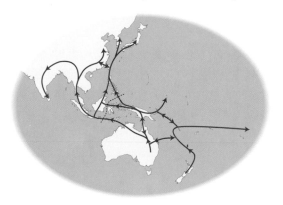

Fig. 5a Theories on the origin of the Dendrobiinae – origin on the Australian plate.

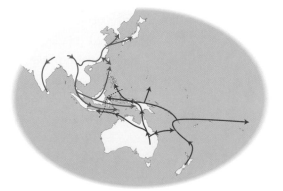

Fig. 5b Theories on the origin of the Dendrobiinae – dual origin in Laurasia and Australia.

islands (e.g. *Distichophyllum, Conostalix, Rhopalanthe*). The endemic sections and genera in New Caledonia and Australia, such as *Cannaeorchis* (section *Macrocladium*) and *Dendrocoryne*, could be considered to be relics of the Gondwana flora which have given rise to groups such as *Grastidium* and *Latouria* in New Guinea.

If an origin from the Australian plate is real, then it would follow that the plants of Malesia and of mainland Asia would have arrived in the last 15 million years. It would also follow that Wallace's Line would have little or no significance and there would be expected to be some attenuation to the west, although this would be obscured by the increasing aridity in areas such as western India and Pakistan. The evidence on Wallace's Line is inconclusive. If the traditional classification of Schlechter is followed, Wallace's Line is of limited importance in orchid distribution, but if recent, but incomplete classifications based on DNA are to be believed, it may be significant.

A problem with this theory is the distribution of the Dendrobiinae along the eastern Australian coast. If the group had an origin in the Australian part of Gondwana, it could be expected that there would be significant numbers of Dendrobiinae in the southern part of Australia and Tasmania where the climates are suitable. This is clearly not the case, as the numbers and diversity reduce markedly from north to south, to the point where there is only one species in Tasmania. Perhaps this can be explained by extinctions caused originally by glaciation and then by increasing aridity as Australia drifts north.

Dual origin on the Indian and Australian plates

This theory has had some recent proponents who see part of the progenitors of the Dendrobiinae moving north on the Indian plate, another part on the Australian plate, with the two parts reuniting some 15 million years ago on the collision of Australia and Laurasia. If this were true, Wallace's Line would be significant, but as mentioned previously our understanding of relationships in the subtribe may not be good enough to examine this productively.

If Australia and South America were linked up to 50 million years ago, it would seem logical that there might be relatives of the Dendrobiinae in South America or relatives of South American groups such as *Laelia* in Australia or New Guineas, but this is not the case. This suggests that the differentiation that led to the evolution of the Laeliinae and the Dendrobiinae occurred after 50 million years ago, when the physical separation of South America and Australasia occurred – possibly some 30 million years ago. By this time the Indian plate had collided with the Laurasian plate, but the Australian plate was some way away from its destiny with the south-east part of the Laurasian plate.

The consequence of this is that the Australian part of the Dendrobiinae must have developed in isolation from the Indian part over the last 75–80 million years, then reunited 15 million years ago. Perhaps evolution proceeded at a similar pace on the Indian plate, but as it had a quite different history to the Australian plate, it seems more likely that the speed and direction of evolution would have been different on the two plates. Therefore it seems hard to believe that after about 60 million years of separate evolution the two parts could come together again and still be so similar that botanists unanimously placed them in the same genus.

Origin on the Indian plate

This theory proposes that the part of the Gondwana flora which was isolated on the Indian plate developed into the Dendrobiinae which, after an original period of rapid diversification as the Himalayas were formed, spread out to the new lands of Borneo and the other Malesian islands and then to New Guinea, Australia and the Pacific, including New Caledonia. It would seem logical that the rapid movement of the Indian plate to moist tropical climates would have been more conducive to the development of epiphytism than the slow progress of the Australian plate through increasingly dry conditions.

A consequence of an early presence of the progenitors of the Dendrobiinae on the Australian plate would be a significant degree of diversity in southern areas, such as southern parts of the Australian mainland and Tasmania. This is clearly not the case, however. The distribution of the Dendrobiinae in the South Pacific and along the east coast of Australia shows a clear tendency to attenuation, the numbers decreasing with distance from New Guinea. Thus Bougainville and the Solomons have 66 species, Vanuatu 31, Fiji 26, Tahiti four and New Zealand one species. The east coast of Australia shows a similar distribution. While the east coast is a continuous land mass (except for Bass Strait) extending 4000 kilometres from north to south, in terms of orchid floras it is more like a series of islands with large, seasonally dry areas acting as barriers to dispersal in the same way that oceans do. A northern flora can be identified, extending from Torres Strait to about 16°S, including 52 Dendrobiinae species. The central flora extends from 20°S to about 33°S and includes 23 species, while Tasmania and Victoria to the south have only three species. The diversity of higher taxa (genera and sections) also clearly attenuates to the south.

If the Dendrobiinae, or part of it, had a southern origin in Gondwana, then moved into Australia, it would be logical to expect more species and more higher taxa in the southern areas. Perhaps ice ages and glaciation, or different sea levels, might have eliminated some of this postulated diversity, but surely some would have survived in southern Australia. In fact, attenuation towards the north should probably be evident if the Dendrobiinae had a southern origin, both in Australia and in the Pacific.

What then of the interesting New Caledonian groups? It seems likely that these New Caledonian endemics represent the survivors of the earliest wave of 'invasion' of the Dendrobiinae from the north-west, which would have occurred about 10 to 15 million years ago. These early arrivals encountered the strange conditions of the *maquis* vegetation and have evolved in unique ways which give the New Caledonian orchid flora its distinctive character. A similar group exists in Australia in the *Dendrobium* sections *Dendrocoryne*, *Australorchis*, *Lichenastrum* and the genus *Dockrillia* (section *Rhizobium*). All these appear to have evolved in Australia from an early invading group and then, Australia being less isolated than New Caledonia, some have secondarily spread out to the Pacific Islands and back to New Guinea.

If the improved understanding of the relationships of the Dendrobiinae does appear to show a correlation with Wallace's Line, does this prove that the groups on either side of the line have different origins? An equally acceptable explanation may be that there were two groups already present, or that the Dendrobiinae, after a period of confinement to Laurasia, were suddenly presented with the opportunity to colonise a new land, the recently emerged island of New Guinea, a place of great topographical diversity, high rainfall and many ecological niches. This resulted in the evolution of a new group, some members of which filtered back to the west, while others moved out to the Pacific and Australia. Thus, rather than southern and northern groups, perhaps we have ancient and recent groups.

The theory that we are favouring here (see Figure 5c and Table 6) is that the Dendrobiinae arose in Laurasia, perhaps from plants rafted north on the Indian plate, or possibly from Africa. They evolved slowly in what is now South-East Asia for several million years, but when the Australasian plate met the Laurasian plate some 15 million years ago, the way was opened for them to move to the east into lands with few, if any, epiphytic species. Directly at their doorstep lay the virgin island of New Guinea with a perfect climate and a vast variety of niches awaiting them. Moving on to the west and south, they encountered numerous small islands as well as New Caledonia and Australia, which were larger land masses but lacked the number and diversity of opportunities in New Guinea. The descendants of this first wave of immigrants today are the peculiar groups typical of these lands. Subsequent to this, as climates fluctuated, sea levels rose and fell and new waves of emigrants moved out into the Pacific and Australia. This must have happened on numerous occasions, and is still happening. Species such as *Dendrobium antennatum* and *D. bifalce*, so typical of lowland New Guinea, occur in small numbers on Cape York Peninsula and represent recent arrivals. Other species have been in situ long enough to evolve into separate species, for example the Fiji species *D. prasinum*, which is closely related to species from New Guinea and the Solomons. These recent arrivals are being superimposed on the earlier plants, forming a diverse array in many areas.

TABLE 6

Proposed timetable for the evolution of the Dendrobiinae (Theory 3, Figure 5(c))

Time*	Plate tectonic events	Possible orchid events
160–140	Southern continents (Africa, South America, Australia, India) all joined in supercontinent of Gondwana.	Angiosperms evolve, most likely in west Gondwana – possibly in Africa. Modern families of flowering plants appear. First orchids differentiate.
120	Gondwana starts to split up.	Generalised orchid flora widespread over Gondwana, including Africa and America.
100–80	India splits off from Gondwana, New Caledonia and New Zealand split from Gondwana. South America and Africa still joined to each other and, through Antarctica, to Australia.	Parts of the Gondwana orchid flora become isolated on Indian plate and on New Caledonian plate.
60	America and Africa separate, India drifts rapidly north, Australia still joined to South America via Antarctica. Climate of Australia, Antarctica and South America moist temperate.	Australia has a generalised orchid flora. No group recognisable as Epidendroid yet present in Australia, South America, Africa or Asia.
50	Australia splits off from Gondwana, moves slowly north. All contact with South America lost.	Orchid floras of South America, Africa, India, New Caledonia and Australia evolve along separate lines.
40	India collides with Asia, with the impact forming the Himalayas. Australia's climate becomes warmer and drier. New Guinea either does not exist or is low-lying land to north of Australia.	Epidendroid groups evolving separately into distinct groups in Africa, Asia and South America. Orchids undergo burst of evolution in Laurasia as the elevation of the Himalayas provides new ecological niches. First recognisable Dendrobiinae appear. The drying climate in Australia is not suitable for the development of widespread epiphytism and some Australian orchids evolve to suit the dry seasonal climate (e.g. tubers).
20–15	Australia collides with Laurasia forming New Guinea, a new land with a wet climate, diverse topography and numerous ecological niches.	Laurasian epiphytic and terrestrial orchids start to move into Australia and New Guinea. The less specialised of the Australian terrestrial orchids move into Laurasia.
15 to present	Climates vary from wet to dry with successive ice ages, particularly in Australia, but also in Malesia and New Guinea. Varying sea levels cause barriers to migration to appear and disappear.	Explosion of evolution of orchids in New Guinea, orchids move into Australia and the Pacific, including New Caledonia. Earliest immigrants to Australia and New Caledonia eventually develop into endemic groups.

* Time in million years before present

CHAPTER 4

Traditional Uses

People throughout the world have been making use of plants, including orchids, from time immemorial. While orchids currently provide but one item of everyday use – vanilla – this was not always so; in the past orchids have been used for a wide variety of both spiritual and material purposes. Local use has been made of many species of the Dendrobiinae described in this book, and in a few cases the use survives to this day.

Within the geographical range of the subtribe, the earliest reports of the use of orchids are associated with religious rites and the shamanistic practices of medicine men. In China orchids were mentioned in the writings of Confucius and were included in ancient Chinese medical herbals. In Sri Lanka the flowers of *Dendrobium maccarthiae* were used to adorn shrines on Buddha's birthday. In Japan *D. moniliforme* was regarded as the plant of longevity and was used to decorate temples. In India *Flickingeria macraei* was used by Ayurvedic medicine men in rites involving prophecy and divination.

In parts of Malesia local species of *Dendrobium* thought to be possessed of magic powers have been used as charms to reunite lovers, to give courage to head-hunters, to make hunting dogs skilful and to exorcise spirits of the dead.

The pseudobulbs of *D. canaliculatum* and *D. speciosum* were used for food by the aboriginal Australians. In Malesia the leaves of *Grastidium salaccense* were steamed in rice to impart a flavour, and a tonic decoction was made from *D. crumenatum* in Vietnam.

In Papua New Guinea the leaves of a species of *Dendrobium* were used to wrap salt cakes. The old stalks of *D. crumenatum* were cut and used as ties in the Andaman Islands. In north Queensland dried strips cut from the canes of *D. discolor* were used to bind traditional weapons. The dried stem of *D. heterocarpum* was used in the Philippines to make a belt to hold up the loincloth.

Juice from the cut stem of *D. affine* is used by the peoples of Arnhem Land and Groote Eylandt as a fixative in bark and rock paintings and in the decoration of ceremonial pieces. The juice is mixed with the pigment, or alternatively may be applied directly to the surface, either beneath or on top of the pigment.

The stems or canes of several species of *Dendrobium* have had local use in various aspects of weaving, basketry and wickerwork. In Indonesia *D. acuminatissimum*, *D. bifalce* and *D. macrophyllum* were used in wickerwork. In the Moluccas *D. faciferum* was used for basketry, mat plaiting and weaving. In the Philippines, *D. crumenatum* was used for straw plaiting and making straw hats, and *D. polytrichum* was used in weaving and basketry.

In some areas within the range of Dendrobiinae, the yellow material used to decorate artefacts is provided by local species of *Dendrobium* or *Diplocaulobium*. This practice is reported from the

Artefacts from Papua New Guinea, making use of yellow dendrobium fibre for decoration and binding.

GEOFF STOCKER, LEN LAWLER

Solomon Islands, Cape York Peninsula, the Torres Strait Islands, Papua New Guinea, Irian Jaya, the Moluccas, Sulawesi, Kalimantan, the Philippines, the Andaman Islands and Manipur. The orchid stems turn yellow on drying, the colour being intensified by exposing the stems to heat from the sun or a fire. The outer covering of the stems is cut into strips which are either woven into artefacts such as mats and armbands, or fixed around objects such as arrows and firesticks. The many types of articles decorated in this way include domestic implements, clothing, body ornaments, ceremonial articles, funerary relics and weapons. While many reports do not identify the species involved, some prominent examples are given below.

In Sulawesi and Kalimantan the stems of *Diplocaulobium utile* are split and dried to a golden yellow colour. The dried strips are used mainly for decorative edging on small items such as baskets and cigar cases. In Sulawesi, because of the rarity of this orchid, its use in baskets and mats was once restricted to royal and noble households. In the Philippines yellow strips made from *Dendrobium crumenatum* were used for decorative purposes in basketry and hat making, and *D. heterocarpum* was used similarly to decorate items of clothing. Also used in the Philippines were *Grastidium luzonense*, to pattern baskets, and *D. tetraedre*, which was used in small hand-woven boxes and in cigar cases. In the Andaman Islands yellow bark from *D. secundum* was used to decorate bows and arrows, personal ornaments and funerary relics. The aboriginal Australians of north Queensland prepared yellow strips from *D. bigibbum* used to decorate clothing, weapons and domestic implements. On the western side of Cape York Peninsula *D. semifuscum* served a similar purpose. In the Solomon Islands *D. gouldii* provided material for yellow decoration on Ulawa and San Cristobal. *D. polysema* was planted around villages in Papua New Guinea to ensure a supply of dried stems for use in weaving armbands, while the long yellow stems of *D. lobbii*, cut into sections and threaded on string, were worn as necklaces.

In Papua New Guinea several species of *Diplocaulobium*, including *D. centrale*, *D. iboense*, *D. pentanema* and *D. regale*, have provided yellow stems that were woven into belts, armbands and girdles, and the last-named species was used also to hold green beetle cases in ceremonial headbands. In Bougainville and the Solomon Islands the yellow stems of *D. solomonense* were plaited into armlets.

In the highlands of Papua New Guinea several species of *Dendrobium* and *Grastidium*, including *Grastidium acuminatissimum*, have provided flowers, leaves and stems for personal adornment and body decoration. To ensure availability of the orchid material, one species was transplanted to villages, while another, together with a species of *Diplocaulobium*, was planted on the roofs of houses to decorate them. The young women of Manipur wore the flowers of *Dendrobium densiflorum* behind their ears, while the dried plant of *D. clavatum* was used in scent. In Sumatra people wore in their hair the dried leaves of *Grastidium salaccense* because of their pleasant odour. On Manus Island, women powder the leaves of *Dendrobium erosum*, soak them in coconut oil and use the mixture as a perfume.

Orchids of subtribe Dendrobiinae have had extensive medical use in China and nearby countries. The drug *shih-hu* has been regarded as a precious drug in Chinese medicine since the Han Dynasty (200 BC–200 AD), and has also been used in Japan, Korea, Taiwan and Tibet.

The drug consists of dried stems of some twenty species of *Dendrobium*, of which by far the most common is *D. nobile*. Several species are cultivated for export to Chinese communities overseas, including Indochina and Malaysia, while *D. moniliforme* is imported from Japan for use as *shih-hu*. *Shih-hu* means 'rock-living', implying that the plant must be hardy, so that, in accordance with the Doctrine of Signatures, it must supply a strengthening medicine. It is traditionally used as such and as a tonic; it nourishes the *yin* system of the body and is considered a drug of longevity and an aphrodisiac. *D. nobile* contains several alkaloids, the chief of which, dendrobine, possesses pharmacological activity. *Shih-hu* is still available in herbalists' shops in China.

In Papua New Guinea the leaves of a species of *Dendrobium* were used to treat cough, and a species from section *Monanthos* has been used to treat internal haemorrhage. In India *D. monticola* and *D. ovatum* have been used as emollients, while *D. moschatum* was used to treat earache. In Malesia *D. bifarium*, *D. planibulbe* and *D. purpureum* have been used to treat various skin disorders. *D. crumenatum* has been used in West Malaysia and Java for earache and ear infections. In Queensland *D. discolor* provides a paste to treat infection and a liniment for ringworm. *D. hymenanthum* was used against dropsy in West Malaysia. *D. subulatum* was used in West Malaysia as a poultice to relieve headache, and in Tahiti the bruised leaves of *D. crispatum* were used to treat headache and acute pain. *D. taurinum* was used in the Philippines to make a wash to remedy falling hair. In Papua New Guinea a species of *Diplocaulobium* has been used to treat infected wounds. *Flickingeria macraei*, often in association with *F. fimbriata*, has had extensive use in India and Sri Lanka against a long list of diseases.

In accord with the notion that orchids have aphrodisiac properties, some of the Dendrobiinae have been used as aphrodisiacs. A species of *Dendrobium* in Papua New Guinea has been so used. Other species used in this way include *D. acinaciforme* in Ambon, *D. chryseum* in India, *D. moniliforme* in Korea and Taiwan, and *D. nobile* in China. The whole plant of *Flickingeria fimbriata*, including the seed capsule, has been used as an aphrodisiac in India.

Not to be forgotten in discussing the uses of these orchids is the contribution made by hobby growers and commercial nurseries, which brings great pleasure and satisfaction to many. The genus *Dendrobium*, in particular the sections *Dendrobium*, *Latouria*, *Phalaenanthe* and *Spatulata*, has been the source of vast numbers of hybrids which support a considerable proportion of the retail orchid trade. One very successful group, known as the 'Pompadour hybrids', is based on *Dendrobium bigibbum*, which has been proclaimed the State Flower of Queensland, the state in which this book has been compiled.

CHAPTER 5

Conservation

During the 1970s and 1980s a debate on the merits of orchid conservation was carried out in the pages of popular orchid journals such as the *American Orchid Society Bulletin* and the *Orchid Digest*. Some writers questioned the generally accepted wisdom that orchid collecting was a major factor in the demise of orchids – in fact, the very idea of a decline in orchids was questioned. In some regards this was something of a popular uprising against conservation laws and in particular the Convention on International Trade in Endangered Species of Wild Fauna and Flora (CITES) which was introduced in 1973.

Much of the debate centred on the removal of orchids in Central and South America by collectors, both amateur and commercial, from the United States. While there are no native Dendrobiinae in the Americas, this debate has implications for the group, as the effectiveness and life span of conservation laws are reduced if the public is opposed to them. In part the opposition was caused by a lack of understanding of the CITES laws as developed in USA, and in part by self-interest. Despite this debate, it is safe to assume that the need for conservation is well accepted in orchid circles, although some reservations remain about the methods of implementation.

Left: *Dendrobium fellowsii*, a vulnerable species, is restricted to the tall open forests on the western margin of the rainforests of north-east Queensland. GERALD MCCRAITH

Above: *Dendrobium antennatum* is an abundant species in New Guinea, but in Australia is restricted to a small area and is in demand by collectors. Therefore the Australian population is considered endagered, but on a world distribution it is not under threat. BILL LAVARACK

Which Dendrobiinae are threatened?

In 1997 the Species Survival Commission (SSC) of the International Union for the Conservation of Nature (IUCN) published the 1997 *IUCN Red List of Threatened Plants*. In this list almost 34 000 species, or 12.5 per cent, of the world's vascular plants are considered threatened. Of these, 1779 species are orchids. This represents about 5.9 per cent of the family's 30 000 species. The only family with more threatened species is the Compositae (Asteraceae), the daisy family, which has 2553 species listed as threatened.

Among the Dendrobiinae, 74 species are listed as threatened, about 5.7 per cent of the total number of species in the group. None is regarded as definitely extinct, but one species, *Dendrobium aurantiacum* Rchb.f., probably is. Six are endangered, 16 vulnerable, 31 rare and

20 indeterminate. The full list of threatened Dendrobiinae is provided in Table 7. The *1997 IUCN Red List of Threatened Plants* is the first global list of threatened plants that has been prepared and it provides a useful summary of the position at one point in time. However, the limitations of such a list must be considered. The data are very variable, with reasonably reliable data from Europe, North America, South Africa and Australia, but very patchy data for most other areas. The data from most orchid-rich areas and most areas where deforestation is a major issue are less reliable. Even the data sets considered more reliable are open to considerable error, as very little data are derived from quantifiable research. Most comes from the subjective observations of local experts.

Dendrobium moorei is restricted to Lord Howe Island and is considered vulnerable because of the limited distribution.
BILL LAVARACK

It is likely that the list underestimates the actual number of threatened species, as there is a natural tendency to concentrate on the more showy species that are threatened by collecting. Less spectacular species are in the majority in the wild and may well be threatened by land-clearing, but this is not so obvious, as many species are small and not well-known.

In addition to the species listed here, many more have been depleted; in fact, few would not have suffered to some extent from the activities of humans. For example, it has been estimated that in the process of clearing an area of about 200 000 hectares of melaleuca woodland on the central Queensland coast, plants of *Dendrobium canaliculatum* numbering perhaps in the hundreds of millions were destroyed, yet this remains a common species, not regarded as being under threat.

Another aspect to keep in mind is that this is a global list which provides a world-wide ranking. Many local populations of species at the extremes of their range are threatened. For example, *Dendrobium antennatum* is a common species throughout lowland New Guinea, but is represented in Australia by only one restricted population on eastern Cape York Peninsula. Australian authorities rate this population as endangered, due to over-collecting, but the species as a whole is under no serious threat.

TABLE 7
THREATENED DENDROBIINAE

[This table is modified from the 1997 IUCN Red List of Threatened Plants. The names used here are those in the Red List. Changes to the newly proposed generic names have not been made.]

Extinct/Endangered

Dendrobium aurantiacum Rchb.f.	Bangladesh, Bhutan

Endangered

Dendrobium flavidulum Ridl. ex Hook.f.	Peninsular Malaysia, Singapore
D. flexile Ridl.	Peninsular Malaysia, Singapore
D. munificum (Finet) Schltr.	New Caledonia
D. pauciflorum King & Prantl.	India (Sikkim, West Bengal)
D. tenuicaule Hook.f.	Andaman Islands
Flickingeria hesperis Seidenf.	India (Uttar Pradesh)

Vulnerable

Dendrobium angulatum Lindl.	Java
D. angustifolium Lindl.	Java
D. aureilobum J.J. Sm.	Java
D. bigibbum Lindl.	Queensland, New Guinea
D. capra J.J. Sm.	Java
D. carronii Lavarack & P.J. Cribb	Queensland and New Guinea
D. clavator Ridley	Peninsular Malaysia
D. fellowsii F. Muell.	Queensland
D. johannis Rchb.f.	Queensland and New Guinea
D. lithocola D.A. Jones & M.A. Clem.	Queensland
D. moorei F. Muell.	Lord Howe Island
D. muricatum Finet	New Caledonia
D. phalaenopsis Fitzg.	Queensland
D. rennellii P.J. Cribb	Solomons
D. spectatissimum Rchb.f.	Sabah
D. tozerense Lavarack	Queensland

Rare

Cadetia collinsii Lavarack	Queensland
C. quadrangularis P.J. Cribb & B. Lewis	Vanuatu
C. wariana Schltr.	Queensland, New Guinea
Dendrobium aegle Ridl.*	Peninsular Malaysia, Sarawak
D. alexandrae Schltr.	Papua New Guinea
D. arachnites Rchb.f.	India–Myanmar
D. ciliatilabellum Seidenf.	Thailand
D. dalatense Gagnep.	Vietnam
D. evaginatum Gagnep.	Vietnam
D. gnomus Ames	Solomons
D. greenianum P.J. Cribb & B. Lewis	Vanuatu
D. jacobsonii J.J. Sm.	Java
D. kuhlii (Blume) Lindl.	Java
D. langbianense Gagnep.	Vietnam
D. lowii Lindl.	Sarawak
D. macropus (Endl.) Rchb.f. ex Lindl. ssp. *howeanum* (Maiden) P. Green	Lord Howe Island
D. macropus (Endl.) Rchb.f. ex Lindl. ssp. *macropus*	Norfolk Island
D. malbrownii Dockrill	Queensland
D. mooreanum Lindl.	Vanuatu
D. paniferum J.J. Sm.	Java
D. ruginosum Ames	Bougainville Island, Solomons

Table 7
Threatened Dendrobiinae (continued)

D. salmonense Schltr.	Bougainville Island, Solomons
D. schneiderae F.M. Bailey	Queensland, NSW
D. toressae (F.M. Bailey) Dockrill	Queensland
D. vagans Schltr.	Samoa
D. vanikorense Ames	Bougainville Island, Solomons
D. wassellii S.T. Blake	Queensland, Cape York Peninsula
Diplocaulobium magnilabre P.J. Cribb & B. Lewis	Bougainville Island, Solomons
Epigeneium chapaense Gagnep.	Vietnam
Flickingeria nativitatis (Ridley) J.J. Wood	Christmas Island
F. punctilosa (J.J. Sm.) A.D. Hawkes	Java

Indeterminate

Dendrobium brachypus (Endl.) Rchb.f.	Norfolk Island
D. brevimentum Seidenf.	Vietnam
D. campbellii P.J. Cribb & B. Lewis	Solomons
D. cruentum Rchb.f.	Thailand
D. deltatum Seidenf.	Thailand
D. erostele Seidenf.	Thailand
D. eserre Seidenf.	Thailand
D. gamblei King & Prantl.	India (Uttar Pradesh)
D. garrettii Seidenf.	Thailand
D. lagarum Seidenf.	Thailand
D. lunatum Lindl.	Philippines (Palawan)
D. maccarthiae Thwaites	Sri Lanka
D. microbulbon A. Rich.	India
D. mucronatum Seidenf.	Thailand
D. normale Falc.	India (Uttar Pradesh)
D. pensile Ridley	Nicobar Island, Peninsular Malaysia, Singapore
D. rechingerorum Schltr.	Bougainville, Solomons
D. sancristobalense P.J. Cribb	Solomons
D. umbonatum Seidenf.	Thailand
D. ypsilon Seidenf.	Thailand

* *D. acgle* is now considered a synonym of the more widespread *D. erosum* (Blume) Lindl. and probably is not under threat over its range.

Definitions of categories used

Extinct	Taxa not definitely located in the wild during the last 50 years.
Extinct/Endangered	Taxa that are suspected of having recently become extinct.
Endangered	Taxa in danger of extinction and whose survival is unlikely if the causal factors continue operating. Included are taxa whose numbers have been reduced to a critical level or whose habitats have been so drastically reduced that they are deemed to be in immediate danger of extinction. Also included are taxa that may be extinct, but have definitely been seen in the wild in the past 50 years.
Vulnerable	Taxa believed likely to move into the 'Endangered' category in the near future if the causal factors continue operating. Included are taxa of which most or all of the populations are decreasing because of over-exploitation, extensive destruction of habitat or other environmental disturbance; taxa with populations that have been seriously depleted and whose ultimate security has not yet been assured; and taxa with populations that are still abundant but are under threat from severe adverse factors throughout their range.
Rare	Taxa with small world populations that are not at present 'Endangered' or 'Vulnerable', but are at risk. These taxa are usually localised within restricted geographical areas or habitats or are thinly scattered over a more extensive range.
Indeterminate	Taxa that are known to be 'Endangered', 'Vulnerable' or 'Rare' but where there is not enough information to say which of the three categories is appropriate.

The threats

What threats do orchids face? How real are these threats? In the case of the Dendrobiinae, they are very real and immediate. The Dendrobiinae inhabit the South-East Asia–Pacific region, a part of the world which supports about 2.5 billion people, almost half the world's population in only a fraction of the world's land area. Until the slump of 1998, the region supported the fastest-growing economies in the world, a position likely to be regained in the near future. There is a huge demand for resources such as timber and minerals and, as living standards gradually increase and health care improves, there is an ever-increasing demand for land. This adds up to enormous pressure on the natural environments of the region, resulting already in the loss of more than half the original rainforests. The threats detailed below all spring from this demand.

While it is convenient to consider these threats one by one, that is not how they operate in nature. The threats all are interrelated and build on each other, so that the end result is greater than the sum of the parts. Thus, while collecting for horticultural purposes may not have been a major problem in the nineteenth century when the habitats were largely intact, it may readily cause extinctions in the twenty-first century when only a fraction of the original habitats remain.

Land-clearing

Whether it is taking place in the developed nations or in the developing nations of Asia and the Pacific, the major threat to orchids, and to all wild plants and animals, is land-clearing. Land-clearing occurs for many reasons, including grazing, agriculture, urban development, timber production and mining.

In some nations such as Australia and India much of the land-clearing is older and we tend to accept it as part of the landscape, but many orchid species must have been affected and it is likely that species have become extinct before they were scientifically described.

Land cleared for grazing on the Atherton Tableland in north-east Queensland. Patches of rainforest remaining along creek lines and even isolated trees can provide habitats for native orchids to retain a foothold. BILL LAVARACK

A recently established residence and agricultural plot in primary forest in Papua New Guinea.
GEOFF STOCKER

Clearing associated with logging No orchid enthusiast can look at the massive clearing for wood products which has occurred in the Philippines and Borneo, and increasingly in New Guinea and the Solomons, without being concerned for the orchids of these areas. Sustainable logging can leave a forest with many of its features intact, but unfortunately the form of logging practised in many Asian and Pacific nations leaves few trees standing and is often followed by fire, resulting in complete removal of the original forest.

Established patterns of shifting agriculture on hillsides in Papua New Guinea. Use here has been heavy and little primary forest remains. BILL LAVARACK

Clearing for agriculture In Australia, extensive clearing of orchid habitat for agriculture occurred in the nineteenth century and early in the twentieth century. Some clearing of orchid habitat continues, but it is mostly on small areas of private land. Much of the remaining land suitable for orchids is now conserved in reserves and land-clearing is slowing. However, this is not the case in other countries. The transmigration schemes in Indonesia, under which large numbers of people are being moved from Java to places such as Sumatra, Kalimantan and Irian Jaya, are having an impact, particularly on lowland rainforests, with natural forest being cleared for agriculture and for urban development. Deforestation in Indonesia was estimated in 1989 at between 7000 and 12 000 square kilometres per year, second only to Brazil on a world scale. Despite this rapid clearing, much forest remains in Indonesia, but this is not true of the Philippines, where the deforestation rate was about 2100 square kilometres per year up to 1988. The rate has since slowed, mainly because so little remains. Similar problems exist in many other South-East Asian nations.

In much of Indonesia, Papua New Guinea, the Solomons and other Pacific islands there is still good forest cover remaining, but the future does not look too promising for the forests and their orchids, particularly in lowland areas.

Clearing for mining Large open-cut mining operations are a rapidly expanding feature of many areas in the range of the Dendrobiinae. Freeport in Irian Jaya, Ok Tedi in Papua New Guinea and Panguna on Bougainville Island are examples. These mines occupy relatively small areas, but tend to obliterate all vegetation in their vicinity and often have major effects downstream. The roads associated with them provide access to shifting cultivators, hunters and orchid collectors and can result in the opening up of otherwise inaccessible areas. While the impact may be limited in area, it is often in highly significant areas such as ridge tops in moderate to high altitude areas, rich in orchids. The total effect is hard to gauge, but is likely to increase.

Habitat modification

Shifting agriculture The indigenous people of many undeveloped nations in South-East Asia and the Pacific practise a form of farming known as shifting agriculture, which involves the clearing and utilisation of a small patch of rainforest for growing crops for a family group or small village. After a few years, as the nutrients in the soil start to decline, the farmer moves on to another area, allowing secondary forest to take over the plot. Shifting agriculture has been a factor affecting South-East Asian, Malesian and Pacific rainforests for thousands of years. The results have been variable, with a degree of sustainability achieved in some areas, but the degradation of forests occurring in other areas resulting in shrublands or grasslands replacing rainforest. The extensive areas of grassland at low and moderate altitudes in New Guinea and many other high rainfall areas in the tropics are evidence of past failures.

Properly carried out, shifting agriculture can be in balance with the rainforest. However, this is a tenuous balance depending on soil conditions, the frequency of use of a particular site and the length of time it is under cultivation. When the human population increases rapidly, the common result is shorter rotations, increased length of usage of a plot and expansion onto less suitable soils. This results in loss of soil fertility, poor regeneration and increases in weeds. The ultimate result is often imperata grasslands, a habitat that can support far fewer orchids than the original forest. A few species have adapted, however, and some of the Dendrobiinae are remarkably able at colonising disturbed habitats. Roadside cuttings in the highlands of New Guinea often support many species that are normally epiphytic, taking root on rock or even clay banks. Other species, such as *Dendrobium terrestre*, have successfully colonised the grasslands, while *D. lobbii* grows in swamps. Small forest remnants are often rich in orchids, but the overall result is a drastic loss in numbers and diversity of orchids in the area.

Logging Since the Second World War, the South-East Asian and Pacific rainforests have been subjected to a massive expansion in logging operations. The use of plywood as a basic construction material developed in USA and Japan in the late 1950s, resulting in an increase in demand for tropical timbers. The lowland dipterocarp forests of western Malesia are particularly suited to logging, as they consist of relatively uniform forests of good quality timber. Many nations have actively encouraged foreign companies to harvest their timber through tax incentives. The boom moved through the Philippines, then to Peninsular Malaysia, Sabah and Indonesia, Papua New Guinea and the Solomons. As an example, the Philippines exported 8 million cubic metres of timber to Japan in 1969, the amount falling to about 1 million cubic metres annually in the early 1980s as resources were used up.

Unfortunately, most of the logging has been based on short-term profit rather than on sound silvicultural principles. A great deal of incidental damage has been done to other vegetation and little effort has gone into practices that will aid the forest to recover. Canopies have been destroyed, allowing the incursion of grasses and weeds which make the forest more susceptible to fire. Often farmers move in, using the old logging roads, and settle in the regenerating forest, practising shifting or permanent agriculture. In short, the end result of logging is often the complete removal of the original rainforest.

There has been a change in approach in the 1980s and 1990s, as the governments of producing nations have sought to gain more control of the operations and a larger share of the profits. This is potentially of some benefit to the forests, as conservation and other long-term considerations are more likely to be considered when the loggers are local citizens, but the trade continues to be a major factor in deforestation.

While this logging has resulted in massive destruction of species of the Dendrobiinae, it has largely been confined to the lowlands on relatively gentle terrain, leaving the higher mountains largely intact. Epiphytes are least diverse in these lowland forests, being more prominent on ridge tops, areas with cliff faces and gorges, and along streams – all areas subject to less logging pressure. Nonetheless, the destruction of orchids is significant and huge numbers are lost in the logging process.

Fuelwood Cutting of timber for fuel by rural populations is an important factor in many Asian and Malesian communities. It is a significant problem in most nations, but it is in India that the problem is most evident. There, fuelwood production has been estimated to be 13 times the quantity of timber harvested for sawlogs, and to be running at three or four times the level of sustainability. The problem is compounded by the level of population, which is currently about 15 per cent of the world's total. About three-quarters of these people live in rural communities and are dependent on natural resources such as fuelwood. Fuelwood collecting, along with shifting agriculture and the large cattle population (also about 15 per cent of the world total), has resulted in a massive loss of forests in India, perhaps as much as 60 000 square kilometres since the Second World War.

Much of this deforestation has occurred in mountain monsoon forests, a notable habitat for dendrobiums, thus the following species are considered threatened in India. Undoubtedly collecting is also a factor:

TABLE 8
INDIAN SPECIES LOCALLY THREATENED

D. darjilingense Pradham	endangered	not seen in recent times
D. pauciflorum King & Prantl.	endangered/extinct	habitat destruction; not in cultivation
D. perula Rchb.f.	endangered	not seen in recent times
D. rhodocentrom Rchb.f.	endangered	not seen in recent times
D. spatella Rchb.f.	endangered	not seen in recent times
D. strongylanthum Rchb.f.	endangered	not seen in recent times
D. tenuicaule Hook.f.	endangered	not seen in recent times

(Taken from: 'Orchids status survey and conservation action plan IVCN)

Top: A logging operation in Papua New Guinea
GEOFF STOCKER

Above: Logs being converted into woodchips at Madang in Papua New Guinea. BILL LAVARACK

Removal of key species Some species of plants and animals may be critical to the continued existence of the rainforest in its current form. If they are removed, changes in forest composition can occur. The cassowary, which inhabits the rainforests of north-east Australia and New Guinea, may be one such species. Cassowaries feed on rainforest fruits and are known to be important in the distribution of many trees. As one of very few large animal species in the rainforest, cassowaries are a sought-after source of protein for native people and are widely hunted in New Guinea. In Australia hunting is prohibited, but fragmentation of the habitat, attacks by dogs, and accidents with motor vehicles are seriously impacting on the population. Predicting the effect on the rainforests if cassowaries are removed is difficult – it is likely that they would change, but how and to what extent is hard to guess. The effect on orchids is even harder to gauge. The situation is not confined to cassowaries and is no better to the west of Wallace's Line, as virtually all large mammals of the rainforest are under threat and their removal must ultimately have an effect.

Fire In late 1997 and early 1998 forest fires in Indonesia in particular, and in South-East Asia generally, became world headline news. The resulting smoke was a problem for months, causing sickness and deaths, ruining the tourist industry and even being blamed for an airline crash and a collision between a cargo ship and a supertanker in the Strait of Malacca. Estimates of the loss of forests due to fires in Sumatra and Kalimantan vary between 80 000 and 690 000 hectares. The fires were largely started by clearing for oil palm and rubber plantations and were exacerbated by the unusually dry conditions of the El Niño weather pattern. One report suggests that over 300 000 hectares in east Kalimantan burned. As well as the destruction in Indonesia, major losses of rainforest occurred in Thailand, the Philippines and New Guinea.

Timber cut for fuelwood, Papua New Guinea highlands. GEOFF STOCKER

No one has attempted to document the effect of these fires on the orchids of these areas. Several of the areas burnt are regarded as extremely diverse rainforests on a world scale, and the orchid populations must be very high. Fires have been an irregular part of the ecology of this part of the world for many years and major fires occurred in the region as recently as 1983. Rainforest will burn only in extreme conditions, normally those associated with El Niño events, perhaps once a century or even less commonly, but this pattern appears to be changing, due to increasing population pressures and perhaps to global warming and associated climate change. In the past, the plant communities and the orchids associated with them have been able to recover over time when normal rainfall patterns reappear. Today, however, many of the damaged forest areas will be cleared by settlers or plantation developers and all plants and animals of the rainforest, including the orchids, will then be lost forever. Even in those areas not settled, the effect is magnified each time as the

Top: Grasslands possibly caused by, and certainly maintained by, regular fires, highlands of Papua New Guinea near Buana. GEOFF STOCKER

Above: Fire effects in open forests near Port Moresby, Papua New Guinea. Fire is a natural part of the ecosystem and is essential to maintain existing plant and animal communities. GEOFF STOCKER

amount of remaining forest dwindles and sources of seed for recolonising are reduced.

In the more seasonal climates such as northern Australia, southern New Guinea and some areas of the South-East Asian mainland, fire has a different meaning to the ecosystems. The vegetation of these areas is strongly adapted to regular fires, which may be started by humans or by lightning. In northern Australia and southern New Guinea these seasonal forests feature several *Dendrobium* species which have learned to live with the fires, including *D. bigibbum, D. williamsianum, D. affine, D. canaliculatum, D. carronii, D. trilamellatum, D. johannis* and *Dockrillia rigida*. Some of these species grow in small patches of vine forest which occur in places where fire cannot penetrate, such as rocky slopes, river banks, and sand dunes behind the beach. Others grow in areas that are regularly burned, but grow high in the trees beyond the reach of fire. These are all species adapted to strongly seasonal climates that are extremely dry for at least half the year, then experience a heavy reliable wet season, and are never found in areas with a high year round rainfall.

In almost all of Australia the indigenous people managed fire over millennia, resulting in a certain mix of forest types. After white settlement, this regime was replaced in many areas by a management style that excluded fire or managed it to suit the requirements of the grazing industry. What had taken millennia to develop was changed in the space of decades, giving plants and animals insufficient time to adjust. A common result, but by no means the only one, has been that rainforests have taken over adjacent open eucalypt forests. In the eyes of some people this has been a good result, as rainforests have more species and are more attractive, but the fact remains that many plants and animals which occur in open forests and not in rainforests have consequently been reduced in numbers. An example of this is *Dendrobium fellowsii*, a species restricted to the narrow band of tall, moist eucalypt forest which occupies the ecotone between the wet coastal and dry inland climates of north-east Queensland. If the delicate balance is upset and the dry inland forests expand towards the coast, or the coastal rainforests move inland, *D. fellowsii* would suffer.

Weeds By and large, weeds have caused few problems for epiphytic species, although weed growth following major disturbances such as fire and logging can significantly alter the regeneration of forests. In northern Australia two climbing species are having a more direct effect. Rubber vine (*Cryptostegia grandiflora*) smothers vegetation, usually in seasonal climates, and can be particularly destructive in fringing forests which support some orchids. In moister rainforest habitats the ornamental climber blue thunbergia (*Thunbergia grandiflora*) has escaped and is showing the potential to smother patches of rainforest, denying the epiphytes the light they need to survive.

Introduced animals In northern Australia, the introduction of cattle, water buffalo, feral pigs and goats is having an effect on tropical savannas and swamps. The effects are usually incremental and not always immediately apparent, but it is certain that the composition and structure of tropical forests and grasslands is changing due to these animals. The effect on epiphytes is harder to document, but it is likely to be significant.

Orchid collecting

The golden age of plant collectors During the golden age of orchid hunting, collectors such as Wilhelm Micholitz, Thomas Lobb, Carl Roebelin and John Gould Veitch roamed the area between India and the Solomons, ever on the lookout for new and spectacular species that would make the fortunes of their employers in Europe. The first of these orchid importers were Messrs

Loddiges, who established a nursery specialising in orchids in 1812. This establishment flourished for 40 years, supplying new species to the eminent botanist John Lindley. It was soon followed by Messrs H. Low, and J. Veitch and Sons. In 1876 Frederick Sander opened his nursery and quickly established himself as 'the orchid king'. He employed Wilhelm Micholitz as his foremost collector in the Asian area from 1882 to 1914.

The golden age of orchid collectors lasted from about 1840 to 1914 and many fortunes were made and lost. Intrigue, deception and occasional violence worthy of a Hollywood epic were acted out in the jungles of Burma, Borneo and New Guinea. These collectors were after a wide range of plants, not just orchids. Conifers, ferns, palms, rhododendrons, pitcher plants and many others were on the list. Among the orchids, the genera *Paphiopedilum, Phalaenopsis, Vanda* and *Cymbidium* species, were all popular. *Dendrobium* species were always near the top of the list, with *D. nobile, D. johnsoniae, D. atroviolaceum, D. spectatissimum, D. schutzei, D. spectabile, D. wardianum, D. sanderae, D. dearei, D. bigibbum, D. superbiens* and *D. phalaenopsis* (now referred to as *D. striaenopsis*) all in demand. The day of the collectors gradually came to an end at the turn of the century as the supply of spectacular new species started to dry up and hybrids rose to prominence.

Unfortunately, these romantic tales had an unpleasant side to them. Attractive species were taken in huge numbers with no regard for the future of the species in the habitat. The voyage to Europe was long and slow in the dark, alternatively stiflingly hot or bitterly cold holds of sailing ships, where the journey was measured in months. The plants were usually in poor condition on arrival and losses of close to 100 per cent were not uncommon. If there were any sparks of life left, the stressed plants would have long since lost their leaves and needed very careful treatment if they were to survive. In the early part of the century, knowledge of the conditions in the natural habitat was negligible and plants from high and low altitude alike were placed in stove-houses with high year-round temperatures, planted in soggy mixtures of rotten wood and the like and kept constantly wet.

By the middle of the nineteenth century the cultural requirements of epiphytic orchids were better understood. A larger percentage survived the voyage and were successfully grown in Europe. The rewards were significant, with sought-after plants often selling for sums from 100 guineas up to 600 guineas, a small fortune in Victorian times.

The number of plants collected sounds horrendous to modern ears, particularly when it is realised that few survived the voyage and even more died soon afterwards in the inappropriate environment of the stove-house. Shipments of thousands of a particular species were not uncommon. However, in the setting of the undisturbed jungles of more than a century ago, the collected plants were probably soon replaced by natural processes, and the attention of the collectors was focused on only a small proportion of the orchid species of an area. Undoubtedly there are many examples where serious damage was done, particularly in the case of the slipper orchids (*Paphiopedilum* spp.), but few dendrobiums would have been threatened by this collecting fever. Another factor operating in the nineteenth century was that orchid growing was the preserve of the wealthy. Few could afford the expensive glasshouses and the heating required in Europe and the northern part of the USA. Thus the market was limited and able to be satisfied by the plants which survived the rigours of the sea trips. This golden age of orchid collecting was brought to an abrupt end by the First World War, which saw unnecessary luxuries, such as orchid collections and heated glasshouses, virtually wiped out in Europe. The tradition had been established, however, and orchids have never lost their popularity.

For all its excesses, this golden age achieved great public popularity for orchids and aroused a great deal of scientific interest in the orchid family. The prominent botanists of the nineteenth century worked closely with the orchid houses and awaited the shipments from the commercial collectors as avidly as the orchid growers. These shipments frequently resulted in new species being described by Lindley, Reichenbach, Hooker, Rolfe and others, providing an important scientific spin-off. Lindley, for example, described more than 100 genera and 3000 species of orchids, including many of the species still popular today. In summary, it is probably fair to say that, while many unfortunate things occurred, the orchid-collecting industry of the nineteenth century may have had some beneficial side-effects for the survival of many orchid species, in that a tradition of scientific study of orchids was established along with a popular public affection for the family.

Wild-collected orchids for sale in a Bangkok market. JIM COMBER

The modern age Since the period between the wars, a change has been taking place in the orchid community. Orchid growing has gradually come within the reach of more people, many of whom are now living in warmer climates such as eastern Australia, California, the southern states of the USA, Latin America and Asia. A heated glasshouse is now more affordable for those living in Europe, Japan and Northern USA than previously. Fortunately for wild orchid populations, however, much of this new demand is satisfied by artificially raised hybrids, although underlying this there has always been a strong demand for species, including many dendrobiums. Increasingly these species collections today are being filled with seedlings from cultivated sources, but from the 1920s to the late 1970s most plants came from the wild and it is likely that considerable damage was done to wild populations during that time. In a randomly selected issue of an orchid journal from that era (*Australian Orchid Review*, September 1947), of 17 paid advertisements six are for orchids which are clearly wild-collected from India and Malaya. One advertisement proclaims '125,000 strong plants ready for shipment'; others from this era proclaim 'we collect in huge quantities' and 'no order too large'. The damage would have been magnified by the fact that it occurred on top of land-clearing and forest degradation in many developing nations. The Convention on International Trade in Endangered Species of Wild Fauna and Flora (CITES) was ratified by many nations in 1973 and there is little doubt that this had a significant effect in reducing the trade in wild-collected plants, thereby encouraging nurseries to grow the species from seed.

Removal of plants from the wild still occurs. There are nations where the removal of plants is permitted or where the laws are not enforced, and plants from the wild are still traded internationally, despite CITES. It is likely that wild-harvested plants are passed off as artificially cultivated by some unscrupulous dealers, although such cases would be less common than they once were. In some areas there is a level of collecting by local people for their own use. In Australia this is a significant problem, which increases in significance as habitats are reduced in area. Most of the removal of Cooktown orchids (*Dendrobium bigibbum*) since the war has been for the local market, an activity over which CITES has no control. New State laws have, however, proved effective in reducing, even eliminating, illegal commercial collecting. A level of illegal private collecting remains, but is reducing as growers turn to artificially raised seedlings.

Case studies

Dendrobium atroviolaceum is a particularly attractive species now known to occur in the D'Entrecasteaux Islands and the Louisiade Archipelago off the eastern tip of New Guinea. It was first introduced to Europe in about 1890 and was described from the first plant to flower in cultivation. For some years there was some doubt about its native habitat, but the collectors from John Veitch and Sons clearly knew, as there are records of 40 000 plants being imported into England, most of which failed to survive more than a year or two.

Top: *Dendrobium atroviolaceum* from the D'Entrecastreaux Islands and the Louisiade Archipelago in eastern Papua New Guinea.
WAYNE HARRIS

Above: *Dendrobium spectabile* from New Guinea.
BILL LAVARACK

Apparently few, if any, plants of *D. atroviolaceum* survived for the long term in England, but in 1962 Hermon Slade reported his surprise on finding a large number of healthy plants growing in a collection in Germany where plants were being raised from seed and sold. These had presumably survived more than half a century in cultivation. Phillip Cribb (1983) mentions large numbers being collected in recent times, but reports suggest the species is still abundant in the habitat. Strict controls on exporting orchids from Papua New Guinea have probably put a stop to most of the collecting, but it occurs in a remote island location and illegal collections are quite possible.

D. atroviolaceum is relatively easy to propagate from seed, and there are now plenty of plants in cultivation, so there is little valid reason for more plants to be removed from the wild.

Dendrobium spectabile was first described in 1855 by Blume but was not encountered again for many years and remained a mystery plant to horticulture in the last half of the nineteenth century. The weirdly shaped large flowers clearly represented potential commercial success to anyone who could successfully import plants to England. Determined to be the first to offer it for sale, the well-known orchid nurseryman Frederick Sander dispatched his most reliable collector, William Micholitz, to the Solomon Islands in 1897 in an attempt to find and collect it. About 1500 plants were collected and dispatched, but all died on the sea trip.

Within a year, however, another large consignment of this species had arrived in England and enough survived to cause great interest in orchid circles.

Dendrobium striaenopsis *(D. phalaenopsis* **var.** *schroderianum)* This spectacular orchid, originally identified as *Dendrobium phalaenopsis* and subsequently known informally as '*D. schroderianum*', was discovered on the Tanimbar Islands south-west of New Guinea in 1882 by the naturalist H.O. Forbes. Micholitz was dispatched by Frederick Sander in 1890 in an attempt to rediscover and collect this species. After considerable difficulty, he discovered them on coastal limestone cliffs used as a cemetery by the local people, where in many cases the orchids were growing among the bones of the dead. A large number was collected, but soon after was destroyed in a fire on board ship. Micholitz was instructed to return and collect more plants. He was almost caught up in a local war on this occasion, but eventually found more plants which this time arrived in England without mishap. The auctioning of one plant attached to a skull caused a sensation. The locality given at the time was 'N E New Guinea' – probably a deliberate error to throw rival collectors off the scent, as the Tanimbar Islands are actually off the south-western coast of New Guinea.

Reading these accounts one can only wonder at the tenacity and personal bravery of the early collectors. Apparently the local people put aside their concerns at the disturbance of the bones of their ancestors when they saw the 'gorgeous handkerchiefs, looking glasses, etc.' which Micholitz offered them. The effect of these two collections, and the others which almost certainly followed, on this species of limited distribution can only be guessed at, although plants remain on the islands today. These plants were the parents of many of the modern hard-cane hybrids. Today the name '*D. striaenopsis*' or '*D. bigibbum* var. *laratensis*' is applied to these plants from Taninbar. They are closely related to *D. bigibbum* from Torres Strait to the east.

The Cooktown orchid – *Dendrobium bigibbum* F.M. Bailey, the Queensland Colonial Botanist, visited Torres Strait in 1897 and wrote, 'The beautiful orchids for which these islands used to be favoured are fast disappearing, at least from anywhere easy of approach from Thursday Island – such is the case with regard to the varieties of *Dendrobium bigibbum* Lindl., which are the kinds most sought after.' The southern form of this species, *D. bigibbum* var. *superbum*, was commonly known a hundred years ago as the 'Cooktown orchid'. Unfortunately it is now absent from the surrounds of Cooktown where, we are told, travellers once marvelled at the sight of the purple flowers along the roads.

As recently as late as the 1970s, advertisements for Cooktown orchids appeared regularly, offering discounts for lots of 100 or 500 plants. Regular shipments of up to 10 000 plants were rumoured to be coming out of Cape York Peninsula and one shipment of 8000 plants was seized by police in 1983. Potential buyers were informed that plants could be supplied in virtually any numbers. All of these were collected, not seed-raised, plants and most were sold through large chain stores in Sydney and Melbourne in totally unsuitable climates and to people with little idea of their cultural requirements. Plants survived for a year on the food reserves stored in the pseudobulbs and responded to their approaching death by producing a last burst of flowers in an attempt to reproduce before dying. This often prompted the owner to purchase a new plant when the original finally died. Clearly the Queensland State laws of the time were ineffective, but fortunately Cape York Peninsula is a wild, remote and often dangerous place, and plants have survived this rash of collecting in out-of-the-way places, often in quite large numbers.

In the last 15 years two factors have combined to reduce this trade in Cooktown orchids. Stronger laws with heavy penalties have been introduced for illegal trading, and plants raised from seed are now available. Although the Queensland laws initially attracted some criticism from orchid growers, they now have general acceptance and it is now uncommon to see wild-collected Cooktown orchids offered for sale. This has provided the breathing space needed for the commercial nurseries to produce plants raised from seed. Previously when they had to compete with large wild-collected plants, there was no market for seedlings which were smaller and more expensive. Now the market is growing and the competition from illegal plants is decreasing, particularly as the seedlings are invariably raised from the best horticultural forms.

Medicinal use

Dendrobiums have long had a prominent place as medicines in many traditional cultures, nowhere more so than among the Chinese. A range of species, mostly in the section *Dendrobium*, are favoured, with *D. nobile* being the most widely used, as detailed in Chapter 4, 'Traditional uses'. The total impact of collection for medicinal use is hard to gauge, but will become more important as natural habitats shrink and human populations expand.

The remedies

How do we conserve orchids?

The desire to conserve expresses itself largely through the actions of governments, as individuals have limited power. Individuals are not completely powerless, however, and with the help of orchid societies there are many ways in which they can contribute.

Some new approaches in conservation are needed in the twenty-first century. While prohibition and restrictions may still be required for certain actions, and complete protection is warranted for a few critically endangered species, an approach that emphasises compromise, sustainable use of resources, and benefits for local people, is much more likely to succeed. Strategies conceived in western nations such as the USA, Australia or the European countries often fail because they do not allow for the complex effects of such issues as traditional cultures and land ownership in many developing nations, for example, Papua New Guinea. They can also fail if they attempt to unreasonably lock up resources necessary for life in areas with an expanding population. On the other hand, in developed countries, laws that totally prohibit the ownership of, or the trade in, horticulturally desirable species can lose public support and fail if they are seen to be poorly thought out and unreasonable.

Conservation goals should involve the retention of as much of the natural vegetation cover of the world as possible. In many nations, the best way to achieve this is by emphasising the value of intact forests and ensuring that standing forests have a value to local communities, in addition to ensuring that such communities have the knowledge to allow them to gain some benefit from this natural resource in a sustainable way.

Conserving orchids or any other form of wildlife in the South-East Asia–Pacific region is tied up with big picture issues such as population growth, quality of life and possibly global warming. There is little that people interested in orchid conservation can do to influence such issues, and their attention is probably best focused on more down-to-earth activities. Conservation strategies in the twenty-first century should be based on three basic principles:

1. making the habitat of the species valuable in intact, or nearly intact, form;
2. encouraging the sustainable propagation of orchids, preferably by local people, making the orchids valuable; and
3. encouraging hobby growers to grow rare species raised from seed and to learn about the plants they grow.

The problem needs to approached at two levels – on site and off site:

On-site conservation

Reserving habitat The aim of on-site conservation is to preserve numbers of a variety of orchid species in their habitat. The most obvious way to do this is to reserve land and place it in a secure tenure, such as national park, where significant clearing cannot occur and where any disturbance of the habitat is sustainable. The difficulty here is that different nations have varying concepts of what should be permitted to occur in a national park. Some allow mining and damaging activities such as shifting agriculture, others prohibit almost all disturbance. From an orchid perspective, what matters is that the habitat remains intact enough to allow the orchids to grow and reproduce naturally.

Most South-East Asian–Pacific nations are signatories to various international treaties and conventions that advocate conservation in one form or another. CITES will be discussed later, but two other treaties dealing with protected areas are of particular interest. These are the Convention Concerning the Protection of the World and Natural Heritage, and the Association of South-East Asian Nations (ASEAN), which has an environment program. Many large reserves in the region are designated ASEAN sites. World Heritage Areas are subject to an international treaty, which is intended to ensure that any use is sustainable, and may represent the best option in many countries.

Table 8 tells a rather sorry story of the destruction of rainforests and the efforts to set aside a series of reserves to conserve them. That rainforests and their orchids should be cleared is certainly inevitable as population increases and as people demand a higher standard of living. What is not inevitable, however, is that all, or even most, of the forests' original species become extinct. In virtually all areas it is not too late to ensure that representative samples of the forests are retained, either as conservation reserves or as production forests, preferably as a combination of both. Table 8 shows that in many areas more than half of the forests remain, and that in some key areas such as Indonesia (69 per cent) and Papua New Guinea (81 per cent), huge tracts of rainforest are still intact. Other orchid-rich areas such as Thailand (42 per cent), the Philippines (22 per cent) and China (7 per cent) tell a less encouraging story, but even there sufficient forest remains to conserve most species if clearing rates are reduced and representative reserves are set aside.

The directions taken in setting up a network of conservation reserves depends to a large degree on the land tenure system of each particular nation. A comparison between two geographically adjacent, but politically very different nations, is an interesting example.

Australia has large areas of state-owned land in the tropics, including most remaining orchid habitats. This makes it relatively easy to create new reserves. Large areas can be set aside, as has been done in the Wet Tropics World Heritage Area, which totals about 9200 square kilometres and includes most of the remaining rainforests. Even privately owned land can be purchased by government and converted to reserve tenure and, while there is sometimes local opposition to such actions, national opinion has, to date, supported them. In Table 8 Australia, a relatively affluent developed nation, has by far the largest proportion of its remaining moist closed forests reserved, at 72.3 per cent. However, it must be remembered that Australia had very little rainforest to start with.

In Papua New Guinea, a young developing nation, the forests are more intact than those of most other areas, but this surely will not last. There are very few reserves – in fact Table 8 shows that Papua New Guinea, with 2.4 per cent of its remaining forests reserved, has one of the lowest percentages in the region. An important reason for this lies in land ownership. Ninety-seven per cent of Papua New Guinea is held in traditional ownership – attempts to create large national parks or other reserves would usually be vetoed by the traditional owners, or they would request prohibitively large compensation. If reserves are to be set up, they must have the support of the local people or they will not survive. Local people will give their support only if they gain benefit from the reserve. This may involve use of the reserve for hunting and gathering, a village-based timber industry or even shifting agriculture. Limits on this use to ensure sustainability could be set by consultation and negotiation. Perhaps there could be zoning, with generous buffer zones, concentric zones of decreasing use and a central core with almost complete protection. Owners must be heavily involved in making these decisions and in any tourist trade that the reserve might generate. They could also be encouraged to raise orchids and other plants from seed for sale internationally. The agreement could exclude large-scale logging or clearing. There have been a few attempts to set up reserves of this type in Irian Jaya with cooperation by local people, but at present the future of the forests of New Guinea hang in the balance and with them lies the fate of the most diverse group of the Dendrobiinae.

Some nations are setting targets such as 5 per cent or 10 per cent of their remaining forests to be set aside in reserves. There is a need to ensure that such programs are targeted at important diverse areas and that there is coordination between neighbouring nations. The program must not fall in the trap of accepting only land of inferior development potential. A range of different reserves is usually appropriate. In some, conservation will be the only use, while in others varying degrees of use and disturbance can be permitted, ranging from tourism to sustainable timber production. With respect to orchids, the only removal from reserves should be from salvage situations or, in certain carefully regulated cases, the collection of stock plants for propagation could be permitted.

It is important that government does not consider its job is completed when an area is formally designated as a reserve. The land set aside must be managed and policed. Repeatedly in the past, reserved land has been logged and even settled illegally. It is important that local people are heavily involved in its management.

How useful are reserves? Clearly the best reserves are both large and diverse. Recognised centres of biodiversity are the heart of orchid conservation. Some such areas are obvious, but it is essential that more work be undertaken to identify and document them. While this is occurring, steps should be taken to ensure that those already known and those to be identified in the future, are never subject to clearing. Fortunately many are in rugged areas which are not likely to be cleared, but there still remain threats from mining, shifting agriculture and wildfires. Clearly the needs of tribal peoples who use these areas for pursuits such as hunting and gathering or shifting agriculture must be met. Where their activities are no longer in balance with nature, developed nations should be providing assistance aimed at allowing them to make the change from shifting to permanent agriculture.

TABLE 9
REMAINING AREAS OF RAINFORESTS AND AMOUNT CONSERVED IN RESERVES*

Nation	Original area of rainforests (sq km)	Percentage of rainforests remaining	Area of rainforests conserved or proposed for conservation (sq km)	Percentage of original rainforests reserved	Percentage of remaining rainforests reserved
Australia (tropical parts only)	11 000	95.6	7 605	69.1	72.3
Bangladesh	130 000	7.5	744	0.5	7.6
Myanmar (Burma)	600 000	51.9	13 040	2.2	4.2
Cambodia	160 000	70.8	25 026	15.6	22.1
China and Taiwan	340 000	7.6	4 155	1.2	16.1
India	910 000	25.1	41 500	4.5	18.1
Indonesia	1700 000	69.3	265 938	15.6	22.5
Laos	225 000	55.3	47 211	21.0	37.9
Peninsular Malaysia	130 000	53.6	12 700	9.8	18.2
Sabah and Sarawak	190 000	68.7	14 951	7.9	11.4
Papua New Guinea	450 000	81.5	9 164	2.0	2.4
Philippines	295 000	22.3	2 395	0.8	3.6
Sri Lanka	26 000	47.1	6 309	24.3	51.5
Thailand	250 000	42.7	56 645	22.7	53.0
Vietnam	280 000	20.2	6 252	2.2	11.0

*This table is modified from *The Conservation Atlas of Tropical Moist Forests – Asia and the Pacific*. The figures quoted were published in 1991, so the current situation may well have changed significantly.

Remnants – or is size important? While large diverse reserves are obviously best, the small remnants which are left after clearing or after the conversion of forest to grassland by fire or shifting agriculture are often very rich in orchids. These remnants, in gullies, along creeks or on very steep slopes, often represent areas naturally rich in orchids prior to clearing and provide a good sample of the original orchid flora of the area, as long as collectors are not permitted to denude them. Maintaining these remnants is important, but there is a problem – most are on land where the law gives the owners the right to clear. Even if the owners choose not to clear, because of logistical problems or other reasons, they are unlikely to spend money or effort in managing unproductive land. In this case, weed growth or uncontrolled fire can eventually lead to the end of the remnant as a useful conservation area. In other areas such remnants can be seriously degraded by fuelwood collecting. There is a need to catalogue these remnants and either add them to the list of conservation reserves, or encourage the owners to manage them, using financial or other incentives.

If land must be cleared, certain things can be done to help the continued existence of orchids. Strips should be left along the streams, patches of forest can be left on steep slopes or on rocky hillsides. Patches can be left in the corner of a block. Perhaps neighbouring landholders can be encouraged to cooperate by leaving adjacent patches so that a larger area is left uncleared. Where possible corridors along streams or boundaries should be left to link larger protected areas. Single trees or groups of trees in a pasture are better than nothing, as long as some forest remains nearby to act as a seed source. Often such lone trees are well stocked with orchids. This is very much a last resort, however. Leaving a few trees in a pasture is better than leaving none – but while it may benefit some orchids it is of limited conservation value generally.

Ecotourism Ecotourism is a rapidly expanding industry with many tourists from Europe, Asia and America interested in seeing natural environments in the tropics. A combination of factors such as a stable and safe political environment and interesting features such as spectacular wildlife, spectacular scenery and an interesting local culture may well provide opportunities for ecotourism. Other factors may include a pleasant climate, opportunities for activities such as fishing, hiking or diving, and the opportunity to see orchids and other interesting plants easily in their habitat – thus ensuring that plants are not removed becomes an important aspect of forest management. Similarly it is important that an appropriate fire regime be maintained, ensuring both that the orchids grow to their potential and that guests are not at risk from wildfires.

Opportunities should be made for local tribal people to be involved in all aspects of such ecotourism ventures as guides, lodge staff and managers, and that they are trained in the interpretive and other skills required.

Off-site conservation

International conventions – Convention on International Trade in Endangered Species (CITES) Of the several international conventions and treaties which seek to control things such as habitat destruction or trade in threatened species, the most important of these, as far as orchids are concerned, is CITES. This Convention was originally created in 1973 and came into force in 1975, with 21 nations ratifying it at that time. By 1995, 128 nations were signatories. The Convention aims at reducing the threats to threatened species of plants and animals through agreed controls on the species in three lists or Appendices. Appendix I includes 'those plants threatened with extinction which are, or may be, affected by trade'. Currently seven species and two genera of orchids are listed on Appendix I – *Cattleya triannaei, Dendrobium cruentum,*

Laelia jongheana, L. lobata, Peristeria elata, Renanthera imschootiana, Vanda coerulea and the genera *Paphiopedilum* and *Phragmipedium*. Plants of these species can be traded internationally only if accompanied by an export certificate and an import certificate from both exporting and importing countries. Generally speaking, the provisions virtually rule out commercial trade in wild-collected plants from Appendix I, although there are exceptions where both exporting and importing nations agree that the trade is not detrimental to the survival of the species and is not primarily for commercial purposes.

Appendix II includes 'those plants (a) which although not necessarily now threatened with extinction may become so unless trade in specimens of such species is subject to strict regulation in order to avoid utilisation incompatible with their survival and (b) other species which must be subject to regulation in order that trade in specimens of certain species referred to in subparagraph (a) of this paragraph may be brought under effective control'. All orchids not on Appendix I are included on Appendix II. Wild-taken plants and propagated plants of these species can be traded only with export certificates issued by the management authority of the exporting country. Plants of Appendix II in flasks, cut flowers from propagated plants, pollen and seed do not require a permit. There is a similar exemption for flasks and sales for Appendix I plants.

It is the responsibility of the nations which have signed the Convention to enact local laws to ensure its provisions are followed in the import and export of orchids and other listed plants. Some nations have elected to be even stricter than the Convention requires under the provisions of these laws, and it is here that some criticism has occurred. On the other hand there have also been examples of corruption or carelessness in the granting of export licences, with wild-collected plants being passed off as propagated plants. Some problems have arisen in interpreting what is meant by 'artificially propagated', particularly the conditions under which 'division' can be an acceptable form of artificial propagation. It seems likely that wild-collected plants are sometimes passed off as divisions, but how large a problem this is, is not known. While in theory it is desirable to allow trade in artificially propagated plants, it is not always possible to determine the origin of a plant from its appearance. Cultivation methods in some tropical countries results in plants that are virtually indistinguishable from plants recently collected from the wild, making it impossible for inspecting officials in importing countries to be certain of a plant's origin.

Another major source of criticism has been the listing of the entire family on Appendices I and II. This was done because it is virtually impossible for customs officers to identify an orchid when not in flower. A better method might be the listing by genus of those plants where trade might be a factor in their conservation. The current situation of all orchids being on Appendix II, when it is obvious that most are under no threat from international trade, has led to a lack of confidence in, and respect for, CITES which may be reflected in local laws. Laws which lack community support rarely succeed in the long term, so it may well be time that a more rational listing for orchids was sought. From another point of view, there has been continuing criticism that the Convention is too focused on spectacular or cute animals and devotes too little time to plants.

Enforcement of the laws relating to the convention is a major problem, being variable from country to country and sometimes between officials from the same country. Many officials are poorly trained, lack understanding of the reasons for the laws and lack the expertise to identify plants. In some poorer developing nations, where actions such as the enforcement of CITES are understandably given low priority, and where officials are both poorly paid and poorly trained, there are many problems in its enaction.

One unplanned beneficial effect that CITES may have had is that administrative fees levied by governments increase the price and thereby reduce the demand for plants from developing countries and, by reducing competition from wild-collected plants, increases the economic viability of propagation from seed in developed countries. If this is the case, CITES has certainly benefited orchid conservation, although not by the intended route.

Deliberate flouting of the provisions of CITES appears to remain a problem for some species. In the 1980s a large number of plants of *Paphiopedilum sanderianum* and *P. rothschildianum* were taken, presumably from national parks in Borneo, and advertised for sale in Europe and the USA at up to $5000 each. Where such large amounts of money are at stake, it is extremely difficult to stop such activities. In the case of these two orchids, their numbers were so small that this incident almost wiped them out in their habitat. Fortunately few, if any, of the Dendrobiinae could command such prices. Such activity is usually limited to a very small number of target species.

In summary, while there are problems and loopholes in CITES and its implementation in some countries, there is no doubt that it has had a major effect in slowing down international trade in wild-collected orchids. To simply abandon CITES and allow open trading in wild-collected plants in this time of habitat destruction would be unthinkable, but there remains scope for improving the its effectiveness by reassessing the provisions for trade in artificially propagated plants, streamlining Appendix II and exploring the possibilities of promoting the use of plants from salvage. An important feature of the Convention is that it encourages trade in artificially raised plants by placing no restrictions on international trade in seed or seedlings in flasks.

Local laws Whatever effect CITES has on international trade in orchids, it does not affect collecting and trade within a nation. Most nations have conservation laws that control the removal of orchids from the wild. Some also control trade and may also limit or even prohibit export of native orchids. As an example, laws introduced by the Australian state of Queensland in 1994 were successful in controlling the removal of orchids from the wild. These laws made it an offence to remove plants from the wild without a licence and also made it illegal to trade in certain plants unless licensed. Licences were to be granted only to those who could demonstrate a legal source of supply, such as plants from salvage. Concessions were granted to those who could demonstrate that they were propagating orchids from seed. Since then trade in wild-taken plants in Queensland has fallen markedly, providing the incentive for nurseries to produce native orchid species from seed.

Recommendations for internal conservation laws In framing laws for conserving orchids the following principles are recommended for consideration.

> **General principles**
> 1. All permitted use of threatened plants from undisturbed habitats must be sustainable.
> 2. Prohibit all collecting from reserves except for scientific research or conservation purposes.
> 3. Protect threatened (especially endangered) species on all land tenures.
> 4. Encourage genuine propagators of threatened plants.
> 5. Make sure illegally collected plants cannot enter the trade.
> 6. Discourage or prohibit collecting of plants from uncleared land.
> 7. Encourage salvage operations from logging or clearing.

- In many nations wild-growing plants are the property of the land-owner, making the framing of laws about the use of the plants difficult. Where possible, threatened plants, in particular endangered plants, should become the property of the State. Whether this is possible or not, the State should retain the right to intervene on private land to ensure the future of such plants and to control (not necessarily prohibit) their use in trade.

- As well as controlling the taking of wild orchids, the law should also control the trading of plants taken from the wild. Controls on trading are required because it is not always possible to prevent the removal of plants from remote areas, and the most effective method of preventing illegal collection is to ensure that illegal plants cannot enter the trade. Only those who can demonstrate a legal source of supply should be granted licences to trade in threatened species.

- The laws should allow for the legal collection and trading in plants from salvage situations such as clearing and logging. The major problem that can arise from this is the 'laundering' of plants taken illegally by passing them off as salvaged plants, and a form of licensing or tagging may be required to control this.

- People propagating orchids from seed and trading in the artificially raised seedlings must not be adversely affected by the laws. For example, those who can show that they are genuine propagators of threatened plants should have any licence fee waived. Where possible active encouragement should be given to genuine propagators of threatened species.

- Because it is virtually impossible to differentiate plants from legal sources from those from illegal sources when they are offered for sale, it may be necessary to have some form of identification for legal plants, such as a tagging system.

- Authorities should not use conservation laws to generate revenue by licence fees and the like. Covering of costs of licensing is appropriate if the law allows plants to be taken from uncleared land, but where the plants are artificially propagated or are from salvage, fees should be much reduced or waived. High licence fees in these situations can be counterproductive to the aims of conservation.

- There should be extremely tight laws with heavy penalties controlling illegal collection from reserves.
- The growing of even the most threatened species in private collections should not be prohibited and should even be encouraged, as long as the plants are obtained legally.
- The laws might contain provisions allowing licensed nurseries to collect stock plants from the wild, under certain conditions such as a prohibition on the sale of any such collected plants, with all trading to be from their progeny.
- The law might allow the taking of a small number of plants from the wild for private use, where it is sustainable and with the consent of the land-owner, but be stricter with respect to commercial collecting. There are several aspects to be considered before such a law is drafted – e.g. does it create a loophole for illegal commercial trading?
- The collection of seed from the wild might be permitted, subject to certain conditions such as where seed may be collected and how much seed may be taken and of which species. A possible condition might be that the collector has a demonstrated capacity to grow plants from the seed and distribute them commercially. Such a provision could encourage people to obtain plants raised from seed rather than obtaining wild-taken plants.
- There should be provisions to encourage land-owners to retain valuable fragments of habitat on their property and, if possible, compensation should be available so that they are not disadvantaged by this action.
- Where encouragement fails, the law should provide for compulsory prevention of clearing on land of any tenure where endangered species are present. Such laws should be used only as a last resort when all other avenues have failed and the future survival of a species is at risk. In such cases owners should be fairly compensated for the land resumed.

These principles and recommendations must be considered in the light of local circumstances. For example, it might be, in some cases, too complex and too demanding of resources for developing nations to administer a licence system for plants taken from salvage, and a blanket ban on commercial taking of orchids from the wild might be the best option. Allowing a harvest from salvage, desirable as it may be, might well result in illegal plants entering the trade where there are not sufficient resources to police the taking. In extreme situations, where enforcement resources are minimal, it is probably best to allow only the export of seed, seedlings in flasks or, perhaps, small seedlings that can clearly be demonstrated to have come from cultivation. However, if there are significant numbers of orchids potentially available for export from logging operations, it might well pay the government to employ inspectors or even collectors to establish a government salvage business, or a strictly controlled private operation.

Clearly a major factor in the usefulness of these laws is the ability to enforce them. Even the best laws are ineffective if there are no trained staff to police them. It is also important that enforcement officers understand the laws and are knowledgeable about the species and the trade that the laws seek to control.

Before such laws can be effective the government needs to know which species occur within their boundaries and their conservation status. The data for many parts of Asia are patchy or lacking and it should be a priority of orchid researchers to produce good inventories of orchid-rich nations in the South-East Asia–Pacific region.

The Orchid Specialist Group of IUCN/SSC The Orchid Specialist Group (OSG) is part of the International Union for the Conservation of Nature (IUCN), Species Survival Commission (SSC). This group comprises members from many nations and at the time of writing is chaired by Dr Phillip Cribb.

The Orchid Specialist Group published a Status Survey and Conservation Action Plan for Orchids in 1996. Compiled by Alec M. Pridgeon, this is the most important publication dealing with the conservation of orchids yet published. All the issues associated with threats to orchid populations, and the methods required to deal with them, are discussed by a range of experienced authors from around the world. It surveys the threats to orchids globally and then provides a series of recommendations for action. These are aimed selectively at (1) scientists and national governments, (2) OSG members and (3) orchid societies.

Members of the OSG should become involved in matters such as the drafting of conservation laws, the development of lists of orchids from important areas, helping societies and others to develop conservation programs, encouraging and assisting with the development of recovery plans for endangered species, encouraging taxonomic and ecological work on poorly known species, helping to develop education programs on orchid conservation.

There is much knowledge that needs to be gained and much research to be carried out. The OSG should be sowing seeds for research projects such as:

- Production of orchid inventories and threatened species lists in developing nations.
- Researching the limits of sustainability for things such as shifting agriculture, fuelwood gathering, hunting wildlife for food.
- Examining how people in developing nations could be encouraged to propagate and sell plants threatened by horticultural collecting (e.g. orchids, cycads).
- Determining how remaining forests can be made valuable as forests rather than as wood chips – possibilities include ecotourism, sustainable harvest of certain plants and animals, payments by multinationals or foreign governments for 'carbon credits' (a procedure where landholders are paid to retain vegetation cover on their land), selective logging rather than clear felling.
- Determining whether natural orchid populations can sustain a level of harvesting. Little is known about recruitment of seedlings to the population. If mature plants are removed are they replaced and, if so, how quickly?
- Management of fire.

Propagation by local indigenous people Papua New Guinea has taken the position of prohibiting the export of their native orchids, and it is hard to argue with this, given the lack of available resources to police any permitted export trade. There have been attempts to involve local people in artificial propagation and export of orchid flasks or seedlings. Orchid gardens can be a part of the propagation activities and could serve the double purpose of providing seed and an attraction for tourists. Such schemes are expensive to set up and may benefit relatively few people, but are still worthy of perseverance, although none has so far been successful. At present Papua New Guinea orchids are being propagated and sold by overseas interests with little benefit to the local people. Nonetheless, the situation has value for orchid conservation in that plants are available to the orchid-buying public and the demand for wild-collected plants is greatly reduced.

Conservation by cultivation Thirty or forty years ago there was only limited interest in 'improving' plant species. Most orchid enthusiasts were interested in the plants as they occurred in the wild, or in hybrids, and in the successful culture of those plants. Recent developments in line breeding mean that many growers today no longer want the 'inferior' wild forms. In terms of conservation this is a mixed blessing. It has certainly resulted in a lessening of collecting pressure – but how useful are the resulting plants for conservation? Could they be used to repopulate an area denuded of some or all its orchids? Sadly, most have been so genetically altered that there is little chance they would survive long in the wild. For a reintroduction to be successful, the largest possible range of genetic variation is needed in the introduced stock. In addition, extreme care has to be taken to ensure the plants go back to an area from which they once came.

For plants in cultivation to be significantly useful in conservation, there is need for long-term security such as can be provided only by an institution such as a botanic garden. Even here there are risks, as botanic gardens change their focus and their expertise waxes and wanes over the years. Only a small number of species can be accommodated in gardens and only a fraction of the genetic diversity will be present.

While conserving plants by cultivation may not be the ultimate solution to orchid conservation issues, it is certainly better to have the plants in cultivation than to lose them entirely. The undoubted benefit of cultivating orchid species is that it takes pressure off wild populations, allowing the public to learn more about rare species and to appreciate them and the need for their conservation.

Role of orchid societies Orchid societies should promote the propagation and growing of native orchids, ensuring that all laws are scrupulously obeyed in obtaining and selling native orchids. Orchid societies should educate their members and the public about the diversity of orchids in their region and their values, through meetings and shows. They should be prepared to extend this education to government where appropriate and should be active in lobbying government about local and national orchid conservation issues.

When the need arises, orchid societies should be able to provide a bank of experienced people for conservation projects such as rehabilitation of local degraded habitats, relocation of plants from an area about to be cleared or the development of an orchid collection in a local botanic garden.

They should support research projects aimed at producing inventories or obtaining data useful for conservation, both in their country and in nearby developing nations.

Code for orchid growers

Several codes have been published to help people interested in studying native orchids without damaging the natural populations. The following are some ideas on the matter:

General

- Be familiar with and obey the relevant laws.
- If you disagree with a law, don't simply flout it and congratulate yourself with getting away with it – rather, lobby to have the law changed.
- Do not purchase wild-collected plants unless you are certain they are from salvage.
- If you see or hear of wild-collected plants being sold without the appropriate tags or documentation, or if you see wild-collected plants being sold as propagated plants, report it to the relevant authorities.
- Give priority to orchids from your particular area in your collection – even if they did not cost anything and have small flowers.
- Avoid plants for which you do not have the correct cultural conditions.
- Learn as much as you can about the orchids from your area, including how to identify them.
- Report any interesting new finds in your area to the appropriate scientific institution.
- If you are able to, collect seeds from your plants, have them propagated and distribute them to other growers.
- If you hear of clearing, see if you can organise your society to salvage plants.
- Never tell people whom you do not know well, the localities of any rare species you find.

When collecting from uncleared land

- Do not collect illegally – always have the relevant permits and the land-owner's permission, and never collect from reserves.
- If you are collecting legally, take only what you need.
- Do not take plants that you know you cannot grow.
- Never take a plant unless there are several other plants of that species in the area.
- Where possible leave part of the plant in situ to continue to grow.
- Collect carefully so that minimal damage is done to the orchids, their hosts and other adjacent plants.

CHAPTER 6

Biology and Ecology

This discussion of the biology of the Dendrobiinae includes an outline of their distribution, morphology, physiology and reproductive characteristics. 'Ecology' is used in the sense of the relationships between a species or group within the Dendrobiinae and its natural physical, chemical and biological environment. For instance, an aspect of the ecology of a species might be the relationship between species distribution within a region and variations in mean annual rainfall. Ecological studies of a particular species can provide the grower with important clues to ways in which the growth of that species in cultivation might be optimised. Finally, there are some observations on how constraints imposed on the dendrobiums by their biology, especially the structure of their seeds, their plant habit and physiology, assist us in understanding not only their ecology but also their distribution, taxonomy and evolution.

General distribution

Dendrobiums are found throughout the western Pacific and East Asian regions, from as far north as Japan to as far south as Tasmania and southern New Zealand; east to Tahiti and west to western India. Within this region they are found from just above the tree line on the highest mountains to the branches of trees overhanging the ocean. They are absent from some of the drier forests and woodlands, deserts and semi-deserts and alpine and other cold temperate environments where special adaptations are required to survive heavy frost and snow. Their distribution is discussed in greater detail in Chapter 3, Distribution and Origins, and shown in Figure 1 (page 12).

Dendrobiums are mainly inhabitants of primary forests, especially the rainforests of South-East Asia and New Guinea. Swamp forests, such as those dominated by *Melaleuca* species, and mangrove forests also often support high populations, both in terms of individuals and of species. In monsoonal forests and woodlands fewer species are generally found, but the number of individuals may be high. Although periodic high-intensity forest fires appear to prevent their establishment in some temperate grassy forests and woodlands, nearby closed forests where fires very rarely occur often have significant populations. The small group of species found in the sub-alpine shrubberies of tropical mountains are noteworthy in that most have brightly coloured flowers. Some species have adapted well to secondary forests and other disturbed environments such as landslides and road cuttings.

Climate

Rainfall In common with most other epiphytes, the dendrobiums are generally restricted to areas of moderate to high rainfall. These could be defined in the tropical lowlands as regions with an annual rainfall of more than 1500 mm and a dry season of less than six months. At higher elevations in the tropics, or in cool temperate regions, suitable habitats may occur in areas with

TABLE 10

SELECTED TEMPERATURE AND RAINFALL DATA FOR LOCALITIES ALONG A LATITUDINAL GRADIENT FROM LAE, PAPUA NEW GUINEA, TO HOBART, TASMANIA*

	J	F	M	A	M	J	J	A	S	O	N	D	ANNUAL
Lae													
Rainfall (mm)	258	254	335	399	423	413	503	484	466	391	328	323	5881
Max. temperature °C	31	31	31	30	29	29	28	28	29	30	30	31	30
Min. temperature °C	24	24	24	23	23	22	22	22	22	23	23	23	23
Cairns													
Rainfall (mm)	421	422	460	264	110	72	39	42	43	50	98	203	2224
Max. temperature °C	32	31	31	29	27	26	25	27	28	30	31	32	29
Min. temperature °C	23	23	23	21	19	17	16	16	17	19	21	23	20
Sydney													
Rainfall (mm)	98	112	125	106	97	126	67	78	63	74	83	77	1106
Max. temperature °C	26	26	25	23	20	17	17	18	20	22	24	26	22
Min. temperature °C	19	19	17	14	11	8	7	8	10	13	15	17	13
Hobart													
Rainfall (mm)	41	40	36	47	37	29	48	49	41	49	45	58	516
Max. temperature °C	22	22	21	18	15	12	12	13	15	17	19	20	17
Min. temperature °C	12	12	11	9	6	5	4	5	6	7	9	11	8

*Data adapted from McAlpine and Keig, 1983, and Australian Bureau of Meteorology climatic tables, 1999.

annual rainfalls as low as 600 mm. Some examples of mean monthly rainfalls, chosen along a latitudinal gradient from northern New Guinea to southern Australia, are given in Table 10. It should be noted that these data are averages and do not illustrate the frequency of irregular (non-seasonal) droughts which might have an important influence on the occurrence and distribution of dendrobiums in this (and other) regions.

Temperature Dendrobiums occur in a wide range of temperature environments, from the hot humid tropical lowlands of South-East Asia and the hot, seasonally dry monsoon environments of northern Australia to the cold alpine shrublands of the mountains of New Guinea and the cool temperate forests of Japan and New Zealand. A few species, such as *Dockrillia striolata*, *Winika cunninghamii* and *Dendrobium speciosum*, can survive mild winter frosts and occasionally snow. In the tropics none appear to grow above the line (at about 4000 m in New Guinea) where frosts occur on most nights, although a few such as *D. brevicaule* may be found in protected microsites near the lower edge of this zone. At the other extreme, some species, especially those usually seen as lithophytes (e.g. *Dendrobium kingianum*) occupy exposed sites where day temperature must be close to lethal levels during hot summer months.

The general pattern of the relationship between temperature and elevation for Papua New Guinea is shown in Table 11. An interesting feature of this table is that the rate of temperature fall from that at sea level, is rather slow until the 1000 m level is reached. In terms of species distribution the effect of this is that species considered typical of the lowlands (e.g. *Dendrobium spectabile*) occur up to about 1000 m. Here there is a short zone where lowland species mingle with species typical of the mountains (e.g. *D. finisterrae*).

TABLE 11
CHANGE IN TEMPERATURE WITH ALTITUDE IN NEW GUINEA*

Altitude (m)	January maximum (°C)	January minimum (°C)	July maximum(°C)	July minimum (°C)
0	32	22	30	20
500	32	20	30	19
1000	29	17	27	16
1500	25	14	24	13
2000	22	12	21	11
2500	18	9	18	9
3000	15	6	15	5
3500	11	4	11	3
4000	7	1	9	0

*Adapted from McAlpine and Keig, 1983

Although it is common knowledge that temperatures are lower at higher elevations and that mean temperature generally decreases with increasing latitude, the decrease in seasonality (differences between summer and winter temperatures) at lower latitudes is not so well appreciated. The magnitudes of these differences are illustrated by the data in Table 10. For example, even though Cairns (north-east Australia) is well within the tropics, seasonal temperature fluctuations become significant enough to influence the growth of many plants originating in more equatorial latitudes. Differences are generally even greater at higher latitudes although they may be moderated by maritime influences.

Day length and light Day length variations are important factors, as the daylight regime typical of a site not only determines the seasonal variation in the amount of light potentially available for plant photosynthesis, but may also provide a mechanism for the timing of phenological events such as growth and reproduction. In equatorial regions there is very little difference in the length of the longest and shortest day. For example, at Lae in Papua New Guinea (6°44'S) the difference is about 58 minutes and is probably too short to exert much of an influence on phenological processes. At Cairns (16°54'S) the difference is two hours, however, and for those plant species which occur in both places the relative lack of seasonal flowering in the Lae environment is quite noticeable. Although other factors such as periods of low temperature may also trigger the initiation of flower buds, day length is suspected as being important in this example. The differences increase rapidly at higher latitudes. For example, further south at Sydney (33°50'S) the difference is 4 hours 43 minutes and at Hobart (Tasmania, 42°53'S) it is 6 hours 36 minutes. It is also suspected that the reluctance of many cultivated, temperate dendrobiums to flower well in tropical montane environments may be due to the lack of an adequate daylight trigger, although this is not as yet thoroughly researched. There do not seem to be any problems with the initiation of flower buds of tropical species when they are grown in temperate climates, although lack of sufficient sunlight may be a problem especially for those species with a continuous growth habit.

Cloudiness, although a very variable characteristic, is an important factor in determining the amount of light available for plant growth. In habitats where most of the rainfall is brought by trade or monsoonal winds, relatively long periods of overcast weather may be experienced. In the equatorial tropics, local topography may be the major control; a common pattern is for the mornings to be clear with storms starting to build about midday, rain falling later in the afternoon and early evening, with the sky clearing before midnight. Although it should be possible to get good data about cloud coverage from satellite images, for the moment this information is not readily accessible.

Microclimates and aspect Published temperature data used to define the environments of orchid habitats are usually screen temperatures taken under the standard conditions adopted by weather observers. While these may provide a good guide for many epiphytes, they can be quite misleading for species such as those growing in gorges, or growing lithophytically on exposed hill slopes. In montane environments the heating of the leaves of plants in sunny locations on ridge tops is particularly noticeable, contrasting with the roots which are in a much cooler environment. Some simple temperature measurements taken near plants of *Dendrobium vexillarius* at an elevation of 2300 m in Papua New Guinea illustrate this point. At midday on a warm sunny day the temperature of the loose dry litter layer at the base of the plants was 28°C; among the roots at a depth of three cm it was 16°C. In some lowland microsites, such as treefall gaps, temperatures can be elevated to levels close to lethal (about 55°C). This helps explain why orchids falling into these gaps in tropical lowland forest usually perish, while those falling into gaps in higher elevation forest not only survive for long periods but also often re-establish.

Aspect may have an important local effect on the distribution of dendrobiums, especially in non-equatorial regions. In temperate latitudes certain topographic sites may offer protection from hot summer suns, drying winds and even forest fires. The significance of aspect recedes in the tropics, for here the weather is influenced mainly by local convectional (rather than frontal) influences and the sun shines from both northern and southern skies. When convectional influences are operating, wind direction is determined more by topography (blowing up slopes during the day and down the valleys at night) than by the relative positions of air masses. The high sun angles in the tropics mean that both north and south facing slopes receive high insolation for at least part of each year. This may not occur in temperate regions, where the slope away from the sun may be in shadow for the greater part, if not all, of the year.

Plant habit

The Dendrobiinae vary considerably in habit from tiny creeping plants less than one centimetre high (e.g. *D. toressae*) to clumped bamboo-like plants over three metres tall (e.g. *D. discolor*). For the most part dendrobiums are epiphytes, with some lithophytes and terrestrials. All, even the terrestrials, have coarse spreading root systems, never having evolved the tuberous root systems so characteristic of terrestrial orchids from temperate climates.

In common with many other plants, the roots of dendrobiums have specialised structures to accommodate mycorrhizal fungi, which may assist them in scavenging nutrients in low fertility environments. Their roots also seem well adapted to absorb free water rapidly. This is a useful attribute for epiphytic species with roots often exposed on the surface of tree branches, as it enables them to make the most of short showers and mists in sites prone to rapid drying.

The stems (pseudobulbs) of the dendrobiums vary greatly. A few are green and relatively succulent (e.g. many of those of section *Dendrobium*); others are long, thin and even wiry (e.g. those of *Grastidium*), while others are swollen and fibrous (e.g. those of section *Spatulata*). In most cases it would seem that those dendrobiums (the majority) with either succulent or swollen stems have a capacity to survive periods of drought and store food supplies to sustain either rapid vegetative growth or flowering. It is noteworthy that most of those with thin stems are terrestrial (where drying of their substrate is not so much of a problem), or occur in habitats where rainfall is very regular in occurrence. Some with thin stems (e.g. *D. malbrownii*) have relatively thick roots that appear to serve as water storage organs. Some have fleshy leaves (e.g. *Dockrillia teretifolia*) that serve the same purpose.

While swollen pseudobulbs may provide protection from drought, they do not offer the protection from fire that buried tubers provide for most terrestrial orchids of temperate zones.

Although the vast majority of the dendrobiums are epiphytes or lithophytes, they may occasionally be found as terrestrials. Where the epiphytic habit is the normal state, the adoption of the terrestrial mode is usually due to adult plants falling from trees and re-establishing on the ground. Species that characteristically commence their lives as terrestrials are relatively few, especially in tropical lowland and temperate environments (examples include *Dendrobium lobbii* and species in the genus *Cannaeorchis* from New Caledonia). At higher elevation in the tropics the distinction between terrestrials and epiphytes blurs and some species, such as *Dendrobium cuthbertsonii*, seem able to develop readily in either habitat. The faces of road cuttings in the wetter areas of Papua New Guinea are often colonised by orchids, including a number of dendrobiums. This is especially noticeable above 2000 m elevation. Among the species occurring in this situation are *D. cuthbertsonii*, *D. subacaule*, *D. rupestre*, *D. amphigenium*, *D. engae* and *D. subclausum*. *D. terrestre* is usually an epiphyte in cloud forest at about the lower end of its altitudinal range (2000 m) but becomes terrestrial at the edge of the tree line (3000–3500 m).

Reproduction

Flowering The flowers of the Dendrobiinae last in perfection anywhere from half a day to a few months. Those with the shortest lives are generally those of the genus *Grastidium*, while the flowers of almost all the species in section *Oxyglossum* last several months. Most have species specific, seasonal flowering patterns, although these tend to break down at low latitudes where some out of season flowering commonly occurs. The most significant exceptions to annual flowering are to be found in those species that have flowers lasting a day or two at the most. *Diplocaulobium* and *Grastidium* are two genera where species with short-lived flowers are the norm (although this characteristic is found among species in other genera and sections). Most of the species with short-lived flowers tend to flower every couple of months or so. One of the most interesting things about this group is that flowering within a species is essentially synchronous.

Although the trigger enabling this to occur is not well understood, it has been postulated that for at least one species, *D. crumenatum*, a sudden temperature drop of about 10°C triggers the development of flower buds. Such a temperature drop can occur in the tropics when a convectional storm sweeps across the landscape during mid afternoon.

Pollination

Unfortunately very little is known of pollinating agents in dendrobiums. However, many species do not seem to have the specialist pollinators characteristic of some terrestrial genera. For example, *D. linguiforme* is reported to have bees (*Euryglossina hypochroma* and *E. lynettae*), flies (*Sryphus viridiceps*) and Thynnid wasps as pollinators. Most of the species with large showy flowers with prominent spreading labellums appear to be pollinated by bees. Birds of the genus *Meliphaga* (honeyeaters) seem to be the main pollinators of the brightly coloured, tubular flowered species, i.e. generally those in sections *Calcarifera, Calyptrochilus, Pedilonum* and *Oxyglossum*. A few species, such as *Dendrobium stuartii, D. rarum* and *D. mirbelianum*, are usually self-pollinating.

The prominence of brightly coloured species in tropical alpine environments was noted earlier. In the South American Andes it was found that at high elevations birds were much better pollinators than insects. Perhaps birds are also the dominant pollinators on the upper slopes of the mountains of New Guinea.

In a collection housed in an open greenhouse on the Atherton Tableland, north Queensland, tubular-flowered species from New Guinea are often pollinated early in the morning by the native honeyeaters, especially the Lewin honeyeater, *Meliphaga noyata*. Unfortunately they do not leave a label on the pod with an indication of either the date of pollination or the name of the pollen parent, and many inter-specific hybrids are accidentally produced! In the same greenhouse, the larger flowered species in section *Latouria* (especially *D. macrophyllum* and near relatives) are pollinated by solitary bees.

Capsule development In most species the ovary begins to swell and sepals, petals and labellum wither within a few days of pollination. A small group of four or five species related to *D. antennatum* (section *Spatulata*) are unusual in that after pollination these flower parts do not die but become greener and more heavily textured, remaining on the capsule during its development.

As capsules approach maturity there is generally a slight change in colour to a more yellowish hue and a decrease in the glossiness of the surface of the capsule. The capsules of some species, especially those from high elevation, split and open rapidly, with the valves separating entirely at the flower end and reflexing. Perhaps this mode allows seeds to disperse during the relatively brief periods when the plants are not enveloped by mist or rain. In other species (e.g. those of section *Spatulata*) the splits remain narrow for at least a few days and gradually extend back along the capsule. The seeds of these species are dispersed over several days.

Seed characteristics The general morphology of the seeds is typical of that for the family. The seeds are very small, usually not more than 0.5 mm long, although there is a small group of three or four species related to *D. antennatum* (section *Spatulata*), which have noticeably larger seeds than most other species. At the centre of each seed is a more or less spherical to ovoid embryo. This is enclosed by a cluster of large thin-walled cells that form wings out to each side which enable the seed to stay airborne in air currents. Seed colour varies from white through cream to yellow or, in the oxyglossums and some related sections, to green.

Physiology

A feature of the orchids is their low metabolic rates. They are just not physiologically capable of growing as rapidly as many other monocotyledons, as for example the grasses. The upside of low metabolic rates is that orchids can survive and grow (albeit slowly) with low levels of nutrients and limited resources in terms of sunlight and/or water.

Since metabolic processes are basically chemical reactions, they are temperature sensitive. Thus temperature is important for plant growth and survival as it controls the rate of photosynthesis (the process where sunlight converts water to organic substances which can be used by the plant for its maintenance, growth and reproduction). Temperature also determines the rate of respiration (the conversion of organic compounds back to carbon dioxide and water vapour, releasing energy for cell growth and maintenance), which is the dominant process when light levels are low. Both day and night temperatures may thus be important to the ecologist and horticulturist.

While ambient temperatures affect the rate of all metabolic reactions, the most sensitive seem to be those involving enzymes. It appears that variations in the concentrations and types of enzymes present in a species largely determine the optimum temperatures for its growth. While these optima can be determined experimentally, the methodology is not straightforward and very few data are available. Orchid growers must generally glean what they can from the environment of the natural range of the species.

Many of the dendrobiums found in relatively dry habitats (e.g. *Dendrobium canaliculatum*) have adopted a metabolic pathway known as crassularian acid metabolism (CAM) in which the complex chemical processes involved in photosynthesis are modified so that gas exchange (absorbing carbon dioxide and releasing oxygen) between cells in the leaf and the air outside can be delayed until nightfall. Gas exchange in all plants is controlled by special pores (stomata), which are generally found on the underside of the leaf. In plants growing naturally in environments with good water availability, these pores open to allow gas exchange and transpiration (water loss) while the sun is shining and photosynthesis is occurring. In CAM plants the pores remain shut during the day even though some photosynthetic reactions may be taking place, opening at night to allow the gas exchange necessary to complete the process. At this time the surrounding air is generally cooler and more humid, thus much less water is lost.

Key biological characteristics

Several key characteristics of the biology of the dendrobiums play a dominant role in determining their distribution, taxonomy and evolution. In contrast to detailed features such as those relating to plant habit and the inflorescence, these key characteristics are uniform and appear to be quite stable (from an evolutionary perspective) throughout the group. They relate to seed size, physiology and general plant morphology.

The ecological significance of the small seed size is fourfold. First, because small seeds have a low unit metabolic cost, enormous quantities can be produced. This increases the chance of their arrival at sites that are favourable for establishment, but are difficult or impossible to reach by larger propagules (e.g. the branches and twigs of forest trees).

Second, because of their light weight, they can be dispersed long distances. In theory at least, this allows them to colonise new sites. However, a new site will not be colonised unless the environment is suitable and includes a compatible fungal species.

Third, their small size means that any resultant seedlings are initially small and very susceptible to fungal and insect attack during the establishment phases. They are also much more vulnerable to unfavourable environmental conditions (such as local or seasonal drought or temperature extremes), than seedlings from plants with larger seeds that can establish more rapidly.

Fourth, in contrast to nearly all other higher plants, the seeds of dendrobiums contain virtually no food reserves. Thus, in nature, germinating seedlings are usually thought not to be able to survive unless they are immediately able to establish an association with a compatible fungus that will supply them with the sugars and other organic compounds needed for survival and growth.

The combination of low metabolic rates and very small initial size means that dendrobium plantlets, even in favourable seasons, may not be able to grow large enough to survive a short period of dry weather or temperature variations occurring as seasons change. This problem has been largely overcome by unrelated, typically temperate, orchid genera such as *Pterostylis* and *Orchis*, in which the aerial parts are deciduous during unfavourable seasonal conditions, the plants regenerating through tuberous roots with the arrival of spring.

Given these factors, it is not surprising that the dendrobiums have reached their greatest diversity in equatorial tropical environments where relatively uniform environments enable establishment through the critical early stages of plantlet development. Although many species are found in the cool environments of tropical mountains, they have not been overly successful in adapting to temperate climates at higher latitudes where they are limited to wetter and milder sites. Their inability to develop root tubers seems to have precluded further development of the terrestrial habit in seasonal and fire-prone environments.

Looked at from another perspective, the dendrobiums are specialists in exploiting niches that have equitable light and moisture environments but which are nutrient poor and relatively inaccessible to species with larger seeds. Although many dendrobiums are able to grow in high nutrient conditions, they are usually excluded because such sites are exploited by more vigorous plant species that grow so rapidly that they overwhelm any orchid which may attempt to establish.

It appears that in the dendrobiums the epiphytic habit evolved well back among the ancestors of the group. The smattering of typically terrestrial species through some of the sections appears to indicate readaptation to terrestrial habitats rather than an expression of a primitive characteristic. Indeed, the distinction between epiphytic and terrestrial species breaks down in the very equitable environment of the mountains of New Guinea, where species normally thought of as typically epiphytic are often found growing on the ground. In this environment the cold nights limit the growth of competitors and dry periods occur at frequencies measured in years rather than the regular annual seasonal droughts experienced in higher latitudes. While frosts and associated fires may be environmental factors in these habitats, they occur at such a low frequency and in such a pattern that plants are either able to re-establish between catastrophic events or avoid destruction in more equitable microenvironments. Another factor permitting the greater adoption of terrestrial mode in these habitats might be that exposed plants do not suffer from the problem of high temperatures encountered by those at lower and warmer elevations and, indeed, may benefit from higher leaf temperatures as compared to epiphytic habitats at the same elevation.

CHAPTER 7

Cultivation

Although cultivation of dendrobiums commenced in the hothouses of Europe during 1819 with the introduction of *D. aphyllum*, a few species had probably been grown by some of the indigenous people of Asia and the Pacific for hundreds, if not thousands, of years. In New Guinea, several *Diplocaulobium* species are grown on the thatched roofs of traditional houses in the highlands. Their stems are regularly harvested to produce a bright yellow fibre that is woven into personal ornaments such as armbands or used for bindings such as those which fasten arrow heads to shafts. *Dendrobium moniliforme*, possibly the first *Dendrobium* in cultivation, is mentioned in Chinese literature as early as the Chin Dynasty (290–307AD), and was certainly grown in Japan several hundred years ago.

Early attempts in Europe to cultivate tropical orchids were not very successful, as few gardeners understood tropical environments and tended to keep their plants in too-hot conditions, with insufficient light and air movement. To compound these problems, soil and rotted wood were widely used as growing media. It was not until the middle of the nineteenth century that people such as Joseph Paxton, the head gardener for the Duke of Devonshire, took notice of the collectors' reports about the plants' habitats and started to gain an understanding of orchids' need for air movement, periods of drying and good drainage around the roots – and that many plants came from cool mountain areas. At last plants were grown successfully and England ceased to be the 'orchid graveyard'. The invention of the Edwardian case, along with faster ships, also allowed a larger percentage of wild-collected orchids to reach Europe alive.

Propagation from seed was also a major problem. For the first fifty years the role of mycorrhizal fungi in seed germination was not really understood, although growers had found through trial and error that seedlings might be established if seed were sown around the base of the parent plant. Around the turn of the century the French botanist Noel Bernard established the link between mycorrhizal fungi and orchid seed germination. Unfortunately the orchid-growing community for a time overlooked his discovery, and it was not until the publication of similar research by the German Professor Burgeff in 1909 and 1911 that the technique was widely adopted. Although more reliable than sowing seeds around the base of a parent plant, this method was still difficult to use, involving the isolation and culture of the appropriate fungi. The next great advance was the publication by Knudson in 1922 of his success in growing orchid seedlings on an agar-based medium (containing essential minerals and sugars) in sterile flasks. This technique rapidly replaced earlier methods for it was easier and far more reliable. Although variations on Knudson's orchid-growing media are periodically announced, the original Formula C remain the mainstay of the propagator.

It will become obvious from discussion in Part II that while cultural techniques for all dendrobiums have not been perfected, every year a wider range of species and hybrids is grown for both pot plants and cut flowers. While *Dendrobium* species remain popular among hobbyists in Europe and North America, very large numbers of hybrids, mainly among species from sections *Spatulata* and *Phalaenanthe*, are grown in Thailand, Malaysia and surrounding countries. These form the basis of a significant cut-flower industry. Flowering pot plants, featuring hybrids mainly among species in section *Dendrobium*, are also widely grown and traded in North America, Asia and Europe.

This chapter, discussing propagation techniques, potting media, out-of-pot cultivation, housing and pests and diseases, should be read in conjunction with Chapter 6, Biology and Ecology.

Propagation

Orchids may be propagated by using either the vegetative or sexual pathway. In vegetative mode, the new plants arise from shoots on the rhizome (divisions) or from dormant buds that lie in the leaf axils along the stems (offshoots). In the sexual mode, flowers are pollinated, a fruit produced and seed sown.

Vegetative propagation

Divisions The general pattern of growth for dendrobiums is that a rhizome grows along the surface of a tree branch or other substrate, producing roots that attach the plant and collect water and nutrients. Stems or pseudobulbs, which support the leaves and inflorescences, are produced at intervals along the rhizome. The rhizome may branch and when the branch is large enough (generally a rhizome with three stems is sufficient), the rhizome may be cut cleanly with a sharp knife and the pieces separated. The plants produced in this way are known as divisions.

Although rhizomes in some species rarely branch, the plant may still be divided by cutting the rhizome behind the third or fourth pseudobulb. The forward piece, the 'lead', is separated from the older canes, the 'backcut'. The loss of the hormonal control exerted by the actively growing lead allows a dormant bud on the backcut to grow.

Offshoots Most *Dendrobium* species will produce offshoots (often called 'anaks', 'kekis' or 'aerials') from buds in the leaf axils. While some adopt this habit only when stressed (e.g. most of the species in section *Latouria*), others appear to produce offshoots as a normal part of their life cycle (e.g. *Dendrobium loddigesii, D. kingianum*). Offshoots are easily removed with a sharp knife and, provided they have roots, will re-establish. Those without roots are better left and the development of roots encouraged by tying a small wad of sphagnum moss immediately below the junction with the mother pseudobulb. Alternatively, it may be more convenient to pin the attached offshoot down to the surface of a small pot filled with fresh mix and detach it as soon as roots have developed enough to hold it firmly in the pot. Offshoots can usually be obtained from older leafless canes if these are detached from the parent plant and laid on a bed of sphagnum moss or other growing medium.

Propagation from seed

Propagation from seed commences with pollination and proceeds through capsule (pod) development to the point where one must decide whether to harvest and culture the immature seeds in the 'green pod' stage or wait until the capsule splits and sow the dry seed.

Pollination   Hand pollination of the larger flowered species is straightforward. The problems come with those which have small flowers and especially where the stigmatic surface is protected by an appressed or folded labellum (e.g. many species in sections *Calyptrochilus* and *Oxyglossum*). A magnifying glass, a clamp to hold the flower steady, and a good deal of patience is needed to pollinate most species within these sections. Cutting flower parts away to gain better access to the stigmatic surface has been tried with mixed results.

The success rate of outcrosses varies, from over 90 per cent in most of the larger flowered species to a frustratingly low 5–10 per cent in some of the small flowered species, such as *D. cyanocentrum*. Outcrossing is preferred over selfing (self-pollination) as seedlings from outcrosses generally appear to be more vigorous.

Occasionally, when the propagation of a rare plant is being attempted, there is no alternative but to try self-pollination, even though the success rate for this technique is often much lower than for cross-pollination. While there is not yet enough documented experience to provide clear guidelines on those species which will self-pollinate, some general trends appear to be emerging. For instance, it is usually possible to self-pollinate species in sections *Latouria* and *Spatulata*, but it is seldom successful in most species in section *Oxyglossum*. A few failed attempts should not lead to the abandonment of efforts to propagate a rare species, however, for there have been cases where repeated attempts over several years eventually yielded viable seed.

Capsule development   The time taken from pollination to capsule splitting is quite variable among the species. There are some consistencies within some of the sections (e.g. six to seven months for the latourias). The species from section *Oxyglossum* seem most variable, with *D. subacaule* taking only six weeks to mature while others take six or seven months.

It is possible to excise and culture the immature seeds from the unripened capsule ('green pod'). Experience suggests they should be allowed to ripen for at least three-quarters of their full term, although sometimes success can be achieved with earlier harvesting. The main advantage of the green pod technique is that the seeds in the intact capsule are sterile and may be sown directly onto the sowing medium. Another is that seed from a batch of capsules can be sown at the same time without the risks associated with seed storage and sterilisation. The downside is that unless the capsules are very close to splitting, the surplus seed cannot be dried without losing viability and is therefore not available for storage or exchange.

Walter Upton, in *Dendrobium Orchids of Australia*, provides a table indicating the interval from pollination to capsule splitting and suggested times for green capsule harvesting for those species endemic to Australia. He does, however, note that ripening times vary greatly between clones and the periods given should only be used as a guide.

Seed sowing   Dendrobiums vary greatly in their ease of propagation from seed. For most, standard aseptic techniques suffice. A few need special media. Unfortunately it has not thus far been possible to propagate successfully some species, especially a few of the brilliantly coloured montane and alpine species from Papua New Guinea. The discussion below centres on the techniques used in the laboratory of one of the authors (GCS). This small facility mainly produces seedling flasks for local use.

Dry seed may be surface-sterilised using standard techniques. Saturated calcium hypochlorite solution is the preferred sterilant. Others, including hydrogen peroxide and sodium hypochlorite, have also been tried but either have not been as convenient or have not produced as consistent results.

The calcium hypochlorite solution is prepared by vigorously shaking 10 g of calcium hypochlorite (granular pool chlorine) with 150 ml water for a minute or so. The mixture is left for about an hour to settle and the clear solution poured off the top. About 10 ml of this solution is shaken for one minute in a 100 ml culture tube with sufficient seed to prepare three or four flasks, and the seeds left in the solution for a further four to six minutes. (Pre-soaking seed for a few hours in water with a tiny amount of wetting agent may be useful if it is suspected that the seed is heavily contaminated, but is not usually necessary.) The seeds are then removed from the tube with a thin stainless steel spatula and spread on the media in the flask. It is often suggested that the seed be rinsed in sterile water at this stage, but for most dendrobiums so far propagated, this step can be ignored without harmful effect.

The seeds of most *Dendrobium* species will float in the decontaminating solution and are easily removed with the spatula. Occasionally a very small-seeded species will be encountered in which the seed remains suspended. In these cases a small hand centrifuge is useful for separating the seed from the solution.

> ## PREVENTING THE SPREAD OF VIRUSES
> Whenever a knife is used on an orchid, either in propagating or for cutting flower stems, the blade should be sterilised before moving on to the next plant, either by heating or by using a suitable chemical sterilising medium. A 1 per cent solution of benzalkonium chloride (100 g/L), as used to clean knives of virus particles in the sugar cane industry, might be tried. The same chemical is used as an algicide in swimming pools. Treatment of all cutting tools is essential if the spread of destructive plant viruses from one plant to the next is to be minimised.

Any of the standard media appear satisfactory for germination of most species. The most difficult have been some of the high elevation oxyglossums, especially *D. brevicaule* and *D. decockii*. To date only small amounts of seed from the wild have been available and it has not been possible to determine whether failure to develop has been due to a very short period of seed viability or an inappropriate medium. From the behaviour of the few protocorms that have developed, both factors may be involved.

The media usually used are Sigma® P6665 for germination and Sigma® P1056 for replating. Some species seem to do better if these are used at half strength. Davis agar (8 g/L) is used to solidify the media. These media are dispensed into ventilated 500 ml polypropylene jars and sterilised in an autoclave at 0.7 kg/cm² for 30 minutes. The pH of these media is generally about 5.5. Both seed and replate cultures are kept in a temperature controlled room (20–22°C) and illuminated with standard fluorescent tubes (36 Watts) at a distance of 15 to 30 cm, for six hours each day.

Traditionally the term for the containers used in the sterile culture of orchids is 'flasks'. This is probably a hangover from the older science of microbiology where the sterile techniques later adapted to the seed and tissue culture of orchids were developed. Flat-bottomed glass Erlenmeyer flasks were often adopted as convenient culture vessels. Although 250 and 500 ml glass flasks of this style are still occasionally seen, a very wide variety of jars and bottles is now used. The main requirements of containers are that they can be sterilised and properly sealed, are sufficiently transparent to allow easy visual inspection of plant growth, and permit sufficient light penetration for the development of the seedlings. Although wide-mouthed polypropylene jars are more expensive and somewhat harder to seal than glass jars, flasks or bottles, they have the advantage of being very light, and provide easy access for sowing, replating and the removal of seedlings without damage.

Flasks are generally vented to allow some gas exchange with the atmosphere. While some species seem tolerant of conditions in airtight containers, most slowly decline. Traditionally venting is through a non-absorbent cotton wool plug. Cellulose and Teflon vent covers, which speed up the process of flask preparation, are now beginning to be widely used.

While these media and conditions give reasonable results for a wide range of species, growers who specialise in particular sections (e.g. *Spatulata*) often achieve better results with other formulations, most of which are closely guarded secrets.

The two problems that occasionally arise with most media are excessive proliferation and the production of dark-coloured exudates from the developing seedlings. Both events seem to suppress further growth.

Proliferation, the tendency for the plantlets to grow into relatively unorganised clumps with several stems, is common among the species of section *Oxyglossum*, especially in *D. subacaule*, *D. sulphureum* and *D. nanoides*, but is also seen in species from other groups such as *D. vannouhuysii* (section *Calyptrochilus*) and *D. spectatissimum* (section *Formosae*). It can sometimes be minimised by using another medium. Lowering sugar levels in the medium, reducing the period of illumination and preventing flask temperatures from becoming too high have also been suggested as methods of prevention. Where the problem cannot be resolved, some seedlings can usually be salvaged by separating large clumps into individual shoots or small pieces. These are replated onto fresh medium and deflasked as soon as any wounding has healed but before further proliferation has occurred.

The production of dark-coloured toxic exudates (apparently phenolics), which stain the agar around the protocorms or seedlings, is an occasional problem best overcome by replating as soon as it becomes apparent. In a few species (e.g. *D. fulgidum*) where the problem is severe the best solution seems to be to deflask the seedlings as soon as they have differentiated. In the case of *D. fulgidum* this can be done successfully when they are about five millimetres high.

Seedling care Dendrobiums vary enormously in their ease of cultivation. For many species and their hybrids, the path from flask to flower is straightforward provided basic criteria are met. A few require experimentation to determine optimal cultural conditions, and close attention must be paid to detail to establish and maintain those conditions. The following notes are based on procedures used to deflask and establish seedlings of species for which we had no previous experience.

The first important consideration is the vigour of the seedlings in the flask. Plants which are yellowish or showing any signs of dying back should be rejuvenated by replating. Weak plants have a greatly reduced chance of survival when removed from the flask. Some growers attempt to harden off seedlings in the flask by removing the lids and adding some water about a week before deflasking. Others place the flasks in a brighter environment. Neither procedure has been found to provide markedly improved survival, although the latter might be tried if the flasks are maintained in a low light environment.

While glass containers may be broken to remove seedlings, wide-mouthed polypropylene jars greatly simplify the process. The seedlings should be separated as gently as possible. Small clumps may be left unseparated, but larger clumps should be discarded, as they appear to provide favourable sites for fungal rots to develop. If the plants are valuable, such larger clumps can be broken up under sterile conditions (long-handled dissecting scissors are ideal) and replated on new medium until wounds are healed (a few weeks is usually long enough).

Generally larger pieces of agar are removed from the roots with a small spatula. Washing is unnecessary unless root development is massive and the agar not easily removed by other means. The small pieces of agar remaining on the roots do not seem to cause any problems.

Grade the seedlings, potting the larger ones individually in 50 mm pots. Smaller seedlings can be planted up to five per 50 mm pot. Large compots are generally avoided, as an outbreak of damping off (due to *Pythium* sp.) will often kill all the seedlings in a pot, where the disease can often be confined to one or a few plants if you have used small pots. Previcure® has been found particularly effective in preventing damping off. Seedlings just out of flask are also sensitive to *Botrytis* fungi; if conditions favouring its development (low light, high humidity and a temperature of about 20°C) occur during the first few months, they should be sprayed with Rovral® (bicarboximide) at the recommended rate.

An overhead fan will provide constant air movement. For most of the year the shading in the seedling house is kept at about 70 per cent. This is reduced a little on the hot bright days experienced during early summer. The seedlings are fertilised weekly with a half strength foliar spray containing a complete array of macro- and micro-nutrients. They are watered heavily once or twice a week depending upon the season. Except in extreme conditions, misting and light waterings are avoided in the relatively humid environment of the eastern coast of North Queensland, for even though high quality water is used, the combination of light waterings, the peat/perlite growing mix and the fertiliser regime can lead to the salinity damage to which some *Dendrobium* species appear particularly prone. For the same reasons care should be taken never to allow the growing mix to dry out completely, as this increases the concentration of any salts which may be present.

The keys to successfully raising seedlings from flask appear to be good vigorous seedlings in flask, minimal damage at deflasking, and cultural conditions that promote rapid development and growth in the greenhouse.

Once well established, seedlings may be managed in the same way as adult plants, with perhaps a little more attention paid to appropriate watering and adequate nutrition.

Basic requirements for growing media
Dendrobiums have been grown successfully on a very wide range of substrates, varying from crumbed car tyres to loquat tree twigs – not surprising, given the wide range of environments in

which they occur naturally. Before looking in detail at the comparative advantages and disadvantages of common and not so common media, let us consider just what a good growing medium should provide.

With the exception of a few species, the dendrobiums are primarily epiphytes or lithophytes. They are usually found in situations where their roots are completely exposed on either a woody stem or a rock, shallowly penetrating the loose, dead outer bark layer of a woody host plant, or are thinly covered with a layer of leaf and twig litter or mosses and lichens. The odd occasions when species normally regarded as epiphytes are found in nature as vigorous terrestrials (see page 80) suggest that perfect simulation of the epiphytic habit may not necessarily be essential for good growth. Indeed, the growing techniques successfully used for over a century of orchid cultivation in many countries support this notion. In our view the most difficult of the dendrobiums to grow are those typically found as twig epiphytes, and their ecology merits close scrutiny. In general the following criteria are relevant.

1 **Water-holding capacity** The medium should have sufficient water-holding capacity to keep the plant from becoming excessively dehydrated between waterings. Many dendrobiums, of course, are able to store water in swollen stems or succulent leaves and/or have metabolic traits enabling them to survive for weeks and even months in a dry medium with minimal water input from the atmosphere (see page 74). Others, such as the species of section *Oxyglossum*, are extremely susceptible to dehydration and irreparable damage is done if the media in which they are grown remains dry for much longer than a day.

2 **Aeration** Water-holding capacity must not, however, be at the expense of aeration. The particles making up the medium must allow sufficient air movement for the roots to absorb oxygen and expel the carbon dioxide and other gases produced during respiration. Where possible all the particles making up a mix should be about the same size, as mixed sizes facilitate packing and consequent loss of porosity.

3 **Nutrition** Although dendrobiums appear to have the ability to absorb nutrients through the leaves when sprayed with a solution of soluble fertiliser, better growth is often observed when the medium also contains nutrients in a form available to the roots. The ability of a medium to retain nutrients despite heavy watering depends on the ion exchange capacity of its components. Organic matter such as peat, and some clays, have a high capacity to retain nutrients whereas they are readily washed out of coarse sand and gravel. Alternatively nutrients may be supplied at low levels at every watering.

4 **Measurement of pH** provides an indication of the acidity or alkalinity of a potting medium. This is important because in a medium outside the optimal range the plants may have difficulty absorbing mineral nutrients. The optimal pH for dendrobiums is generally a little on the acid side of neutral. If necessary the pH of potting mixes may be adjusted by adding dilute acid to too alkaline a mix, or powdered limestone or dolomite to one too acid.

5 **Clean potting media** A potting medium free of pathogens and weed seeds is very desirable, especially if it is to be used for establishing seedlings out of flask. Where necessary, media can be pasteurised with heat (e.g. by using solarisation or steam) or fumigants such as methyl bromide. Some components of potting mix may be purchased in a sterile state (e.g. peat and perlite) and if care is taken in storage and mixing to prevent contamination, no other treatment is required. Other media, such as tree fern fibre, might not be so clean and it is difficult to ensure they are pathogen free.

The benefits of using clean media may be short-lived if plants are repotted in dirty pots or contaminated water is used. Hygienic practices should be followed in the greenhouse, for example, avoiding splashing plants with water from the floor or other pots when watering. Wire-mesh bench tops also help slow down movement of pathogens from an infected pot.

6 **Potting medium stability** The potting medium should also have good stability. Ideally it should still be in good condition when the plant has outgrown its container. The physical, chemical and microbiological changes occurring in media that have started to break down will not usually provide optimum conditions for growth and survival.

Three factors affect the stability of growing medium, the first being the gradual accumulation of dead roots. While unavoidable to a degree, this problem can be minimised by ensuring that unhealthy and dead roots are clipped off during repotting and that cultural conditions favour the development of a healthy root system. In particular, the medium should be well aerated, over-fertilising should be avoided and the water supply should be free from the spores of root-rot fungi.

The second factor is the breakdown of some or all of the components of the medium over time. A direct effect is that the medium begins to hold more water and fertiliser. When this occurs cultural management needs to be adjusted to compensate. Acidity may also increase and become high enough to interfere with nutrient uptake. Some growers attempt to alleviate this problem by adding marble chips, shell grit or powered limestone to the mix. Occasionally the breakdown products appear to be quite phytotoxic (see note on tree fern slabs, below).

The third problem is the gradual accumulation of salts in the media from low-grade water supplies and/or over-fertilising. In severe cases this can alter the physical and chemical properties of the mix to the degree that the plant either dies or has to be repotted well before it has outgrown its container. The sensitivity of some dendrobiums to this problem was discussed earlier. Early symptoms include root tip dieback, the death of roots and yellowing and premature loss of leaves. Occasionally over-watering is blamed for these symptoms, but reducing watering to salt-affected plants makes the problem worse as it increases salt concentrations in the root zone.

The best treatment is to implement a program of regular heavy watering, flushing out the pots to remove accumulated salts. In locations where the water quality problem is severe, the best solution may be to buy a storage tank and use rainwater as often as possible. Reverse osmosis or ion exchange units can also effectively remove dissolved salts. Unfortunately their capital and running costs are relatively high, but if it means the difference between being able or unable to grow some of the delightful miniatures such as the oxyglossums, then the expense is well worth while.

Potting materials

Opinions among orchid growers as to what constitutes the best potting medium for dendrobiums vary widely. To some degree the grower's choice is based on historical factors and individual cultural techniques, especially watering and fertilising regimes. There are, however, some broad trends. The most noticeable is that organic materials are rarely used in the tropics because of their accelerated decay rates in hot, wet environments. The use of very coarse materials is also more common in the tropics than in temperate environments.

Bark Since most dendrobiums grow on the bark of trees, bark may appear to have some desirable chemical and physical properties when used alone or as the major constituent of potting mixes. Indeed, bark is probably the most popular potting medium in the USA and Australia and is widely used in mixes elsewhere. Various grades based on size are generally available. The small sizes (0.5 to 1 cm) are used for seedlings; larger sizes (2 to 3 cm) for mature plants. Although broken pieces of virgin bark from the cork oak are very useful, that from conifers, such as radiata pine, redwood and Douglas fir, is generally preferred. Ideally the bark used should be decay resistant, thick, not too fibrous and be able to be broken up to regular-sized chunks. Species that have very resinous or flaky bark are to be avoided.

The main advantage of bark is that, although it holds some water, it is free draining and provides the roots with excellent aeration. It is also readily available, light and easy to use in potting. It may, however, be difficult to wet until it weathers. A significant problem, especially in tropical environments, can be its relatively rapid decay rate and the consequent need to repot as often as annually. Bark has virtually no capacity to retain nutrients so they should be added regularly either in the irrigation water or in a foliar spray.

Bark is often treated before use by boiling or partial composting, mainly to make it easier to wet. Lime may be added to promote composting and reduce its acidity. Bark may be sterilised to kill weed seeds and pathogens by heating or fumigation.

Perlite/peat mixes Although perlite and peat are hardly ever used individually, various combinations are becoming increasingly popular. Raw perlite is a strongly hydrated mineral formed when certain lavas are extruded beneath ice caps. When ground to the consistency of sand and heated to 900°C, it expands to form the perlite commonly used in horticulture. While it does hold some water, it has no nutrient-holding capacity or value. It is essentially neutral in pH, stable and inert. Perlite from some manufacturers does, however, contain fluorine, which can be damaging to sensitive seedlings. This is easily removed by washing the perlite in water before use. Some manufacturers produce two grades, medium and coarse. The latter is preferred for use in orchid potting mix.

Good quality, fibrous sphagnum peat is much more durable than other forms, particularly sedge peat and that made from coconut husk. Most peat is rather acid and powdered dolomite should be added to lift the pH to between 5 and 6. While the amount of dolomite required will

PART TWO

The Dendrobiinae

In this chapter 413 species and varieties are illustrated and described. The subtribe Dendrobiinae has been subdivided into a number of genera including the large genus *Dendrobium*, which itself has been split into many sections. The species in this book have been arranged under these genera and sections. This has resulted in 48 groups (44 if the old classification is followed). While the classification of Schlechter has been generally accepted for many years, there is little doubt that it has many shortcomings and changes are already under way. In this book the genera and sections of the Dendrobiinae have been arranged alphabetically. This has the disadvantage that related groups are often not placed next to each other, but the advantage that any particular group or species is more easily found.

There is a further complication in that at least two revisions of the subtribe are under way. Some sections have been raised to generic status and others clearly will also suffer this fate in the near future. This means that some groups are listed below as genera while other very closely related groups are listed as sections. For example, *Grastidium* is a genus, according to the latest classification, while the closely related *Monanthos* remains as a section. While these changes have not received universal acceptance, partly because supporting evidence has not yet been published, they have been accepted here as an interim measure because it appears likely that the groups so far elevated to generic level do represent distinct groups. Probably the only real question is whether the new genera are too narrow and whether other groups should have been included. In all cases the alternative name is given and readers are invited to make up their own minds.

Recent revisions have been published in the species *Dendrobium speciosum*, *D. tetragonum*, *D. bigibbum* and *D. canaliculatum*, in which existing well-known species have been split into several separate species. These revisions have received mixed reception both inside Australia, where all the species occur, and outside Australia, where several are popular horticultural subjects. In all the cases mentioned above the old classification has been used in this book, partly because it is more familiar and partly because there remains some level of controversy with many questions still unanswered at the time of writing. As with the new genera, both names are given and readers can decide for themselves.

Within the genera *Cadetia*, *Diplocaulobium* and *Flickingeria* there are recognised sections, but the species have not been listed under these, as they have not had the same general degree of use and are not as well known as are the sections of *Dendrobium*.

Each species description includes the name of the person who originally described it. Details of distribution and habitat are included, along with an idea of the size of the plant and of the leaves and flowers, characteristics not always obvious from the colour illustration. Detailed descriptions of the flowers, including colour and shape, are not given, as much of this can be seen in the illustrations. Synonyms in common use are listed.

Dendrobium capituliflorum
PHILLIP CRIBB

In the second paragraph of each description, specific information on cultivation is provided. These parts should be read in conjunction with Chapter 7, Cultivation, which describes some of the general principles underlying dendrobium cultivation.

The terms 'warm', 'intermediate' and 'cool' are used to describe the temperatures recommended for the cultivation of each species. Experience in greenhouses of the cool temperate climates of the northern hemisphere has shown that, depending upon season, a cool greenhouse should be maintained at between 8 and 14°C during the day and 6 and 12°C at night. Intermediate houses should be run at 12 to 18°C (day) and 10 to 16°C (night) while warm houses should be maintained at 16 to 22°C (day) and 14 to 19°C (night). During sunshine, temperatures are permitted to become about 20 per cent higher.

In warmer temperate and tropical climates, it has been found possible to grow most species within wider extremes. For example, in the Cairns area (temperature data, Table 10, page 74), warm species and many intermediate species can be successfully grown in shadecloth covered greenhouses or even on trees in gardens.

Section *Amblyanthus* Schltr. (Genus *Dendrobium*)

This is a poorly known section with some 14 described species, but it seems likely that the number will reduce when synonyms are allowed for. All are from New Guinea except for one species in Borneo and Peninsular Malaysia and one in the Solomons. They grow at low to moderate altitudes in cloud forests, often low down on trees with stems growing out, then hanging down from the trunk. It is uncertain where the affinities of this section lie, perhaps with *Breviflores* or *Distichophyllum*.

The stems are crowded, usually erect then pendulous with leaves in 2 ranks along the apical half of the stem. The flowers are lateral, in a short raceme of a few flowers. and last for up to a week or two. There is a peculiar scaly covering to the flowers and the lip has an appendage pointing backwards.

Dendrobium squamiferum J.J. Sm.

This medium sized to large epiphyte is widespread throughout Irian Jaya and Papua New Guinea at altitudes of about 150 to 500 m. They grow in trees overhanging rivers or on ridge tops, often forming large clumps in fern baskets. The habitat in many areas features a rather drier period, but rainfall overall is heavy. The pseudobulbs are slender, 25 to 75 cm long and 5 to 10 mm in diameter, initially erect, then pendulous as they lengthen, with leaves along their apical half or along their entire length. The leaves are deciduous, lanceolate, 7 to 10 cm long and 2 to 3 cm wide, with wavy margins. The inflorescences are borne on the apical part of the leafy, or occasionally leafless, stems. There are several inflorescences per stem and they consist of 2 to 8 flowers, each about 17 mm long and about the same across. They are slow to develop and open only briefly. Flowering has been recorded from April to July in the habitat.

In cultivation, warm conditions with bright light are required. The plants should be watered regularly throughout the year, but a slight decrease in winter may be beneficial. A hanging pot or basket or slab to accommodate the pendulous growth is recommended.

Dendrobium sp. aff. *D. squamiferum* J.J. Sm.

The species illustrated is apparently undescribed. It is from lower montane forest at an elevation of about 1000 m in the ranges south of Lae, Morobe Province, Papua New Guinea. Mature plants grow to 30–40 cm high. The leafy habit is somewhat unusual for a *Dendrobium* and it has some resemblance to certain *Eria* species. The pseudobulbs are almost circular in cross-section and 7 to 10 mm in diameter. Each has 8 to 12 broad, relatively thin leaves about 15 cm long and 45 mm wide. The green clasping leaf bases are sparsely covered with brown scales. The flowers are borne in tight clusters from the nodes on the upper two-thirds of the pseudobulbs. They have scattered brown scales on the backs of the petals and sepals. This species flowers every few months and the flowers last for about two weeks.

This species is easily grown in intermediate conditions using any of the standard epiphyte potting mixes. The single clone found will not self-pollinate.

Section *Aporum* (Blume) Lindl. (Genus *Dendrobium*)

This section includes about 45 species occurring from India to New Guinea with the centre of distribution being South-East Asia and the Indonesian Islands. Myanmar (Burma) has about 25 species and Borneo has 24. They are mostly small epiphytes of lowland situations, but some species are found at altitudes up to 1600 m. The section is closely related to sections *Rhopalanthe*, *Oxystophyllum* and *Strongyle*. *Aporum* lacks the swollen basal nodes of *Rhopalanthe*, and also lacks the small projection under the apex of the lip which is present in *Oxystophyllum*, while the leaves of *Strongyle* are terete as opposed to the flattened leaves in *Aporum*.

Most are small plants, initially erect, then pendulous, with short to moderately long leafy stems with flattened, usually sharp-pointed, fleshy leaves in 2 ranks. The leaves are usually closely spaced or overlapping at their bases. The flowers are borne laterally, usually singly from a cluster of chaffy bracts. Some species have an elongated terminal extension of the stem that lacks leaves and bears the flowers. The flowers are small and last a few days.

WAYNE HARRIS

Dendrobium acinaciforme Roxb.

Synonyms: *Dendrobium spatella* Rchb.f., *D. banaense* Gagnep.
This medium sized epiphyte is widespread across South-East Asia, from north-east India through Myanmar (Burma), Thailand, Laos, Cambodia, Vietnam and southern China. It grows in montane forests at altitudes of about 800 m to 2000 m in areas that mostly have a distinct dry season in winter. The stems are up to 33 cm long with a basal leafy part and a slender leafless apical part on which the flowers are borne. The leaves overlap at the base and are fleshy, narrowly triangular, about 3 cm long and 5 mm wide. The flowers, which are about 5 mm across, are borne singly along the leafless apical part of the stem. Flower colour is variable and different colour forms often grow together. The form originally described as *D. banaense* has purple flowers while the flowers of most other forms are greenish-yellow.

Intermediate to cool conditions are recommended for this species, and the plants can tolerate very cold conditions if dry. The plants should be given a dry resting period in winter when waterings are a week or so apart and the plants dry out thoroughly. A slab is best to accommodate the growth habit, although a small, well-drained pot is also successful.

B ▬▬ LAVARACK

Dendrobium aloifolium (Blume) Rchb.f.

Synonyms: *Dendrobium serra* (Lindl.) Lindl., *D. micranthum* (Griff.) Lindl.
This widespread species occurs from Myanmar (Burma) through Indochina, Thailand, Malaysia and Indonesia to New Guinea. It is a reasonably compact epiphyte occurring at low altitudes, usually below 600 m, on rainforest trees. It forms small clumps of tangled stems with numerous aerial growths. The stems are up to about 60 cm long, but usually much shorter, with overlapping leaves in 2 rows along most of the stem. There is a slender apical part of the stem bare of leaves or with some short leaves. The basal leaves are up to 2 cm long, and the leaves decrease in size towards the apex of the stem. The flowers are tiny, about 4 mm across, and borne from a cluster of bracts on the leafless part of the stem or from the leaf axils of the smaller apical leaves. The sepals and petals bend backwards a few days after opening to give the flowers their distinctive appearance. The flowers are borne throughout the year and last about 2 weeks.

While the flowers are not attractive, the plant form is interesting and it rapidly grows into a large clump. It requires warm conditions and a well-drained mixture in a small pot or on a slab. It should be given bright filtered light and watered throughout the year.

JIM COMBER

Dendrobium distichum (Presl.) Rchb.f.

Synonym: *Dendrobium indivisum* Naves, [non *D. indivisum* (Blume) Miq.]
This medium sized, pendulous epiphyte is restricted to the Philippines where it has been recorded in numerous localities. It occurs from sea level to about 900 m, growing on mangroves and on trees in swamps in areas with a dry season in winter. The stems are up to 40 cm long with flattened triangular leaves in 2 ranks along their length. The leaves are triangular, overlapping and fleshy. The flowers are borne in a dense bunch from a group of small bracts at the apex of the stem. Flowering is more or less throughout the year, perhaps with an emphasis in spring.

While a slightly drier period may be useful in winter, plants are probably best kept reasonably moist throughout the year. They should be given warm humid conditions with bright filtered light all year. The pendulous habit makes the plants best suited to a slab, but a hanging pot with a well-drained medium is also suitable.

Dendrobium indivisum (Blume) Miq.

Synonyms: *Dendrobium incrassatum* (Blume) Miq., *D. eulophotum* Lindl. This medium sized epiphyte occurs over a wide area in South-East Asia, being recorded from Myanmar (Burma), Thailand, Peninsular Malaysia, Laos, Vietnam, Borneo, Java, the Moluccas and the Philippines. It grows from sea level to about 1600 m in coffee plantations, mangroves and lower montane forests. Several varieties have been recorded, the one shown here being the type variety from west Java. The stems are pendulous, up to 40 cm long and leafy throughout. The leaves are triangular, overlapping, fleshy, usually flattened, but some almost terete leaves have been recorded. They vary in size, but are commonly about 2.5 cm long. The flowers are produced singly at the base of the leaves. They are about 9 mm across and last several days. There are several variations in flower colour and labellum shape. Flowering in the habitat may occur at any time of the year.

The pendulous habit makes this species more suited to a slab or hanging pot. The plants should be kept moist throughout the year, particularly if on a slab, although plants from some regions may grow in areas where there is a pronounced dry season in winter. Warm conditions are probably best with year-round high humidity and bright filtered light.

Dendrobium keithii Ridl.

This is a medium to large epiphyte which is restricted to Thailand. It grows at low altitudes in areas with a strongly seasonal climate. The stems are pendulous, up to 40 cm long and covered along their length with succulent, flattened, sharp-pointed leaves up to 5 cm long in 2 distinct rows. Aerial growths are produced regularly. The single flowers are borne prolifically along the centre line of the stems, mostly near the apex of the stems. They are about 1.5 to 2 cm across and last about 2 weeks. The main flowering season is late winter and spring, but occasional flowers may appear at any time. This species is very similar to the more widespread *D. anceps* Sw. from which it differs only in the details of the lip, which is bilobed in *D. keithii* and with a shallow notch in *D. anceps*.

The heavily pendulous habit makes slab culture best, but a hanging pot of well-drained medium is also effective. It should be given warm conditions, but will tolerate intermediate temperatures, if given a resting period in winter and early spring when watering is reduced, but not stopped. Filtered sunlight is best, but flowering may be inhibited if the light levels are too low. The plant may be propagated from the aerial growths that can be removed when they have roots attached.

Dendrobium leonis (Lindl.) Rchb.f.

This is a small epiphyte with wide distribution from Thailand, Peninsular Malaysia, Singapore, Cambodia, Laos, Vietnam, Sumatra and Borneo. It is a lowland species, although plants have been recorded from as high as 1400 m. In Borneo it has been reported growing as a lithophyte on limestone cliffs. The stems are up to 25 cm long, erect or pendulous, with leaves along their length. The leaves are fleshy, about 2 to 3 cm long and the same across, in 2 ranks, overlapping at the base. The flowers are fleshy, about 1.5 cm across, fragrant and borne singly or in pairs at the apex of the stem. Flowering is throughout the year.

Warm conditions with year-round high humidity are required. Watering should be maintained throughout the year, although it may be slightly decreased in winter in cooler climates, provided the plants are not dry for long periods. A slab is best to accommodate the growth habit. A pot of well-drained medium is also successful.

WAYNE HARRIS

Dendrobium lobulatum Rolfe & J.J. Sm.

This is a medium sized epiphyte from Java, Sumatra, Borneo and Ambon. It occurs in lowland to mid-montane forests at altitudes of 500 to 1200 m. In some locations there is a distinct dry season in winter, but in other areas there is year-round high rainfall. The stems are up to 50 cm long, the young stems covered for their length with the overlapping leaves, while the older stems have a leafless portion of up to 10 cm at the end. The leaves are triangular, varying in size up to about 2.5 cm long, but much smaller near the apex. The flowers are borne on the apical leafless part of the stem and are about 7 mm across. Flowering can occur at any time of the year.

A slab or hanging pot of well-drained medium is best to accommodate the pendulous habit. The plants should be watered throughout the year and given intermediate to warm temperatures with bright filtered sunlight.

JIM COMBER

Dendrobium mannii Ridl.

This small epiphytic species occurs in India, Thailand, Indochina and Peninsular Malaysia. It grows at low to moderate altitudes in seasonal forests where rainfall is low during winter and early spring. The stems are up to 25 cm long, pendulous and covered with 2 ranks of succulent, overlapping leaves that are often tinged with purple and deciduous after 2 or 3 years. The flowers are about 1 cm across and are borne terminally in clusters of a few flowers and laterally along the old leafless stems. The flowering season is variable, but seems to concentrate on winter, with the flowers lasting about 2 or 3 weeks. There is some confusion between this species, *D. nathanielis* Rchb.f. and *D. terminale* Par. & Rchb.f.

This species is easy to grow in a small pot of well-drained medium. It should be grown in filtered light and watered heavily during the growing season with a dry resting period in winter and early spring. It does well in warm to intermediate conditions.

BILL LAVARACK

Dendrobium patentilobum Ames & Schweinf.

This medium sized epiphyte is restricted the lower slopes of Mt Kinabalu in Sabah on the island of Borneo. It grows in lower montane forest and in low forest on ultramafic substrate. It has been recorded as an epiphyte on *Gymnostoma sumatrana*. The altitude range is 800 to 1500 m, in areas with a high year-round rainfall. The stems are up to 40 cm long, erect or pendulous, with leaves along most of the length, but with a slender, leafless portion at the apex on which the flowers are borne. The leaves are fleshy, narrowly triangular, in 2 ranks, about 4 to 8 cm long and 1 cm wide. The flowers are about 1 cm across, borne singly along the leafless part of the stem and opening successively.

Warm to intermediate temperatures and high humidity levels are required throughout the year. Watering should be regular throughout the year, with the plants remaining constantly moist. Their habit makes the plants suited to a slab, but a hanging pot of well-drained medium is also suitable.

WAYNE HARRIS

Dendrobium prostratum Ridl.

This medium sized epiphyte occurs in Peninsular Malaysia and Borneo. It grows at altitudes below 1000 m in lowland and foothill forests, being recorded on mangroves in the southern part of Peninsular Malaysia. The stems are creeping and branching with roots at regular intervals, the plant reaching about 30 cm in length. The leaves are broadly and bluntly triangular, about 7 mm long and 4 to 5 mm wide, in 2 rows along the length of the stem. The flowers are borne singly or in groups of a few flowers at the apex of the stem. They are about 1 cm across and have a vanilla-like fragrance. The labellum is pink with a prominent yellow, hairy callus.

The creeping habitat of the species makes it suited to slab culture, but a pot with a well-drained medium is also suitable. The plants require warm conditions with year-round watering and high humidity.

JIM COMBER

Dendrobium pseudocalceolum J.J. Sm.

This medium sized to large pendulous epiphyte is restricted to New Guinea and some small nearby islands. It is widespread in both Irian Jaya and Papua New Guinea, growing from a few metres above sea level to about 500 m, in seasonally dry forest, usually hanging over streams. The stems branch and produce numerous aerial growths, which eventually form a tangled mass. The older stems are leafless, while the younger stems have 2 rows of succulent, narrowly triangular, well-spaced leaves about 4 cm long and 5 mm wide, overlapping at the base. The flowers are produced apically in groups of 1 to 3. They are about 2.5 cm long and are white with a few red stripes on the reverse of the petals and sepals. Flowering occurs about 12 to 13 days after heavy rainfall and all plants in an area flower at the same time. The flowers last about 2 to 3 days and have a faint sweet scent.

In cultivation, this species requires constantly warm conditions with year-round high humidity. Watering may be decreased slightly in winter, but should generally be frequent throughout the year. The pendulous, tangled habit of this species makes it best suited to a slab or, if the climate is suitable, to being tied firmly to a tree. It should be given filtered sunlight.

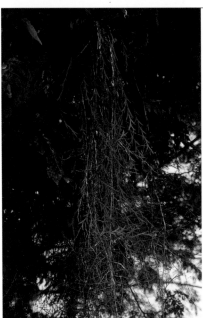

GEOFF STOCKER

JIM COMBER

Dendrobium sagittatum J.J. Sm.

This is a medium sized epiphyte, which occurs in Java and Sumatra. It grows in open forests at altitudes of 700 to 1500 m in areas with a seasonal climate and is subject to regular dry periods. The stems are up to 30 cm long, flattened, pendulous, with leaves along their length. The leaves are overlapping, triangular, about 50 mm long. The inflorescence consists of a single flower, usually borne at the apex of the stem. The flowers are about 1.2 to 1.4 cm across, opening widely.

In cultivation, this species requires warm to intermediate temperatures with bright filtered sunlight. This species will withstand longer dry periods than most others in the section and should be given a distinct dry period in winter when watering is reduced, although it should not be withheld for more than a few days. The pendulous nature of the plants makes them suited to a hanging pot with well-drained medium or a slab.

Section *Australorchis* (Brieger) Dockrill (Genus *Dendrobium*)

The name *Monophyllaea* Benth. is also used for this section. It is a group of only 3 species, all restricted to eastern and north-eastern Australia. They are epiphytes, or occasionally lithophytes, from low to moderate altitudes, occurring in open forests and rainforests. This section is perhaps closest to *Dendrocoryne*.

The plants form dense mats made of pseudobulbs that are short and thick and often well spaced. There are 1 or 2 leaves, which do not have a sheathing base, at the apex of each stem. The long inflorescence is apical, with several small flowers, which are cup- or star-shaped. There is a prominent mentum and the lip is 3-lobed.

GERALD McCRAITH

Dendrobium carrii Rupp & C.T. White

This small, creeping, mat-forming epiphyte or occasionally lithophyte, is restricted to the wet tropical mountains of north-eastern Queensland in Australia. It occurs from 900 to about 1400 m in cloud forests where there is year-round high humidity and rainfall. It often grows on the outer branches in windy, exposed conditions. The pseudobulbs are egg-shaped, 1.5 to 3.5 cm long and 0.8 to 1.5 cm wide. They are separated by as much as 5 to 8 cm along a slender rhizome. There are 2 strap-like leaves at the apex, 5 to 10 cm long and about 1 cm wide. The inflorescence is apical, usually solitary, but occasionally 2 or 3, with 5 to 10 flowers, each about 1 cm long. The flowering season is spring.

The mat-forming habit of this species makes it unsuited to pot culture. A slab of cork or similar material is recommended, but it is important that the plants are tied tightly to the substrate while establishing. Intermediate to cool conditions with constant humidity, year-round watering and filtered sunlight are recommended.

Dendrobium monophyllum F. Muell.

This creeping, mat-forming epiphyte or lithophyte occurs in eastern Australia from northern New South Wales to the base of Cape York Peninsula. It grows in rainforests and open forests from the coast to areas 100 kilometres inland at low to moderate altitudes (up to 900 m). The climate is often seasonal and the plants usually grow in strong sunlight. The pseudobulbs are short, thick, almost conical and about 6 to 8 cm long and well spaced, with a single or occasionally 2 leaves, oval and about 5 to 13 cm long. The inflorescences are terminal, long and slender with up to 20 fragrant cup-shaped flowers each about 7 to 8 mm across. The flowering season is spasmodic with an emphasis on late winter and spring.

This species is not well suited to pot culture due to its creeping habit. A slab of weathered wood or cork is best and the plants must be tied firmly to the slab. They should be placed in a moist, but well-lit position. Watering should be reduced in winter and increased towards the end of spring. They tolerate warm to intermediate conditions.

BRUCE GRAY

WAYNE HARRIS

Dendrobium schneiderae F.M. Bailey

This is an epiphytic species occurring in eastern Australia. There are two varieties – the type variety, which occurs from northern New South Wales to central Queensland, and variety *major* Rupp, which occurs in the Clarke Range in central Queensland. Both varieties occur in rainforests at low to moderate altitudes (up to 1000 m), usually on the upper branches where there is good light and air movement. They often grow in dense moss. The pseudobulbs are short and almost globose, usually less than 1 cm long. They are closely packed together and have 2 leaves 2.5 to 7 cm long and about 5 mm across. The inflorescences are long and pendulous with up to 25 fragrant flowers, each less than 1 cm across. The flowering season is autumn. Its more robust habit and longer raceme distinguish the variety *major*.

In cultivation, these plants are difficult to grow. They should be tied tightly on a slab of cork or similar material and should be watered throughout the year, making sure the plants dry out between watering. When first attaching to the substrate some moisture-retaining material is useful. They are best given intermediate conditions with strong light.

Section *Bolbidium* Lindl. (Genus *Dendrobium*)

This is a small section of about 6 or 7 species which occurs from India to Borneo. There is one doubtful record from New Guinea. Peninsular Malaysia, with 5 species, may be the centre of distribution. They are epiphytes of low to moderate altitudes, often in areas with a seasonal climate. The section is related to section *Dendrobium*.

The pseudobulbs are small with the pseudobulbs crowded close together. There are 2 leaves, without leaf sheaths, apparently opposite each other at the apex. The flowers, which are ephemeral, are produced singly from a group of bracts between the leaves. The lip is entire and there is a long mentum.

BILL LAVARACK

Dendrobium hymenanthum Rchb.f.

Synonym: *Dendrobium quadrangulare* Parish & Rchb.f.
This is a miniature species from Myanmar (Burma), Thailand, Indochina, Peninsular Malaysia, the Philippines and Borneo. It grows as an epiphyte in hot, steamy, lowland rainforests, often in fairly open situations and in areas with a drier season in winter and spring. The stems are densely crowded, up to 10 cm long, club-shaped, with a very slender base and prominently 4-angled. There are 2 fleshy oblong leaves 2 to 3 cm long at the apex of the stem. The flowers are borne singly from the apex of the stem. They are about 1 to 2 cm long, fragrant and last only a day or two. The flowers are produced several times a year, a week or two after a sudden drop in temperature.

In cultivation, this species requires warm, humid conditions throughout the year. It is best grown in a small pot with a standard well-drained medium. A drier resting period in winter is recommended, but the plants should not be allowed to dry out for longer than a day or two. Bright filtered sunlight is recommended.

Dendrobium pachyphyllum (Kuntze) Bakh.f.

Synonyms: *Dendrobium pusillum* (Blume) Bijdr., *D. carnosum* Teijsm. & Binn., *D. borneense* Finet, *D. pisibulbum* Guillaumin, *Flickingeria pumilum* (Roxb.) A.D. Hawkes

This widespread, miniature species occurs from north-eastern India to Myanmar (Burma), Thailand, Vietnam, Peninsular Malaysia, Sumatra, Java and Borneo. It grows epiphytically in areas of high light intensity such as on roadside trees and in plantations, from sea level to about 1500 m. There is a branching, creeping rhizome and the plants rapidly form a dense mat. The pseudobulbs are club-shaped, very slender at the base, with the upper part swollen and 3 to 6 cm long. There are 2 succulent oblong leaves, less than 1 cm long and up to 5 mm wide. The flowers are borne singly at the apex of the pseudobulb and are about 1 cm long. They are fragrant and last only a day or two. Flowers are produced sporadically throughout the year, with all plants in the area flowering at the same time, probably in response to a drop in temperature some time previously.

The mat-forming habit means that the plants are best suited to slab culture, but they can also be grown in a pot of well-drained medium. The plants require strong light and grow well in warm to intermediate conditions with year-round watering and high humidity.

Section *Breviflores* Hook.f. (Genus *Dendrobium*)

This small section occurs from India to Borneo and Java. There are about 12 species in the section with the centre of distribution being in mainland South-East Asia with about 11 species. The plants grow as epiphytes, mostly at low to moderate altitudes in areas with a markedly seasonal climate. It is not a clear-cut section, and those with a fringed lip are sometimes placed in section *Stuposa*. The section appears related to sections *Dendrobium*, *Stachyobium*, *Calcarifera* and *Pedilonum*.

The plants mostly have slender stems that may be swollen and pseudobulbous in the apical part, with leaves along most of the length of the stem. The leaves are deciduous after 2 or 3 years. The inflorescences are short with 3 to 10 flowers, rather small and usually in shades of pink or yellow. The base of the lip (mentum) is saccate and the lip is 3-lobed and usually hairy along the margin.

Dendrobium aduncum Wall. ex Lindl.

This small epiphytic species is widespread in much of South-East Asia, including India, Myanmar (Burma), Thailand, Vietnam and south-west China. It grows at altitudes of about 300 to 1300 m in open montane forests in areas with a distinctly seasonal climate featuring a dry season in winter. The pseudobulbs are slender and pendulous, 40 to 60 cm long, with 4 to 6 leaves on the apical part. The leaves are elliptic–lanceolate, deciduous, 5 to 9 cm long and thin-textured. The inflorescences consist of about 3 to 5 fragrant flowers each 2.5 to 3.5 cm across and borne from the apical third of the leafless stems. Individual flowers last a few weeks and, as the flowers on individual pseudobulbs open successively, a large plant may be in flower for a month or more. Flowering is in spring. This species is very closely related to *D. hercoglossum* Rchb.f., but can be separated by the pseudobulbs, which are club-shaped in that species and cylindrical in *D. aduncum*.

The pendulous habit makes this species suited to a slab or a hanging pot of well-drained medium. It requires intermediate to warm temperatures and bright filtered light. The plants should be given a dry resting period in winter when water is much reduced and the plants dry out thoroughly between waterings.

Dendrobium dantaniense Guillaumin

Synonym: *Dendrobium alterum* Seidenf.
This medium sized species has been recorded from Vietnam and Thailand where it grows as an epiphyte in montane forests at altitudes of 700 to 1800 m. In these areas there is a distinct dry season during winter. The pseudobulbs are up to 55 cm long, slender at the base and swollen in the middle. There are 4 to 6 deciduous leaves, about 6 to 10 cm long, oblong to lanceolate, on the apical part of the pseudobulb. The inflorescences consist of 3 to 6 tightly crowded flowers and are produced on the leafless pseudobulbs, laterally and near the apex. The flowers are fleshy and 5 to 10 mm across. Flowering is in spring and summer. The flowers last about 2 weeks.

In cultivation, the plants may be grown on a slab or in a pot of well-drained medium. Intermediate temperatures are best with a drier resting period in winter and early spring when the plants are allowed to dry out completely between watering. Filtered light or semi-shade are recommended.

Dendrobium hercoglossum Rchb.f.

Synonyms: *Dendrobium vexans* Dammer, *D. poilanei* Guillaumin, *D. wangii* Tso
This small to medium sized epiphyte occurs in Thailand, Indochina, southern China, Hong Kong, the Philippines, Sumatra and Peninsular Malaysia at low to moderate altitude. It grows in rainforest, but the climate is seasonal to some extent, with a drier period in winter and spring. The pseudobulbs become pendulous as they lengthen. They grow to about 20 cm long and are club-shaped with a narrow basal part expanding to an apical section about 1 cm in width. The leaves are narrow–linear, 5 to 10 cm long, and are in 2 ranks along the swollen part of the stem. They are deciduous after 1 or 2 years. The inflorescences are short and are borne laterally on leafy or, more commonly, on leafless stems. Each has about 5 waxy flowers each about 2.5 cm in diameter. The flowers last about 2 weeks and are borne in spring. This species is closely related to, and often confused with, *D. aduncum* and

BILL LAVARACK

Cadetia collinsii Lavarack

Section *Cadetia*

This is a miniature species forming dense clumps. It grows as an epiphyte at low altitudes in shady conditions in the rainforests of the McIlwraith and Iron Ranges of Cape York Peninsula in north-east Australia. The stems are 0.5 to 6 cm long and 1 to 2 mm wide with a single fleshy leaf, 1 to 3 cm long and 0.5 to 1 cm wide. The flowers are about 6 to 8 mm across and are borne singly at the apex of the stem. The ovary and the seed capsules are covered with fleshy green hairs. Flowering may occur at any time with an emphasis on summer and autumn. They last about a week.

Both pot and slab culture have proved successful for this species. It should be given semi-shade and warm moist conditions with watering throughout the year. A small pot with a mixture that retains a little moisture is recommended.

PETER O'BRYNE

Cadetia karoensis Schltr.

Section *Cadetia*

This miniature species occurs in the Bismarck Archipelago and the Solomon Islands. It grows at low altitudes in coastal forests forming small clumps on tree trunks, often in rather open situations, in areas with a high year-round rainfall. The stems are erect, 6 to 10 cm long and 2.5 mm wide at the widest near the apex. The single leaf is 3 to 5.5 cm long and 8 to 10 mm wide and fleshy. Flowers are borne successively, one at a time (occasionally 2 at once) from a bract at the stem apex. The flowers last several weeks and flowering is continuous throughout the year. The ovary and seed capsule are covered in fleshy hairs.

This species does best in a small pot of well-drained medium. It should be watered throughout the year and kept in warm conditions in semi-shade or filtered sunlight. It does well in cultivation and is always in flower.

GERALD McCRAITH

Cadetia maideniana (Schltr.) Schltr.

Section *Cadetia*

Synonyms: *Dendrobium hispidum* sensu F. Muell., *D. maideniana* Schltr.

This miniature epiphytic or lithophytic, tufted species grows in the rainforests of north-east Queensland, Australia, and possibly in New Guinea. It grows in shaded rainforest conditions, often low down on tree trunks, mostly at altitudes below 1000 m. The slender stems are 2 to 7 cm long and 1 to 2 mm in diameter, slightly swollen at the base. The single terminal leaf is ovate or oblong, about 3 to 6 cm long and 10 to 15 mm wide. The solitary flower is about 6 mm in diameter. The ovary, and subsequently the seed capsule, is covered with short fleshy hairs. Flowering is erratic and can occur at any time of the year. The flowers last about a week.

This species requires warm to intermediate conditions with semi-shade and a humid atmosphere. It should be kept evenly moist throughout the year. A slab or a small pot of well-drained medium is recommended. If grown on a slab, care must be taken that the plants do not dry out for long periods.

Cadetia quinquecostata (J.J. Sm.) Schltr.

Section *Ptero-Cadetia*
Synonym: *Dendrobium rumphiae* Rchb.f. var. *quinquecostata* J.J. Sm.
This miniature species has been recently reported from the Kokoda area of Papua New Guinea, where it grows in the outer canopy of trees lining streams, but is probably much more widespread and has been recorded from Irian Jaya. The erect stems are 2 to 7.5 cm long and 3 to 5 mm wide at the widest near the apex. The single leaf is 4.5 to 9.5 cm long and 8 to 14 mm wide. The flowers are about 8 mm by 10 mm long and are borne successively one at a time from a bract at the leaf apex. The flowers last 10 to 14 days and flowering is probably spasmodic throughout the year.

This species should be grown in a small pot with good drainage. It requires warm conditions and should be watered throughout the year and kept in humid conditions with good air movement. Bright light is recommended.

PETER O'BYRNE

Cadetia taylori (F. Muell.) Schltr.

Section *Ptero-Cadetia*
Synonyms: *Dendrobium uniflos* Bailey, D. *hispidulum* sensu Fitzgerald
This miniature species occurs in north-eastern Australia including Cape York Peninsula and possibly New Guinea. It grows on trees and rocks from low to moderate altitudes (up to 1200 m) in semi-shaded areas with year-round rainfall and warm to intermediate temperatures. The plants grow into dense clumps which can consist of up to 100 closely packed, slightly swollen stems, each about 3 to 10 cm long and 3 to 5 mm in diameter. The single leaf is about 3 to 4 cm long and 1 cm broad. The flowers are borne singly from a bract at the apex of the stem and are about 1 cm in diameter. They last about a week and may appear at any time, although they are more common in summer and autumn.

In cultivation, the plants should be kept evenly moist, but not soggy. They will tolerate dry periods. They are best grown in a small pot or on a slab and should be given semi-shade and warm to intermediate conditions.

BILL LAVARACK

Cadetia transversiloba (J.J. Sm.) Schltr.

Section *Ptero-Cadetia*
Synonyms: *Dendrobium transversilobum* J.J. Sm., *Cadetia heterochroma* Schltr.
This small species is widespread but uncommon throughout Irian Jaya and Papua New Guinea at low altitudes below 500 m, in montane rainforest. In these areas there is year-round rainfall and high humidity. The stems form small clumps and are erect, 1 to 8 cm long, 7 to 10 mm wide at the widest near the apex, prominently 4-winged. The single leaf is erect, fleshy, 7 to 10 cm long and 2 to 3.5 cm wide. The flowers are borne successively, one at a time, from a bract at the apex of the stem. They are about 8 mm across, last about 10 days and flowering is probably throughout the year.

A small pot with a well-drained medium is best. The plants should be kept moist throughout the year and given semi-shade and humid warm conditions.

PETER O'BYRNE

Cadetia wariana Schltr.

Section *Sarco-Cadetia*

This is a miniature mat-forming species from New Guinea, the islands of Torres Strait and Cape York Peninsula in north-east Australia. It grows on trees or rocks in filtered light in areas with a predominantly wet climate but may be subject to a drier period through winter and spring. It occurs from about 200 to 800 m altitude. The plant forms a dense mat of closely packed stems each about 1 cm long. The glossy green leaf is a similar length. The flowers are a crystalline white, about 5 mm across and borne singly from a bract at the apex of the stem. They last a week or two and are borne at any time of the year.

The creeping habit means that this species is best suited to a slab of wood or cork or similar material. They should be given filtered sunlight and watered throughout the year, although a drier period in winter causes no problems. Warm conditions are required.

Cadetia sp. ex April River

Section *Sarco-Cadetia*

This small tufted species was found in tall foothill forest dominated by the conifer *Agathis labillardieri*, at about 400 m altitude in the vicinity of April River, East Sepik Province, Papua New Guinea. It was growing epiphytically on small trees and understorey shrubs. Only a few plants were seen. They were 3 to 4 cm high and 2 to 5 cm across.

As far as is known this species is not in cultivation. The habitat and environment in which the plants were found suggest that it should be grown in a warm, humid, shady situation. An occasional short dry period may not do the plants any harm.

Cadetia sp. ex Mt Gahavesuka

Section *Sarco-Cadetia*

A colony of this species was found growing on shrubs and small trees on the summit of Mt Gahavesuka at about elevation 2500 m, Eastern Highlands Province, Papua New Guinea. Individual plants are tufted, 3 to 5 cm across and from 2 to 3 cm high. Unfortunately this colony was badly affected by the widespread El Niño drought and subsequent fires of 1997. While damaging fires were not widespread in this region, the drought has had a major impact on the orchid flora. Although some recovery was evident by mid-1999 at this site, it has been slow and surviving plants have not yet regained their pre-drought vigour.

As far as is known this species is not in cultivation. Similar species have grown well in a small pot that is kept moist and placed in a bright spot in a greenhouse maintained at intermediate temperatures.

Section *Calcarifera* J.J. Sm. (Genus *Dendrobium*)

This section was originally described by J.J. Smith in 1908, but was largely ignored, with the species being allocated to the closely related section *Pedilonum* until J.B. Comber resurrected it in his work on the orchids of Java (Comber 1983, 1990). Most of the mainland Asian species previously placed in *Pedilonum* are now placed in *Calcarifera*. Borneo with 21 species seems to be the centre of distribution, while Java has 10 and mainland Asia a similar number. The island of New Guinea has only one member of this section (*D. lancifolium*), and there are no members further east. A total of about 50 to 60 species in the section seems possible.

Most members of the section are medium sized epiphytes with fleshy stems or pseudobulbs and leaves in 2 ranks along the length of the stem, deciduous after a year or two. The flowers have a long mentum that is directed away from the pedicel and ovary. The lip is moderately wide and narrows abruptly at the base, where there is usually a small protuberance on the upper surface. The flowers are borne singly or in short, often pendulous, inflorescences that are borne laterally along the stems. The species are recorded from low and moderate altitudes, but usually in areas of year-round rainfall.

WAYNE HARRIS

Dendrobium amethystoglossum Rchb.f.

This is a moderate sized epiphyte or lithophyte from Luzon in the Philippines. It is reported from mossy limestone cliffs at moderate to high altitudes (about 1500 m) where there is year-round humidity and a drier period in winter. The stems are up to 90 cm long and 1.5 cm in diameter with deciduous leaves in 2 ranks along the upper half of the stem. The leaves are oval, pale green and about 8 to 10 cm long. The flowers are fragrant and borne in pendulous racemes about 10 to 15 cm long, from the apical part of the stem, with up to 15 flowers each about 4 cm across. The flowering season is winter and the flowers last about 3 to 4 weeks.

The plants grow well in an open mixture in strong filtered light. They should be given a dry resting period through winter into early spring, but should not be kept totally dry for long periods. They do best in intermediate temperatures, but tolerate tropical climates as long as there is a slightly cooler winter.

GEOFF STOCKER

Dendrobium arcuatum J.J. Sm.

This is a medium sized, free-flowering species from east Java, where it grows from sea level to about 800 m altitude. It is an epiphyte in the lower parts of mountains, often on slopes facing the sea. The stems are slender, up to 70 cm long and 6 mm wide, with broad leaves about 10 cm long and 3 cm wide along most of the stem. Several inflorescences, each of 2 to 6 flowers, are borne along the apical two-thirds of the leafy or leafless stems. The flowers, which feature a long narrow mentum, are about 4 to 4.75 cm long.

In cultivation this species is best grown in a pot of well-drained medium or on a slab to accommodate the growth habit, which is often horizontal. A drier resting period, when the plants are allowed to almost dry out, is recommended in winter. The plants should be given bright filtered light and warm temperatures.

Dendrobium auriculatum Ames & Quisumb.

This medium sized species is restricted to Luzon and Mindanao Islands in the Philippines. It grows as an epiphyte or lithophyte at about 1000 m in montane rainforests. The stems are unbranched, 30 to 80 cm long with leaves along the lower part and the apical part bare. The linear–lanceolate leaves are 8 to 12 cm long and 4 to 8 mm wide, the leaf base with large ear-like lobes extending across the stem. These structures have given rise to the name 'auriculatum'. The flowers are borne singly on the leafless apical part of the stem. They are about 6 to 6.5 cm across and flowering occurs in winter and spring.

Intermediate conditions are required, with year-round high humidity. The plants should be watered throughout the year, and although a slight reduction in winter is probably beneficial, the plants should not be permitted to dry out for long periods. A pot with well-drained medium is best and the plants should be given filtered sunlight.

Dendrobium calicopis Ridl.

This medium sized epiphyte occurs at low altitudes in Peninsular Malaysia and doubtfully Peninsular Thailand. It is recorded from the Langkawi Islands, which are on the west coast of the Malay Peninsula close to the Malaysia–Thailand border. The pseudobulbs are long and slender, to about 40 cm long and less than 1 cm wide. The leaves are acuminate, about 9 cm long and 12 mm wide, in 2 ranks along the length of the stem. The inflorescences consist of up to 6 flowers each about 3 cm across. They are borne laterally on the leafless stems.

This species is not well known in cultivation. It presumably requires warm to intermediate temperatures. A slightly drier resting period in winter is suggested, but the plants should not be permitted to dry out for long periods. A pot of well-drained medium or a slab should be equally suitable.

Dendrobium chameleon Ames

Synonyms: *Dendrobium longicalcaratum* Hayata, *D. randiacnse* Hayata
This is a medium sized epiphyte or lithophyte, which occurs on Luzon Island in the Philippines and on Taiwan. It grows at altitudes of 600 to 1000 m, often in shady conditions in montane rainforests. The pseudobulbs are branched, pendulous, 15 to 60 cm long, thickened towards the apex with leaves along the apical half of the final branches. The ovate leaves are about 3 to 6 cm long and 7 to 15 mm wide. The inflorescences are borne on the apical part of the stem and consist of 1 to 4 flowers, each 3 to 4 cm across. The flowers start white, sometimes with a lavender tinge, and turn yellow as they age. Flowering is in summer and autumn in the wild.

Intermediate to warm conditions with high humidity are required for this species in cultivation. In winter the plants should be permitted to dry between waterings, but should not to remain dry for long periods. A slab or hanging basket is best to allow for the pendulous growth habit. Semi-shade or filtered sunlight is recommended.

Dendrobium cumulatum Lindl.

Synonym: *Dendrobium eoum* Ridl.

This is a medium sized epiphyte from low to moderate altitudes in India, Myanmar (Burma), Indochina and Borneo, usually growing in lower montane forest. This widespread species mostly grows in areas with a seasonal rainfall and a reasonably distinct dry season. The pseudobulbs are 45 to 60 cm long, laterally flattened and pendulous, with about 6 leaves near the apex. The leaves are deciduous and about 7 to 10 cm long and 2.5 cm wide. The inflorescences are crowded, about 10 cm long, arising from the nodes on leafy or leafless stems, with 3 to 6 flowers, each 3 to 4 cm across. The flowering season is summer, the flowers last 2 or 3 weeks and have a vanilla-like fragrance

In cultivation, this species requires a cool dry resting period in winter for good flowering. It should be grown on a slab or in a hanging pot to accommodate the pendulous pseudobulbs and should be watered and fertilised regularly when in active growth from late spring onwards.

BILL LAVARACK

Dendrobium epidendropsis Kraenzl.

This medium sized epiphyte occurs on Luzon Island in the Philippines and also in Japan. In the Philippines it grows at about 900 m altitude in montane rainforests. The slender, spindle-shaped pseudobulbs are about 60 cm long with leaves on the apical half. The oblong–lanceolate leaves are 7 cm long and 1.5 cm wide, leathery. The flowers are borne on a pendulous inflorescence, which arises near the apex of the stem and includes about 15 waxy, glossy flowers each about 6 cm across. The flowers are fragrant and flowering is in autumn and winter.

Warm to intermediate temperatures are required with high humidity and good air movement. The plants should be given a slightly dry period in winter when watering is reduced, but should not be permitted to dry out for long periods. Bright light is recommended. Pot or slab culture is equally useful. If a pot is used, the medium should be well drained.

WAYNE HARRIS

Dendrobium fairchildae Ames & Quisumb.

This medium sized species occurs in the Philippines on Luzon where it grows epiphytically at altitudes of around 1000 to 1500 m. There is a report of plants growing on exposed rocks on the road to Bontoc. The stems are from 60 cm to almost 1 m long and very slender, becoming pendulous, with leaves on the apical third. The thin, lanceolate leaves are 13 to 17 cm long and 1.5 cm wide, deciduous. The flowers are about 6 cm long and are borne on short lateral inflorescences of 2 to 4 flowers, crowded on the apical part of the stem. The flowering season is late autumn and spring.

The plants grow well in a hanging pot of well-drained medium. They are best in intermediate conditions, but also tolerate hot tropical conditions as long as there is a winter with cooler nights. A rather drier period in winter is suggested, but the plants should not be allowed to dry out for long periods. Regular fertilising in the growing period is recommended. Bright light and high humidity are required.

WAYNE HARRIS

applied to an orange-flowered species from higher altitudes.

These plants are easily grown under intermediate or warm conditions, in a well-drained pot or on a slab. They should be watered throughout the year and not permitted to dry out. Bright filtered light is recommended.

Dendrobium sp. aff. *D. oreodoxa* Schltr.

The species has been seen on several occasions in the mid-montane rainforests of Papua New Guinea. It is usually found growing low down on the trunks of both small and large trees along ridge tops within the elevation range of 1500 to 2500 m. The rhizome is short and typically bears a few slender (2.5 mm thick), sparsely branched, semi-pendulous stems to 50 cm in length. The leaves are mainly on the apical half of the stems. They are moderately thin, ovate, about 6.5 cm long and 1 cm broad at the widest part. The short inflorescences arise at intervals of about 7 cm along most of the length of the leafless stems. They each bear 1 to 3 flowers. The colour of the flowers varies from pale orange to red. Each is about 2 cm long.

Seedlings of this species have been relatively easy to grow in intermediate temperature conditions. Plants should be kept moist. Moderate to low light levels are recommended.

Dendrobium sp. ex Kuper Range

This species has been seen only in *Nothofagus* forest at about 2200 m near the crest of the Kuper Range south of Lae, Morobe Province, Papua New Guinea. The rhizome is short. The pseudobulbs are about 40 cm long, about 1 cm wide at the thickest point near the middle and tend to be pendulous. The leaves are ovate, 8 cm long and 2 cm wide, and green with a purple flush. The flowers arise from the upper third of the older, leafless stems.

The species is very slow-growing in flask and has so far proved difficult to establish in cultivation. The original habitat indicates that intermediate to cool temperatures, a moist, well-drained potting medium and moderate light would be good starting points.

Dendrobium sp. ex Freeport

Little is known about the origin of this species except that it originally came from near the Freeport copper mine in West Irian, presumably at moderate altitude. The rhizome is short. The pseudobulbs are thin (3 to 5 mm thick), up to 40 cm long and erect to arching. The leaves are ovate, 5 cm long and 1.7 cm wide and quite reddish, especially when young. The leaf sheaths clasping the pseudobulbs remain dark red. Each short inflorescence usually consists of only 2 or 3 long-lasting flowers, generally borne towards the ends of the leafless stems. The flowers are about 1.5 cm long.

This species has been relatively easy to grow (albeit slowly) in a range of well-drained potting media in a greenhouse providing moderate light and intermediate temperatures. The potting medium should not be allowed to dry out.

Genus *Cannaeorchis* M.A. Clem. & D.L. Jones

Synonym: Section *Macrocladium* Schltr.

This genus of about eleven large terrestrial species is restricted to New Caledonia. They grow at low to moderate altitudes in areas of scrubland where there is high light intensity and a seasonal climate. They are largely confined to the *maquis* vegetation and the margins of stunted rainforest. Their tall slender habit has resulted in the common name 'cane orchids'. This genus is related to the *Grastidium* group, in particularly to *Pleianthe* and to the New Caledonian section *Kinetochilus*. It has only recently been elevated to the status of a genus.

The stems are cane-like, up to 4 or 5 m tall with leaves in 2 ranks along their length. The old stems are covered with the persistent leaf sheaths. Some species have granulose roots. The flowers are borne in lateral inflorescences that are erect or pendulous, with one to many small to medium sized flowers. The lip is entire or obscurely 3-lobed and there is a prominent mentum.

Cannaeorchis fractiflexum (Finet) M.A. Clem. & D.L. Jones

Synonym: *Dendrobium fractiflexum* Finet

This very large terrestrial species is restricted to the southern part of New Caledonia. It grows in areas with a year-round rainfall, from sea level to about 800 m altitude, often in shaded conditions in hillside forests, along creek banks. The stems range from 50 cm to 3 or 4 m tall, with blue-green leaves about 10 cm long in 2 ranks concentrated towards the apical part of the stem. The inflorescences arise laterally from the upper part of the stem. They are pendulous with 3 to 15 flowers, each 3 to 5 cm long. The flowers last a few weeks. The flowering season is throughout the year.

In cultivation, this species responds to a sandy soil, rich in organic material and well drained. Warm to intermediate conditions with semi-shade is recommended. Watering should be reasonably even throughout the year, with the medium being allowed to dry out between waterings.

Cannaeorchis sarcochilus (Finet) M.A. Clem. & D.L. Jones

Synonyms: *Dendrobium sarcochilus* Finet, *D. megalorhizum* Kraenzl.

This is a large, bamboo-like terrestrial species which is restricted to New Caledonia, mostly in the south of the island. It grows from sea level to about 1000 m altitude in maquis forests and along forest margins, in areas with year-round rainfall. The stems grow in clumps and are slender, reaching 5 m tall. There are 8 to 15 linear-lanceolate leaves, about 12 cm long, grouped at the apical third of the stem. The inflorescences are erect and produced from the upper nodes between the leaves. They are up to 10 cm long with as many as 15 flowers, each about 1.5 cm long, opening successively. The flowering period is summer and autumn.

In cultivation, a well-drained, sandy mixture with added organic material is recommended. The temperature should be warm to intermediate with year-round watering. The plants should be allowed to dry out almost completely between waterings. Filtered sunlight is recommended.

Cannaeorchis verruciferum (Rchb.f.) M.A. Clem. & D.L. Jones

Synonym: *Dendrobium verruciferum* Rchb.f.

This slender terrestrial species is restricted to New Caledonia where it occurs mostly at the southern part of the island with one record from the north. It grows from sea level to about 500 m (occasionally to 900 m) altitude in scrubland between boulders, often in disturbed sites, or in low forest in areas of bright light or even full sunlight. This is an area of year-round, but not extremely high, rainfall. The stems are long and slender, reaching 1 m tall, but commonly about 30 cm. The leaves are 2 to 5 cm long, unequally bilobed at the apex, mostly concentrated on the apical third of the stem. The flowers are about 4 to 5 cm long and are borne singly or occasionally in pairs, from the upper nodes. The colour of the lip varies from yellow to red. Flowering occurs throughout the year.

In cultivation, warm to intermediate conditions are required. Watering should be throughout the year, with the plants allowed to almost completely dry out between waterings. High humidity and bright light are recommended. The medium should have a sandy loam with organic material and must be very well drained.

Section *Conostalix* Kraenzl. (Genus *Dendrobium*)

This is a small section of about 10 species occurring from Myanmar (Burma) to New Guinea and Australia. Borneo, with 8 species, is clearly the centre of distribution. Most are terrestrial species of low to moderate altitudes. This section is related to sections *Grastidium* and *Distichophyllum*.

The stems are usually long and slender with narrow leaves that have hairy leaf sheaths enclosing the stem. The flowers arise from the leaf axils singly or in pairs and are usually held upside down. The lip is 3-lobed. Not many species in this section are popular in cultivation.

Dendrobium lobbii Teijsm. & Binn.

Synonyms: *Dendrobium calcaratum* Lindl., *D. tiejsmannii* Miquel, *D. conostalix* Rchb.f.

This is a widespread terrestrial species of swampy or sandy soils or on stream margins at low altitude. It was first described in 1853 and has been recorded from Thailand, Indochina, Peninsular Malaysia, Sumatra, Borneo, the Philippines, New Guinea, the Solomons and north-east Australia. The stems are brittle, long and slender, up to 70 cm with alternate leaves that are held erect close to the stem in 2 ranks. The leaves are unequally bilobed at the apex and about 1 to 2.5 cm long. Aerial growths are produced from the stem and help in propagating the plant. The flowers are about 1.5 cm long and are borne singly or in pairs, on the upper half of the stem, usually facing downwards in such a way that the underside of the lip is the most visible part. The flowers last about 2 or 3 weeks and are produced at any time of the year.

Cultivation is difficult, but plants have been grown in a moisture-retaining mixture which is never allowed to dry out. Stagnant conditions should be avoided. They should be kept warm year-round and strong light is required.

Dendrobium pachyglossum Parish & Rchb.f.

Synonyms: *Dendrobium abietinum* Ridl., *D. fallax* Guillaumin
This medium sized epiphyte or lithophyte occurs in many localities in South-East Asia, including Myanmar (Burma), Thailand, Peninsular Malaysia, Laos and Vietnam. It occurs at 600 to 1200 m growing on mossy rocks where it usually consists of tufted, erect stems, or as an epiphyte low down on tree trunks where it is usually pendulous. The stems are slender, up to 50 cm long, but often shorter, particularly in plants growing on rocks, with leaves along most of the length. The leaves are long and narrow, up to 10 cm long and 2.5 cm wide, with the leaf sheaths covered in long black or dark brown hairs. The flowers are about 1 to 1.3 cm long and are borne in pairs or occasionally 3 or 4 per inflorescence, which arises opposite the leaves. Flower colour varies from white to yellowish or greenish or occasionally almost pink, with stripes of orange or brown in the petals and sepals. The lip varies from white to yellow-green. The flowers last about 8 to 10 days.

In cultivation, the pendulous nature of many plants makes them more suited to a slab or hanging pot of well-drained medium. If grown on a slab the plants must be kept moist and watering should be maintained all year round. Warm temperatures with high humidity and semi-shade are recommended.

Dendrobium pinifolium Ridl.

Synonym: *Dendrobium squarrosum* J.J. Sm.
This small terrestrial species is restricted to Borneo where it is recorded from Kalimantan, Sarawak and Sabah. It grows at altitudes between 300 and 600 m in lowlands and hill forest, often in low forest with *Dacrydium*. The stems are erect, 15 to 20 cm long, covered with dark hairs. The numerous leaves are linear, fleshy, dark green, about 6 cm long and 1 cm wide. The inflorescences consist of 1 to 3 flowers each about 1 cm across.

This species requires warm conditions with year-round watering and high humidity. It should be given bright filtered light. A slab or pot of well-drained medium is recommended. In the tropics the plants do well tied to a suitable tree.

Dendrobium villosulum Lindl.

Synonym: *Dendrobium melanochlamys* Holttum
This is a large slender terrestrial species from Peninsular Malaysia and Borneo. It grows at altitudes of 400 to 1700 m, in decaying leaf litter, on rotting logs, moss forests and damp places near waterfalls, often growing in shade or semi-shade. These are areas of high year-round humidity and rainfall. The stems are up to 100 cm tall and about 50 mm wide, with leaves in 2 ranks along most of the length. The leaves are up to 5 cm long and 6 mm wide, unequally lobed at the apex and with distinctive long black hairs on the leaf sheaths. The flowers are held upside down so that the labellum is facing the ground. They are from 1 to 1.5 cm long and borne singly, opposite the leaves.

The plants should be potted in a well-drained, organically rich terrestrial medium. They should be kept moist throughout the year and not permitted to dry out between waterings. Intermediate to warm temperatures with semi-shade and a humid atmosphere are required.

Section *Cuthbertsonia* Schltr. (Genus *Dendrobium*)

This small section consists of 3 species and is regarded by some authorities as being part of section *Oxyglossum*. The species can be distinguished by the lip, which has upturned sides and a blunt apex, somewhat similar to *Calyptrochilus*, while the stems are much shorter. There are two species in New Guinea, one of which extends as far as Vanuatu with another species in Fiji.

The plants are small with short, thick pseudobulbs and a few leaves at the apex. The flowers are large in relation to the plant, brightly coloured and long-lasting. Colour is variable in some species. The flowers are borne on short inflorescences of 1 or 2 flowers at the apex of the pseudobulbs. The flowers are held in such a way that the lip is usually uppermost. In common with *Oxyglossum*, the ovary is angled or otherwise ornamented in cross-section. Members of this section are proving very popular in cultivation due to the large flower size in relation to the size of the plants and to the fact that the species are suited to cool climates.

WAYNE HARRIS

Dendrobium cuthbertsonii F. Muell.

Synonyms: *Dendrobium sophronites* Schltr., *D. agathodaemonis* J.J. Sm.

This colourful miniature species features flowers that are often larger than the plant. It occurs in highland areas from about 750 to 3400 m, but mostly above 2000 m, throughout the island of New Guinea and on New Ireland. It grows as an epiphyte or a terrestrial, being recorded from road cuttings and mossy rock ledges and short alpine grassland, but more commonly growing on trees and moss-covered shrubs, in areas with cool to intermediate temperatures and year-round high rainfall, constant high humidity and semi-shaded to very exposed positions. The pseudobulbs are about 1 to 8 cm long and less than 1 cm in diameter, often spheroid, forming small clumps. There are 1 to 5 leaves grouped near the apex of the pseudobulb, up to 4 cm long and 1 cm wide, with prominent black warts on the upper surface. The under surface is often purple and only occasionally has warts. The flowers are borne singly at the apex or occasionally from the nodes. They are up to 3.3 cm across and 5 cm long, extremely long-lasting (up to 10 months) and are very variable in colour with yellow, orange and purple combinations recorded, although red is most common.

This species requires cool to intermediate temperatures and will not tolerate lowland tropical conditions. It should be grown in a well-drained pot, but with a medium which retains some moisture. The use of sphagnum moss in the medium is recommended. It requires humid, semi-shaded conditions with excellent air movement and should not be allowed to dry out.

Dendrobium laevifolium Stapf

Synonym: *Dendrobium occulatum* Ames

This miniature epiphytic species occurs in several islands to the east of New Guinea, including the Louisiade Archipelago, Bougainville and the Solomon Islands, Santa Cruz Islands and Vanuatu. It grows from about 300 to 2300 m altitude, in damp moss forest where it often occurs low down on tree trunks. The pseudobulbs are commonly 2.5 to 8 cm long, but occasionally up to 14 cm long, and usually about 1.5 cm wide. The remains of the leaf sheaths are evident as persistent upright bristles arising from the nodes. There are 2 (or occasionally 3) leaves, 5 to 14 cm long and 0.5 to 2.5 cm wide at the apex of the pseudobulb. The inflorescences are borne apically and consist of 1 or 2, or occasionally up to 4, flowers. The flowers are large for the size of the plant, being 2 to 4.5 cm long, and somewhat variable in colour in shades of cream, pink and purple. The flowers last more than a month.

While this species can be grown in warm conditions, cool to intermediate temperatures are preferable. It can be grown on a slab, but a pot of well-drained mixture is best, as the plants must not be allowed to dry out. Year-round heavy watering and shaded conditions with high humidity are necessary.

Dendrobium prasinum Lindl.

This is a miniature species with relatively large flowers, which occurs on the Fijian Islands. It grows epiphytically in mossy forests from 600 to 1100 m altitude, in areas which have year-round high humidity and rainfall and intermediate temperatures. The pseudobulbs are shortly ovoid, up to 5 cm long and 2 cm wide, with bristles formed from the persistent veins of the old leaf sheaths. There are from 1 to 3 leaves, from 2 to 14 cm long and 0.5 to 1.7 cm wide, at the apex of the pseudobulb. The inflorescences are terminal with usually 2 flowers, each up to 4 cm across. The flowers last 6 to 7 weeks and are predominantly white, with varying degrees of a green tinge. Flowering may occur at any time of the year.

In cultivation, this species requires cool to intermediate conditions, although plants have been grown at sea level in the tropics. It should be potted in a small well-drained pot; the inclusion of sphagnum moss on the surface to keep humidity levels high is useful. It needs semi-shade, high humidity, good air movement, and should not be allowed to dry out.

Section *Dendrobium* (Genus *Dendrobium*)

This is the type section for the genus as it includes the type species *D. moniliforme*. It is a large section of 50 to 60 species occurring from India to New Guinea and Australia in the east and Japan and Korea in the north. The centre of distribution lies in the area from India to Indochina including China and Thailand. This area is home to about 50 species, while Borneo has only 4, New Guinea 2 or 3 and Australia 1. They are mostly epiphytic plants of low to moderate altitude in areas with a distinct dry season. This section is related to *Calcarifera*, *Pedilonum* and *Formosae*.

The stems are of moderate length and often swollen into club-shaped pseudobulbs. The leaves are borne along the upper two-thirds of the stem and are usually deciduous after a year. There is a leaf sheath. The flowers are produced from the apical part of the stem on long or short inflorescences in the dry season. The lip is entire and there is a short mentum. The flowers are often large and showy – many of the most popular species in cultivation are in this section.

WAYNE HARRIS

Dendrobium albosanguineum Lindl.

This is a medium sized species from Thailand and Myanmar (Burma) where it grows high up in the upper branches of tall trees. It occurs at low to moderate altitudes in mountainous areas near the Myanmar–Thailand border and other areas with a drier winter. The pseudobulbs are up to 25 cm long and about 1.5 cm in diameter, with leaves in 2 ranks along the length of the stem. The lanceolate, deciduous leavea are 8 to 15 cm long and about 2 cm wide. The inflorescences are borne on the apical third of the leafy or leafless pseudobulbs. They are short with 2 or 3 flowers up to 8 cm across. The flowering season is late spring and the flowers last about 2 or 3 weeks. It is regarded as being under threat due to habitat clearing and collecting.

This species requires copious watering and fertilising during the growing season, but the medium must be exceptionally well drained. A slab may be best, but the plants also do well in a well-drained pot. A dry resting season is required for good flowering during winter and spring, but the plants should not be completely dried out and a little watering during this time is required. Good light and warm to intermediate conditions are recommended. The aerial growths on the stem can be used for propagation.

DAVID TITTMUSS

Dendrobium amoenum Wall. ex Lindl.

Synonyms: *Dendrobium egertoniae* Lindl., *D. mesochlorum* Lindl.
This medium sized epiphyte occurs from northern India, Sikkim, Nepal and Bangladesh to Myanmar (Burma) in the foothills of the Himalayas. The plants have been recorded at altitudes of 1000 to 2000 m, often growing at the base of trees. The pseudobulbs are 30 to 60 cm long, initially erect, becoming pendulous as they lengthen. The leaves are 6 to 10 cm long and 1 to 1.7 cm wide, deciduous and distributed along most of the length of the pseudobulb. The inflorescences arise laterally on the apical half of the leafless pseudobulbs and consist of 2 to 3 fragrant flowers, each about 4 to 5 cm across. Flowering occurs in spring and early summer.

The pendulous habit requires a slab or a hanging pot of well-drained medium. Intermediate to cool conditions are recommended with bright filtered light. A dry period of around 3 to 4 months in winter is required for good flowering. During this period the plants should be allowed to dry out for about a week between waterings.

BILL LAVARACK

Dendrobium anosmum Lindl.

Synonyms: *Dendrobium superbum* Rchb.f., *D. leucorhodum* Schltr., *D. scortechini* Hook.f., *D. macrophyllum* Lindl., *D. macranthum* Hook.f.
This is one of the most widespread species in the subtribe, occurring from India through Thailand to Peninsular Malaysia, the Indonesian Islands, Borneo, the Philippines and New Guinea. It occurs primarily in lowland areas but does extend to above 1000 m in some areas. In most of its habitat the climate is seasonal with a distinct dry season in winter, although in some areas it is wet all year. The stems are long, slender and pendulous, up to 3 m long, but commonly 50 cm to 1 m in cultivation. The deciduous leaves are variable in size, 12 to 18 cm long, oblong–lanceolate and occur along most of the length of the stem. The inflorescences are lateral, along the length of the leafless stems and bear 1or 2 flowers, each 5 to 10 cm across. Flowering

is mainly in the dry season, although it can occur at any time in New Guinea. The flowers last about 2 or 3 weeks.

The long, pendulous stems make this species unsuited to a pot. It can be tied to a slab or grown in a hanging basket. The plants must be given a dry rest during the colder weather if they are to flower well. During the growing season it should be watered copiously. It does best in strong to filtered light, good air movement and humid conditions. The aerial growths on the stem can be used to produce new plants.

Dendrobium aphyllum (Roxb.) Fischer

Synonyms: *Dendrobium pierardii* Roxb. ex Hook., *D. cucullatum* R.Br., *D. madrasense* A.D. Hawkes

This is a medium sized epiphyte, or occasionally a lithophyte, from India, Myanmar (Burma), Thailand, Indochina and southern China. It grows in seasonal forest from about 200 to 1800 m altitude. This was one of the earliest dendrobiums to be grown and flowered in England, with records of it flowering in the botanic gardens at Liverpool in 1821. The stems are pendulous, long and slender to about 70 cm long and 8 mm in diameter. The leaves are in 2 ranks along the length of the stem and are deciduous. They are 10 to 13 cm long, linear to ovate. The flowers are fragrant and are borne in pairs laterally along the leafless stems. They are about 3 to 5 cm across and last about 3 weeks. The flowering season is spring. The plants produce numerous aerial growths that can be used to propagate new plants.

The pendulous habit makes this species unsuited to pot culture, but a slab or hanging basket with well-drained medium is suitable. The plants must be kept dry during winter and early spring with only very occasional light watering. During summer when the plants are growing they should be watered heavily. Strong light and good air movement are recommended. This species is tolerant of a wide range of temperatures.

Dendrobium chrysanthum Lindl.

Synonym: *Dendrobium paxtonii* Lindl.

This medium sized to large epiphyte is widespread in the foothills of the Himalayas, occurring in north-east India, Nepal, Myanmar (Burma), Thailand, Laos, Vietnam and the Yunnan Province of southern China. It grows in seasonal foothill forests at altitudes between 1000 and 2000 m. The pseudobulbs are up to 3 m long, but usually shorter, and about 1.5 cm wide with leaves along their length. The leaves are 10 to 18 cm long and about 4 or 5 cm wide, deciduous. The flowers are solitary or in short inflorescences of 2 to 6 and, unlike other species in this section, are borne on the leafy pseudobulbs. They are fragrant, 4 to 5 cm across and last about 1 to 2 weeks. Flowering can occur throughout the year, with the main season being summer and autumn. This species is closely related to *D. ochreatum* Lindl., but differs in the more rounded petals and sepals.

This species does best in intermediate conditions. It seems to require more water in winter than most other species in this section and, while watering should be somewhat reduced in winter, the plants should not be permitted to dry out entirely for more than a day. It is best grown on a slab or in a hanging basket. It requires bright filtered sunlight and good air movement.

Dendrobium crepidatum Lindl. & Paxton

Synonyms: *Dendrobium lawanum* Lindl., *D. actinomorphum* Blatter & Hallb.
This medium sized epiphyte is widespread in South-East Asia, from the Deccan region of India through the Himalayas in north-east India, Myanmar (Burma) and Thailand to Laos, Vietnam and the Yunnan Province in southern China. The plants grow as epiphytes in deciduous montane forests with a distinctly seasonal climate, at altitudes of 600 to 2100 m. The pseudobulbs are rather thick and usually pendulous, up to 45 cm long, but usually shorter, and about 1 to 1.5 cm wide. There are a few thin, deciduous leaves, 5 to 13 cm long, linear–lanceolate, on the apical half of the stem. The inflorescences are borne laterally on the leafless stems and consist of 2 to 3 fragrant flowers, each 3 to 4 cm across. The flowers are variable in size and colour and some forms do not open fully. Flowering occurs at the end of the dry season in spring and the flowers last from 1 to 3 weeks.

To grow and flower well, this species must be given intermediate to cool conditions with a dry resting period in winter and early spring. During this period watering should be much reduced with the plants drying out and remaining dry for several days between waterings. Plants should be watered and fertilised copiously during growth. A hanging pot or a slab is recommended to cater for the pendulous growth habit. Bright sunlight or light shade are recommended.

Dendrobium crystallinum Rchb.f.

This medium sized, pendulous epiphyte occurs from Myanmar (Burma) and Thailand through Indochina to China. It grows in montane forest with a distinct dry season at moderate altitudes (900 to 1500 m). It often occurs in exposed situations in full sunlight. The slender stems are up to 60 cm long and 8 mm wide. The thin-textured, linear–lanceolate leaves are restricted to the apical third of the stem and are about 10 cm long. They are deciduous, dropping when the dry winter season commences. The inflorescences are lateral and short, with 1 to 3 flowers borne on the leafless stems. The flowers appear in spring, are fragrant and about 5 cm in diameter. The name comes from the unique anther cap that is covered with crystalline papillae.

D. crystallinum will grow in warm climates, but is better suited to intermediate conditions with a definite resting period when water is virtually withheld during winter. The long pendulous stems make the plants well suited to a hanging pot, which should contain a standard well-drained medium. Bright light conditions are suggested.

Dendrobium devonianum Paxton

Synonyms: *Dendrobium pictum* Griff., *D. pulchellum* Lindl.var. *devonianum* (Paxton) Rchb.f., *D. brevifolium* Hort. ex Lindl.
This medium sized to large epiphytic species occurs across the Himalayas from north-east India through Myanmar (Burma), Thailand, Laos and Vietnam to the Yunnan Province in southern China and Taiwan. It grows at altitudes of 550 to 2000 m, mostly above 1000 m, in deciduous forests with a distinct dry season in winter. The stems are long and very slender, branching, up to 1.5 m long and just a few millimetres wide, with leaves in 2 ranks along their length. The leaves are thin, soon deciduous and up to 10 cm long and

8 mm wide. The flowers are borne singly or in pairs along the upper part of the stem. The flowers are about 5 cm across and last about 2 weeks. Flowering is in late spring and summer. The flowers are variable in colour with varying amounts of pink and purple tinting.

Cool to intermediate conditions are required if this species is to grow and flower well. It should be given a dry resting period in winter and early spring when watering is reduced and the plants allowed to dry out for several days between waterings. Plants should be watered and fertilised copiously during the growing season. The pendulous nature of the plants makes it necessary to mount them on a slab or to grow them in a hanging pot. They should be given light shade or lightly filtered sunlight.

WAYNE HARRIS

Dendrobium dixanthum Rchb.f.

This medium sized to large species occurs in northern Myanmar (Burma), Thailand and Laos. The plants grow as epiphytes in tall trees at about 800 m altitude, in deciduous forests where there is a distinct dry season. The stems are slender, 60 to 90 cm long and a little less than 1 cm wide, erect or semi-pendulous. There are several narrow–linear, deciduous leaves 8 to 18 cm long on the apical third of the stem. The inflorescences, which consist of 2 to 5 flowers, are produced laterally on the leafless stems. The flowers are about 3 to 4 cm across.

In cultivation this species is best grown in intermediate temperatures with a dry resting period in winter when the plants are allowed to stay dry for several days between waterings. A hanging pot or a slab is best to accommodate the pendulous habit. Bright filtered sunlight is recommended and the plants should be watered and fertilised copiously during growth.

GEOFF STOCKER

Dendrobium falconeri Hook.f.

Synonym: *Dendrobium erythroglossum* Hayata

This is a medium sized to large epiphyte, spectacular when in full flower. It has a wide distribution from north-east India across South-East Asia to southern China and Taiwan, growing at altitudes of 1000 to 2300 m, high up in forest trees in areas with a distinct dry season. The pseudobulbs are very distinctive in this species, being 30 to 120 cm long, slender, pendulous, branched, with prominent swellings at the nodes. There are several narrow–linear deciduous leaves about 2.5 to 8 cm long, grouped near the apex of the pseudobulbs. The flowers are solitary, fragrant and about 5 to 10 cm across, occurring on the leafless pseudobulbs. They last about 2 weeks (more in some forms) and flowering is in spring and early summer.

Intermediate to cool conditions are required with bright light and high humidity. A slab or hanging pot is best to accommodate the pendulous habit. A resting period for 3 or 4 months in winter is required for good flowering. During this period, plants should be allowed to dry out thoroughly for several days between waterings, even remaining dry for extended periods with only occasional light misting.

Dendrobium fimbriatum Hook.f.

Synonyms: *Dendrobium paxtonii* Paxton, *D. fimbriatum* var. *oculatum* Hook.f. This large robust epiphytic species is widespread in South-East Asia in India, Nepal, Myanmar (Burma), Thailand, Laos, Vietnam, southern China and Peninsular Malaysia. It grows in deciduous, seasonal montane forests at altitudes of 500 to 1500 m, with some records from as high as 2400 m. The pseudobulbs are up to 2 m long and about 1 cm wide, erect, then becoming pendulous as they lengthen. The leaves are borne in 2 ranks along the upper half of the stem. They are lanceolate, 8 to 15 cm long and are deciduous after about 2 years. The inflorescences arise from the apical part of the leafless stems and consist of 7 to 12 flowers each 5 to 8 cm across. Most of the forms in cultivation have a dark maroon area at the base of the lip and are known as 'var. *oculatum*'. Other forms have pure yellow flowers. The flowers last 7 to 12 days, but large plants produce flowers very prolifically and plants with 100 or more flowers are quite common. Flowering is in late winter or early spring.

When well grown, this is a large plant requiring room in the orchid house. It will grow in warm, intermediate or cool conditions, but does best where there is a cooler winter. A cool, dry resting period is required for good growth and flowering. During this time, plants should be allowed to dry out, but only for a day or two, between waterings. Semi-shade or dappled sunlight is recommended.

Dendrobium findlayanum Parish & Rchb.f.

This species is a small to medium sized epiphyte or lithophyte from Myanmar (Burma), Thailand and Laos. It grows in mixed montane forests at altitudes of 1000 to 1700 m. The pseudobulbs are up to 70 cm long and about 1 cm wide, erect or pendulous, according to length. Each internode has a long narrow base and a more or less globular apex, giving the pseudobulb the appearance of a string of beads. There are several deciduous oblong–lanceolate leaves 8 to 10 cm long along the stem. The flowers are produced usually in pairs, laterally on the apical part of the stem. They are 5 to 7 cm across, fragrant and long-lasting. Flowering occurs in late winter.

A dry resting period with watering frequency decreasing throughout late autumn and winter is required. Heavy watering and fertilising is required in the growing season. The plants may be grown in a pot of well-drained medium or on a slab to accommodate the pendulous habit. Bright light and intermediate to cool conditions are recommended.

Dendrobium friedericksianum Rchb.f.

Synonym: *Dendrobium friedericksianum* var. *oculatum* Seidenf. & Smitinand. This is an epiphytic species of the hot steamy lowlands of southern Thailand, a region with year-round high temperatures and a drier period in winter. The pseudobulbs are up to 45 cm long, erect, then somewhat pendulous, and about 1 to 1.5 cm in diameter. The leaves are about 10 to 18 cm long and 2 cm wide and are borne in 2 ranks on the apical two-thirds of the pseudobulb. They are deciduous after a year. The flowers are about 5 to 6 cm across and are borne in short inflorescences of 3 or 4 flowers from the upper part of the leafless stems. The flowering season is spring and the flowers last about 5 weeks.

In cultivation, this species does best if temperatures are kept high, but it will tolerate cooler temperatures if it is not kept too moist during cold weather. It should be given a drier resting period during winter if the plants are to flower well. It is best grown in a mixture that retains a little moisture without becoming soggy, but is well drained. Good strong light and high humidity are required.

Dendrobium guangxiense S.J. Cheng & C.Z. Tang

This medium sized plant is rare and not well known in cultivation. It occurs in Gungxi, Guizhou and south-east Yunnan Provinces in China, where it grows as an epiphyte or lithophyte. It is believed to occur at moderate elevations in an area that has a markedly seasonal climate. The pseudobulbs are up to 60 cm long, erect, becoming pendulous, slightly zigzag. The deciduous leaves are oblong–lanceolate, about 4 to 6 cm long and 1.5 to 2 cm wide, mostly on the upper third of the stem. The flowers are borne singly or in pairs on the leafless or occasionally leafy stems. The flowering season is uncertain, but probably spring.

Although virtually unknown in cultivation, it is assumed that this species would require intermediate temperatures and a drier resting period in winter. A well-drained medium and bright light conditions should be best.

Dendrobium gibsonii Lindl.

Synonyms: *Dendrobium fuscatum* Lindl., *D. fimbriatum* var. *gibsonii* (Lindl.) Finet

This large robust epiphyte or lithophyte occurs in the Himalayan region in Nepal, north-east India, Myanmar (Burma), Thailand and the Yunnan Province of southern China. It grows in montane forests in areas with a distinct dry season at altitudes of 700 to 1600 m. The pseudobulbs are up to 120 cm long and less than 1 cm wide, erect, becoming pendulous as they age. There are about 10 leaves, about 15 cm long in 2 ranks along the upper two-thirds of the stem. The leaves are deciduous after 2 or more years. The inflorescences are borne from the upper part of the leafless stems and consist of up to 15 flowers, each 3 to 5 cm across and very fragrant. The flowers last about 2 weeks and flowering is in summer.

Intermediate temperatures are recommended. There should be a slightly drier period in winter when the plants are permitted to dry out between waterings, but they should not remain dry for more than a day or two. Bright light, but not direct sunlight, is suggested. The plants are large and require plenty of room in the bush-house. A hanging pot or slab is best to accommodate the pendulous habit.

Dendrobium heterocarpum Lindl.

Synonyms: *Dendrobium aureum* Lindl., *D. rhombeum* Lindl., *D. atractodes* Ridl., *D. minahassae* Kraezl.

This is a medium sized epiphytic species that is one of the most widely distributed species in the subtribe. It occurs from Sri Lanka and India through South-East Asia as far north as southern China, in Sumatra, Java, Borneo, the Philippines and Sulawesi. It grows at moderate to high altitudes but in cooler areas may occur below 500 m. While it occurs in a range of habitats over its extensive range, in most places it grows in strong light in areas with a distinct dry season. The pseudobulbs are erect or pendulous if long, up to 60 cm long, but usually shorter. The leaves are in 2 ranks along the pseudobulb, about 10 cm long, oblong to linear–lanceolate, deciduous and light green in colour. The flowers are borne from the upper nodes of the leafless pseudobulbs, in groups of 2 or 3, and are 6 cm across. They are fragrant, open widely and last several weeks. The flowering season is spring. The species is variable over its range, but all have a narrow lip, which is an unusual feature in this section.

This species does best in intermediate conditions with a dry resting period in winter and early spring. It should be potted in a well-drained medium. The plants should be watered and fertilised heavily when the new growths appear. A hanging pot, basket or a slab is best to accommodate the stems, which become pendulous as they age.

Dendrobium linawianum Rchb.f.

Synonyms: *Dendrobium alboviride* Hayata, *D. moniliforme* Lindl. not Sw.

This small to medium sized species occurs in Taiwan and the Kwangsi Province of southern China where it grows at altitudes below 1000 m in forests with only a slightly drier period in winter. The pseudobulbs are 30 to 40 cm long, somewhat flattened and sparsely branched, with leaves along their apical third. The leaves are narrow-elliptic, 4 to 7 cm long, 2 to 2.5 cm wide and deciduous or persistent. The inflorescences are borne on the apical part of the leafless stems and consist of 2 or 3 flowers, each 4 to 5 cm across. Flowering is in spring and the flowers last about 2 weeks.

A slab or pot of well-drained medium may be used. Filtered light or semi-shade with high humidity and warm to intermediate temperatures are recommended. A resting period when watering is somewhat reduced in winter is recommended, but the plants should not be permitted to dry out completely.

Dendrobium lituiflorum Lindl.

Synonym: *Dendrobium hanburyanum* Rchb.f.

This medium sized epiphyte occurs in north-east India, Myanmar (Burma), Thailand, Laos and south-west China, where it grows at altitudes ranging from 400 to about 1700 m. Most plants are probably from the altitude range 400 to 1200 m. They grow high up in trees in areas with a distinct dry season. The pseudobulbs are slender, more or less pendulous, and 40 to 60 cm long and about 1 cm wide. The leaves are quickly deciduous, fleshy, oblong and about 8 to 13 cm long. The flowers are borne laterally along the leafless stems in short inflorescences of 2 to 5. They are 6 to 10 cm across, fragrant and vary in colour from white to deep purple. Flowering is in spring and the flowers last about 2 weeks.

It is best grown in a hanging pot or basket of well-drained medium or on a slab. It should be given warm to intermediate temperatures, bright light and a dry season in winter, when the plants are allowed to dry out completely, but not for long periods. They should be kept moist while in active growth.

Dendrobium loddigesii Rolfe

Synonyms: *Dendrobium seidelianum* Rchb.f., *D. pulchellum* Lodd. non Roxb. This small species grows in Laos, southern China, Hainan Island and Hong Kong, in areas with a distinct dry season at altitudes of 400 to 1300 m. This species was well known in cultivation for many years before the details of its natural occurrence were known. The stems branch freely by means of aerial growths complete with roots, and form dense tangled clumps or mats on trees or rocks. The stems are slender, up to 15 cm long and 5 mm wide, with small, deciduous leaves along their length. The leaves are fleshy, oblong–lanceolate, 4 to 6 cm long. The solitary flowers are about 4 to 5 cm across, fragrant and are borne laterally on the leafless stems. Clumps of this species may be covered in flowers. The flowers last about 3 weeks and are produced in spring and summer.

The scrambling habit makes this species unsuited to pot culture and it is best mounted on a slab of weathered wood or cork or similar material. The plants must be given a dry resting period in late autumn and winter if they are to flower well. Strong light, good air movement and intermediate to warm conditions are recommended. The aerial growths on the stem can be used for propagation.

Dendrobium maccarthiae Thwaites

This is a medium to large sized, pendulous epiphyte from southern Sri Lanka where it has been reported from near Point de Galle. It grows at low altitudes in wet tropical rainforests with year-round rainfall and high humidity and temperatures. The pseudobulbs are 15 to 60 cm long, pendulous, greyish-white, purplish at the nodes, with a slightly thickened base and slender and terete above the base. There are a few linear–lanceolate leaves, 4 to 10 cm long, near the apex of the pseudobulb. The pendulous inflorescences have 2 to 5 flowers, each about 8 to 10 cm wide, usually opening widely. They last 6 to 8 weeks and flower in spring.

The pendulous growth habit makes the plants more suited to slab culture than to pot culture, although a hanging pot with a well-drained medium is suitable. It has a reputation for being hard to grow in glasshouse conditions. The plants should be watered throughout the year, although there are suggestions that two slightly drier periods in late winter and late summer may be beneficial. Semi-shade to filtered sunlight, but with good air movement, are recommended and warm temperatures are required.

WAYNE HARRIS

Dendrobium moniliforme (L.) Sw.

Synonyms: *Dendrobium japonicum* (Blume) Lindl., *D. monile* (Thunb.) Kraenzl. and several others
This is the type species for the genus *Dendrobium*, being first described as *Epidendrum moniliforme* by Linnaeus in 1753. It is a small species occurring on the Japanese islands of Honshu, Shikoku and Kyushu, and many small islands south of Japan including the Ryuku Islands. It is also in Korea, China and Taiwan. It grows epiphytically or lithophytically in forests from 800 to 3000 m in areas where the climate is temperate and moist throughout most of the year, but with a drier period in winter when temperatures regularly reach freezing. The pseudobulbs are slender to about 40 cm long and 0.5 to 1 cm in diameter with deciduous leaves in 2 ranks along the upper half. The leaves are linear–lanceolate, 5 to 13 cm long. The inflorescences, which consist of 1 or 2 flowers, are borne on the apical third of the leafless pseudobulbs. The flowers are strongly fragrant, about 5 cm across and last about 2 or 3 weeks. Flowering occurs in spring.

The plants do best in cool to intermediate conditions, in a small well-drained pot. They should be watered throughout the year with watering being somewhat reduced during winter, but the plants must not be completely dry for extended periods. Bright filtered light is recommended.

BILL LAVARACK

Dendrobium moschatum (Buch.-Ham.) Sw.

Synonyms: *Dendrobium calceolaria* Carey ex Hook.f., *D. cupreum* Herbert
This is a large robust epiphytic species from the foothills of the north-eastern Himalayas including India, Myanmar (Burma), Thailand, Laos and Vietnam. It grows at altitudes of 300 to 2000 m in deciduous forests with a seasonal climate, bright light and good air movement. The pseudobulbs are slender and up to 2 m long, erect, becoming pendulous as they lengthen. The leaves are 8 to 15 cm long, oblong–lanceolate, deciduous after about 2 years and tend to turn a purple colour in bright light. They are arranged in 2 rows along most of the length of the pseudobulb. The inflorescences arise from the upper nodes of the 2-year-old stems. They are pendulous with 7 to 15 flowers, each 5 to 8 cm in diameter. The lip is slipper-shaped and hairy. The flowers last only a few days and the flowering season is late spring.

The large size of the plant can be a disadvantage in cultivation and it needs plenty of room. Plants may be tied to a tree in intermediate to warm climates. In a pot it requires a well-drained medium. A dry resting period is required from late autumn to spring. During this period the plants should be allowed to dry out for at least several days between waterings. The plants do best in bright filtered sunlight and good air movement.

WAYNE HARRIS

Dendrobium nobile Lindl.

Synonyms: *Dendrobium coerulescens* Wall, *D. lindleyanum* Griff., *D. formosanum* (Rchb.f.) Masamune

Dendrobium nobile is one of the most popular orchids in cultivation. It occurs naturally in the foothills of the Himalayas in India, Myanmar (Burma), Nepal, China, Vietnam and Thailand, growing epiphytically in seasonal deciduous forests, often in full sun, mostly at moderate altitudes (200 to 2000 m). It is a widespread variable species with many forms and varieties. The pseudobulbs are initially erect, then pendulous, up to 60 cm long, swollen at the nodes and about 1.5 to 2 cm wide. The leaves are in 2 ranks along most of the length of the pseudobulb, 7 to 10 cm long, strap-shaped, and are deciduous. The flowers are borne on short inflorescences of 2 to 4 flowers from the nodes. The flowers are about 6 to 8 cm across, waxy, fragrant and variable in colour. The variety *virginale* is white with a yellow-green patch on the lip. They last 3 to 6 weeks and the flowering season is late winter and spring.

This species is noted for its ease of culture. It is best grown in a hanging pot or basket with a mixture that retains some moisture but is free-draining. It should be kept dry in winter and spring until the new growths start. At this stage it should be watered and fertilised freely. It should be given strong sunlight and does best in intermediate temperatures, but will tolerate hot climates as long as there is a distinct winter. The plants often produce aerial growths that can be used for propagation.

DAVID TITMUSS

Dendrobium ochreatum Lindl.

Synonym: *Dendrobium cambridgeanum* Paxton

This is a medium sized epiphyte or lithophyte from north-east India, Myanmar (Burma), Thailand and Laos. It grows at altitudes between 1200 and 1600 m in areas with a distinct dry season. The pseudobulbs are pendulous, 15 to 70 cm long, but commonly around 30 cm, with leaves in 2 ranks along most of their length. The leaves are deciduous, ovate–lanceolate, 5 to 13 cm long. The inflorescences consist of 1 to 3 flowers each 5 to 7 cm across, and are borne laterally on the apical two-thirds of the pseudobulb. The new growths start in winter and flowering occurs in late spring and summer while the pseudobulbs are still developing and leafy. The fragrant flowers last about 2 weeks. This species is closely related to *D. chrysanthum* Lindl., differing in the shorter pseudobulbs and more pointed petals and sepals.

Intermediate to cool conditions with bright light and good air movement are recommended. The species has proved difficult to flower and this may be related to the unusual nature of the flowering, which occurs on the developing pseudobulb. A dry resting period is required, but perhaps this may be at a different time to most other species in this section. A slab or hanging pot is best to accommodate the pendulous habit.

BILL LAVARACK

Dendrobium parishii Rchb.f.

This is a compact epiphyte from north-eastern India, Myanmar (Burma), Indochina and Yunnan and Gweizhou Provinces in south-western China. It grows in deciduous forests at moderate altitudes (250 to 1500 m), where the climate is strongly seasonal with a dry period in late winter and spring. It is very closely related to *D. rhodopterygium* Rchb.f. and the two names may represent one species. The pseudobulbs are short and thick, often curved or misshapen, about 30 cm long and 2 cm thick. In shaded conditions the stems may be longer and more slender. The oblong–lanceolate leaves are 5 to 15 cm long and are soon deciduous, leaving the stem covered in white leaf bases. The flowers are borne on short inflorescences of 1, 2 or 3 flowers, along the leafless pseudobulbs. They are variable in colour, fragrant, about 4 to 6 cm across and last about 3 or 4 weeks. The flowering season is spring.

In cultivation, this species requires warm to intermediate conditions with bright light. It may be grown in a pot or on a slab. It should be watered and fertilised heavily during the growing season, but requires a dry resting period in winter if it is to flower well.

WAYNE HARRIS

Dendrobium primulinum Lindl.

Synonym: *Dendrobium nobile* var. *pallidiflora* Hook.f.

This medium sized species is widely distributed through the foothills of the Himalayas, from north-west India through Nepal, Myanmar (Burma), Thailand, Vietnam to southern China. It occurs at altitudes of 300 to 1600 m in deciduous forests in areas with a distinct dry season. The pseudobulbs are erect or pendulous, up to 45 cm long, but usually shorter. The deciduous leaves are lanceolate to oblong, 8 to 13 cm long, in 2 ranks along most of the pseudobulbs. The inflorescences consist of 1 or 2 flowers and are borne laterally on the leafless pseudobulbs. The flowers are fragrant, 4 to 8 cm across and last about 2 weeks. There is some variation in the colour of the petals and sepals, which vary from pink, mauve, purple to white, with a cream to yellow lip.

This species will grow in warm to intermediate climates, but must have seasonal changes in temperature and moisture to grow and flower well. It should be given a dry resting period of 3 or 4 months in winter when the plants are allowed to dry out thoroughly between waterings. Bright light and good air movement are recommended. A slab or hanging pot is best to accommodate the pendulous habit.

WAYNE HARRIS

Dendrobium pulchellum Roxb. ex Lindl.

Synonym: *Dendrobium dalhousieanum* Wall.

This large epiphytic species occurs over a large area of South-East Asia including north west India, Myanmar (Burma), Thailand, Laos, Peninsular Malaysia and Vietnam. It grows from 200 to 2000 m altitude, usually in open forests where there is bright light, good air movement and a distinct dry season in winter. The pseudobulbs can be up to 2 m long, although most are much shorter. There are characteristic stripes on the internode areas. The leaves are deciduous after a few years. They are linear–oblong, borne along the upper half of the pseudobulb and are 10 to 20 cm long. The pendulous inflorescences are 15 to 20 cm long with up to 12 flowers and are borne on leafy or leafless pseudobulbs. The flowers are 5 to 10 cm across. There are many variations of colour with white, lemon, apricot and orange having been reported. They last 1 to 2 weeks and have a slight musky fragrance. The flowering season is late spring and early summer. Old stems continue to produce flowers for several years.

Plants of this species are relatively easy to grow in intermediate or warm conditions with a cooler, rather drier period in winter required for good flowering. They may be grown in a pot of well-drained medium or tied to a tree in suitable climates. They should be watered and fertilised heavily during the growing season.

BILL LAVARACK

Dendrobium regium Prain

This epiphytic species occurs in southern India at altitudes of about 600 m. In this area there is a distinct dry season in winter. The pseudobulbs are up to 45 cm long, erect, or tending to become pendulous as they lengthen. The leaves are deciduous, lanceolate, 10 cm long and about 1 to 1.5 cm wide. They are borne in 2 ranks along most of the length of the pseudobulb. The inflorescences consist of 2 or 3 flowers and are borne laterally, usually from the leafless pseudobulbs. The flowers are about 7.5 cm across and last about a week. This species is closely related to *D. nobile*, differing in that it lacks the purple marking at the base of the lip. The flowering period is late spring and summer.

This species requires warm to intermediate temperatures, with strong light and good air movement. It should be placed in a well-drained pot with standard medium or tied tightly to a slab. A dry resting period in winter and early spring is necessary for good flowering.

BILL LAVARACK

Dendrobium rhodopterygium Rchb.f.

This species is very closely related to *D. parishii* Rchb.f. and may eventually be shown to be a synonym of that species. It has been recorded from near Moulmein in Myanmar (Burma). The pseudobulbs are stout, about 30 cm long and 2 cm in diameter, and covered with the white bases of the deciduous leaves. The leaves are 5 to 8 cm long, lanceolate or oblong. The pseudobulbs are less likely to be curved or misshapen than those of *D. parishii*. The flowers are borne on short lateral inflorescences of 1 to 3 flowers along the stem. The flowers are about 6 to 7 cm across and variable in colour. They last about 3 weeks and are fragrant. The flowering season is late spring.

Slab or pot culture are equally successful. Bright filtered light and warm to intermediate humid conditions are recommended. A dry resting season is required during winter and early spring to produce good flowering. Heavy watering and fertilising are required during the growing season. Aerial growths are often produced and may be used for propagation.

Dendrobium ruckeri Lindl.

Synonym: *Dendrobium ramosum* Lindl. ex Wall.
This medium sized epiphytic species occurs in Sikkim, Bhutan, the Khasi Hills and other areas in north-east India, where it grows at altitudes of 1300 to 1700 m in areas with a seasonal climate. Some reference books from the nineteenth century give the location as the Philippines, but it is now known to be restricted to India. The pseudobulbs are long, slender, branched, pendulous and from 30 to 90 cm long. The leaves are linear–lanceolate, 8 to 12 cm long and 12 to 25 mm wide, deciduous and borne along the upper half of the pseudobulb. The inflorescences are borne from the upper nodes and consist of 1 or 2 flowers, each about 4 cm across. The flowers are fragrant and the flowering season is spring.

The pendulous habit makes this species more suited to a slab or a hanging basket with an open medium. It requires a dry resting period in late autumn and winter when waterings are infrequent, with the plants remaining dry for extended periods. Bright filtered sunlight, intermediate temperatures and good air movement are required.

Dendrobium senile Parish & Rchb.f.

This is a small epiphyte from Myanmar (Burma), Thailand and Laos where it grows at altitudes of 500 to 1500 m, in areas with bright light and seasonal rainfall. The pseudobulbs and leaves are distinctive, being covered with a dense layer of white hairs, which gave rise to the name 'senile'. The pseudobulbs are short and thick, 5 to 15 cm long and less than 1 cm wide. There are 5 or 6 ovate–lanceolate leaves on the apical part of the pseudobulb. They are more or less deciduous and about 5 cm long. The flowers are borne singly from the upper nodes. There are about 3 flowers, each about 5 cm across, on each pseudobulb. They last about 3 weeks and are lemon-scented. The flowering season is late winter and spring.

This species has a reputation for being difficult to cultivate. It is best grown on a slab such as a piece of weathered wood. It requires intermediate or warm temperatures and must be given a dry season of about 3 months with little water if good flowering is to be achieved. It does best in bright filtered sunlight and good air movement.

Dendrobium signatum Rchb.f.

Synonym: *Dendrobium hilderbrandii* Rolfe
This attractive species is common in many collections, usually under the name *Dendrobium hilderbrandii*, which was the accepted name until some 10 years ago. To complicate the matter further there is a school of thought that *D. signatum* should be considered synonymous with *D. tortile*. It occurs in Myanmar (Burma), Thailand, Vietnam and Laos, usually at low to moderate elevations in the mountains. Captain Bartle Grant in his book *The Orchids of Burma* (1895) sheds some light on the history of *D. hilderbrandii*: 'A handsome species collected in the Shan States by H.H. Hilderbrand Esq., in April 1893 ... Mr. Hilderbrand collected three different forms, one with sepals and petals pale green and lip sulphur yellow, one with sepals and petals creamy pink and the lip yellow and a third like the last, with the addition of

two dark chocolate blotches in the throat. He observes that it grows in magnificent huge masses, and on one of the plants he counted upwards of 1,500 blooms.' The pseudobulbs grow to about 50 cm long, becoming pendulous as they lengthen. The leaves are lanceolate, about 10 cm long and deciduous after a year or two. The flowers, which last about 3 weeks, are borne in spring on the leafless pseudobulbs and are about 4 to 6 cm across.

The plants do well in a standard dendrobium mix of bark in a small pot or basket under shadecloth or on a tree in partial shade in warm or intermediate conditions. It needs a dry resting period through winter to flower well and appreciates frequent applications of fertiliser during the growing season.

Dendrobium stricklandianum Rchb.f.

Synonyms: *Dendrobium tosaense* Makino, *D. pere-fauriei* Hayata
This medium sized epiphyte occurs on Shikoku and Kyushu Islands in Japan, the Ryuku Islands, Taiwan and China. It grows epiphytically and on rocks at altitudes of 300 to 1200 m. The pseudobulbs are up to 40 cm long and about 4 to 7 mm in diameter with leaves along their length. The leaves are deciduous, elliptic–lanceolate, about 2 to 6 cm long and 1.5 to 2.5 cm wide. The inflorescences arise from the upper nodes of the leafless stems and consist of 3 to 8 flowers. The flowers are green, turning greenish-yellow, and are about 3 cm across. Flowering occurs from autumn to spring.

The plant grows best in intermediate temperatures with a dry resting period in late autumn to spring. It is best grown in a pot of well-drained medium and should be watered and fertilised copiously in late spring and summer. It requires bright filtered light.

Dendrobium stuartii F.M. Bailey

Synonym: *Dendrobium whiteanum* T.E. Hunt.
This species is also sometimes referred to as *D. tetrodon*, but current thinking is that *D. tetrodon* is restricted to Java and *D. stuartii* is a widespread species occurring from Thailand and Peninsular Malaysia to Java, New Guinea and northern Australia. It is typically a species of lowland savanna areas with a distinct dry season. It often grows in gallery forest along streams. The stems are long and slender to about 35 cm long and 5 mm in diameter. The leaves are thin and deciduous covering most of the length of the stem in 2 ranks. They are lanceolate to ovate, 2.5 to 7 cm long. The flowers are borne in short lateral inflorescences of 1 to 3 flowers, each about 2 cm in diameter, fragrant, lasting about 10 days. The flowering season is summer. Many plants are self-pollinating and the flowers do not open fully.

This species is best grown on a slab of cork or weathered wood or in a small pot with a medium that is excellently drained. It should be watered heavily during the growing season, but kept reasonably dry during winter and early spring. It is best grown in a humid environment with strong light. It requires hot conditions to grow well.

Dendrobium tortile Lindl.

Synonyms: *Dendrobium dartoisianum* Wildeman, *D.haniffii* Ridl.
This medium sized epiphyte is widespread in the Himalayan area, occurring in north-east India, Myanmar (Burma), Thailand, Laos, Vietnam and Peninsular Malaysia. It generally grows at low to moderate altitudes (about 1200 m) in deciduous forests in areas with a seasonal climate. The pseudobulbs are slender and up to 40 cm long, not swollen at the nodes. The leaves are deciduous, about 4 per pseudobulb, and up to 10 cm long. The inflorescences consist of from 1 to 3 flowers borne laterally from the upper nodes. The flowers are about 7 cm across, with twisted petals and sepals, and are borne on the leafless pseudobulbs. They last several weeks, are fragrant and somewhat variable in colour. The flowering season is spring. It is closely related to *D. signatum* Rchb.f., but has less robust pseudobulbs.

In cultivation, this species does well in a pot or basket of well-drained medium or on a slab. It requires a dry period in winter when water is only sparsely applied so that the plants dry out for long periods. It requires warm to intermediate temperatures and bright filtered sunlight and good air movement. Watering should be regular in the growing season.

Dendrobium unicum Seidenf.

This is a spectacular species with unusually shaped bright orange flowers. It is a medium sized species, which occurs in northern Thailand, Laos and Vietnam. It grows at altitudes of 800 to 1500 m, growing on low shrubs and on rocks, in areas with seasonal rainfall and strong light. The pseudobulbs are erect or pendulous up to 25 cm long, turning a dark colour with age. There are about 3 narrow, deciduous leaves, about 6 cm long, at the apex of the pseudobulb. The inflorescences are borne laterally from the upper nodes and consist of 2 to 4 bright orange, sometimes twisted, flowers about 4 to 5 cm across. They have a tangerine-like fragrance. The flowering season is winter and spring.

Plants of this species should be allowed to dry out gradually through winter into early spring. They should be given bright filtered light and good air movement. Plants may be tied firmly to a slab or potted in a pot of well-drained medium.

Dendrobium vesiculosum M.A. Clem. & D.L. Jones

This is a medium sized epiphyte from the Waria River valley in Morobe Province in Papua New Guinea, where it has been recorded at about 500 m altitude. It grows on trees in disturbed rainforest. The pseudobulbs are about 25 to 35 cm long and about 1 cm thick, with about 8 leaves grouped on the apical third of the stem. The leaves are deciduous, 8 to 10 cm long and 2 cm wide. There are several inflorescences consisting of 1 to 3 flowers, borne laterally on each leafless pseudobulb. The flowers are about 2 cm across and last about 5 to 10 days. They flower throughout the year. This species was first described in 1996.

In cultivation, the plant requires warm conditions with constant high humidity and year-round watering. The plants should not be allowed to dry out entirely, although a little less frequent watering in winter may be appropriate. Bright filtered light is probably best. A pot of well-drained medium or a slab is recommended.

Dendrobium wardianum Warner

This large epiphyte or lithophyte occurs in north-east India (Assam), Myanmar (Burma), Thailand and south-west China. It grows in deciduous forests at altitudes of 1000 to 2000 m, in areas with a distinct dry season. The pseudobulbs are pendulous, swollen at the nodes and up to 100 cm long and 2 cm wide at the widest point. The leathery, deciduous, oblong to linear–lanceolate leaves are about 8 to 15 cm long and are spread along the apical half of the stems. The waxy, fragrant flowers are borne in groups of 2 or 3 near the apex of the leafless stems and are about 7 to 10 cm across. Flowering is in late winter and spring and the flowers last about 2 weeks.

This species does well in a hanging pot or basket in bright light and intermediate temperatures. It should be given a brief dry season in winter if it is to flower well. During this time humidity should be low and the plants should dry out completely.

Section *Dendrocoryne* Lindl. (Genus *Dendrobium*)

This section is distributed in Australia and adjacent Pacific islands. There about 12 species in Australia, with 2 species on Lord Howe Island, 2 on Norfolk Island and 1 species, *D. comptonii*, extending from New Caledonia through Vanuatu to Fiji. There have been no substantiated records from New Guinea. In Australia their distribution is confined to regions along the eastern seaboard from western Victoria in the south through New South Wales and into the tropics of Queensland.

Plants in this section are characterised by having pseudobulbs up to 1 m in length with several nodes and 2 to 6 leaves at, or near, the apex. The leaves do not have sheathing bases. The inflorescences are sub-apical, racemose and with a distinct peduncle. They are rarely 1- or 2-flowered. The labellum is trilobed with the lateral lobes more or less erect and is attached to the column foot apex. The lip is not strongly hinged so that the disc or its keels are not in close contact with the column. The disc has 1 to 3 keels which are not usually high. The less fleshy flowers and the loose attachment of the lip distinguish this section from the closely related *Latouria*. Members of this section are popular subjects in cultivation in Australia and increasingly in other areas.

Dendrobium adae F.M. Bailey

Synonyms: *Dendrobium palmerstoniae* Schltr., *D. ancorarium* Rupp
This species is confined to the eastern tropics of Australia from Cooktown to Townsville at altitudes of more than about 800 m. It grows as a lithophyte or epiphyte forming small clumps up to about 60 cm high. The pseudobulbs are thin and wiry and are topped by 2 to 4 ovate leaves, about 6 to 7.5 cm long. Inflorescences carry 1 to 6 flowers about 2.5 cm in diameter and individual flowers last about 2 weeks. The colour ranges from white to greenish, pale yellow and apricot. The labellum is narrow–triangular with a prominent central ridge. The flowers have an attractive perfume similar to orange blossoms. Flowering time is late winter to spring.

This species is most suited to cool or intermediate conditions with high humidity and semi-shade. It may be grown either mounted or in a pot of well-drained medium. It does not appear to be cold sensitive.

WAYNE HARRIS

Dendrobium aemulum R. Br.

This is an extremely variable epiphytic orchid occurring from north-eastern Queensland to south-eastern New South Wales in Australia. They grow at a range of altitudes from sea level to 1000 m. Several forms have been recognised, depending on which host tree the plants occupy. The pseudobulbs are narrow, hard and dark coloured, forming small clumps, and may be up to 30 cm tall. The apex of the pseudobulb bears 2 to 4 ovate to oblong leathery leaves, about 5 cm long. The racemes are up to 10 cm long, free-flowering, and bear from 2 to 12 crystalline white flowers up to 2.5 cm across. The labellum is trilobed and has a prominent wavy yellow ridge. Flowers last a week or two and often turn pink as they fade. Flowering time is mid-winter to spring.

This species is best suited to slab culture, preferably on hardwood or natural cork. They tolerate a wide range of environmental conditions, but are best in intermediate temperatures. They can be grown in a bush-house or glasshouse. They can also be attached to garden trees in suitable climates.

BRUCE GRAY

Dendrobium callitrophyllum B. Gray & D.L. Jones

Synonym: *Dendrobium aemulum* R. Br. var. *callitrophyllum* (B. Gray & D.L. Jones) Dockrill

This small epiphyte is restricted to a few localities in the tablelands of the north-east coast of Queensland. It grows mostly on *Callitris macleayana* trees in the tall open forests on the western margins of the rainforests at altitudes between 750 and 1250 m, in areas with a slightly drier season in winter and spring. The pseudobulbs are 5 to 30 cm long and about 2 or 3 mm wide, with 2 leaves about 4 cm long and 2 cm wide, at the apex. The inflorescence is short and consists of 1 to 6 flowers each about 2 cm across. The flowers last about a week, changing colour from greenish-yellow to apricot as they age.

This species does well in cultivation if given an intermediate to cool climate, with a drier period in winter and spring when the plants are allowed to dry thoroughly between waterings. It should be grown in a small pot of well-drained medium in bright filtered light.

WAYNE HARRIS

Dendrobium falcorostrum Fitzg.

This epiphyte forms medium to large clumps almost exclusively on the Antarctic beech (*Nothofagus moorei*) in highlands above 800 m altitude in south-eastern Queensland and northern New South Wales. This species is one of the most desirable in this section and is highly prized for its spectacular floral displays. The pseudobulbs are up to 50 cm high, narrowed at the base, but then becoming cylindrical or fusiform and becoming ribbed with age. There are 2 to 5 dark green, leathery obovate leaves 6 to 15 cm long, arising near the apex. The inflorescences are up to 16 cm long with 4 to 20 crystalline white flowers up to 3.5 cm across. The flowers have a distinct and strong spicy perfume, especially in the warmer parts of the day. Sepals and petals are a snowy glistening white and the labellum is white with orange and purple markings. Flowering time is spring and the flowers last about 2 weeks.

This species is readily grown in a cool, humid bush-house with good air circulation using a coarse potting mix. Plants can also be grown mounted, preferably on tree fern slabs that should be kept moist. Plants can withstand temperatures down to 0°C.

DAVID TITMUSS

Dendrobium finniganense D.L. Jones

This small terrestrial or lithophytic species has been recorded from several peaks in the vicinity of Mt Finnigan in north-east Queensland, Australia, where it occurs in cloud forest above 1000 m altitude. It usually grows in exposed situations amongst granite boulders, in an area with a high year-round rainfall. The pseudobulbs are from 2 to 24 cm long and 3 to 4 mm in diameter, with 3 to 4 elliptical to elliptical–lanceolate leaves, 5 to 8 cm long and 1.6 to 2 cm wide, at the apex. There are numerous aerial growths. The single fragrant flowers are borne terminally and are 2.5 to 3.5 cm across. Flowering is in late spring and summer and the flowers last about a week. This species is closely related to *D. fleckeri*, but has white, fragrant flowers, while *D. fleckeri* has apricot-coloured, unscented flowers.

In cultivation this species should be grown in intermediate to cool conditions in bright light and extremely good air movement. The plant should be grown in a pot of open medium or on a slab. It should be allowed to dry somewhat between waterings, but never to dry out completely, and should be watered heavily in summer and autumn.

WAYNE HARRIS

Dendrobium fleckeri Rupp & C.T. White

Vegetatively this species is very similar to *D. adae* and it, too, is a common species of the cooler highland rainforests of the Queensland tropics (Cooktown to Innisfail). The species is usually a lithophyte forming small to medium sized clumps of pseudobulbs to about 40 cm high. These are narrow and slender and are covered by brown papery bracts when young. There are 2 or 3 ovate leaves 3 to 8 cm long, borne near the apex. Racemes are about 40 mm long and bear 1 to 3 apricot coloured flowers, 30 mm in diameter. The segments are widely spreading and are thick-textured. The labellum is suffused with purple-red markings and the margins of the mid-lobe are densely ciliate, a feature which distinguishes it from *D. adae*. Flowering time is late winter through to early summer with most flowers appearing in the spring.

This species is readily grown in a cool, humid bush-house with good air circulation using a coarse potting mix. Plants can also be grown mounted, preferably on tree fern slabs that should be kept moist. Plants can withstand temperatures down to 0°C for short periods.

WAYNE HARRIS

Dendrobium gracilicaule F. Muell.

Synonyms: *Dendrobium elongatum* A. Cunn., *D. brisbanense* Rchb.f., *D. macropus* (Endl.) Rchb.f. subsp. *gracilicaule* (F. Muell.) P. Green
This widespread and common species ranges from the Hawkesbury River in New South Wales to the Bloomfield River in northern Queensland. It grows as a lithophyte or epiphytically in both rainforests and more open eucalypt woodlands, from sea level to about 1000 m (usually above 600 m in the northern part of the range). The pseudobulbs are slender, to about 80 or 90 cm long, cylindrical, and when young are covered with brown papery bracts. There are 3 to 6 ovate–lanceolate leaves, 5 to 13 cm long, at the apex. The inflorescences are up to 12 cm long with 5 to 30 flowers each 1.5 cm in diameter. The segments are heavily textured and may be green, yellow or orange inside and are irregularly blotched reddish-brown on the outside. Flowering time is late winter to spring.

This species is very easy to grow under intermediate to cool humid conditions. Plants can be grown either on a slab or in a pot with coarse potting medium. They can also be attached to garden trees in suitable climates.

Dendrobium jonesii Rendle

Synonyms: *Dendrobium speciosum* Sm. var. *fusiforme* F.M. Bailey, *D. ruppianum* A.D. Hawkes, *D. fusiforme* (F.M. Bailey) F.M. Bailey
This very showy species, which may form medium to large clumps, occurs in north-eastern Queensland, Australia, where it grows on rocks and on trees in the open forests and rainforests from the lowlands to the highlands. It is a very variable species, occurring from sea level, where it is uncommon, to about 1500 m altitude. One form with stout pseudobulbs has flowers up to 5 cm across and occurs at higher elevations. The species is very distinctive and can be readily recognised by its hard brown fusiform pseudobulbs up to 50 cm tall with inflorescences up to 40 cm long bearing numerous cream to white flowers that are strongly perfumed in the mornings. The flowers are up to 2 cm in diameter and the labellum is white with purple markings. The flowers last about 7 to 10 days.

D. jonesii is a very much sought-after plant for cultivation because of its easy culture and because of its spectacular display in late winter to spring. It can be grown either mounted on slabs or in pots with a well-drained medium. Minimum winter temperatures should not fall below about 5°C and at this time of year watering should be reduced. Plants benefit from heavy watering in summer. Intermediate temperatures are best.

Dendrobium kingianum Bidwill ex Lindl.

This is probably one of the best-known *Dendrocoryne* species. It is easily grown and is a very rewarding subject. It extends from northern New South Wales to south-eastern Queensland from sea level to 1200 m. As a lithophyte it can form large clumps, often growing in full sun, and it is rarely seen as an epiphyte. Vegetatively it is a very variable species with pseudobulbs ranging in size from as small as 3 or 4 cm to more than 50 cm. The pseudobulbs are generally broadest at the base and taper upwards with 2 to 7 tough, ovate to obovate leaves near the apex. The inflorescences are up to 20 cm long and carry up to 15 flowers of good texture. Flower colour ranges from white through various shades of pink to deep mauve. The labellum may be white or it may be heavily marked with red or purple. The flowers last up to 2 weeks. Flowering time is late winter through spring.

Considerable line-breeding of the various forms has resulted in many sought-after clones. This species has been used more than any other *Dendrocoryne* species in hybridisation of Australian native orchids.

Because of its adaptability, this species can be grown in a wide range of situations. It makes an excellent rockery plant in semi-shaded positions, it does very well in shallow terracotta pots with a coarse mix and it can also be grown on slabs or on trees in the garden. Ample water should be provided over the spring and summer months, with a drier period in winter, when temperatures should not fall below about 2°C. It grows well in intermediate to cool conditions.

Dendrobium moorei F. Muell.

This species is restricted to Lord Howe Island where it is common and grows both as a lithophyte and an epiphyte in humid rainforests. The plants are relatively small with pseudobulbs up to 25 cm tall. They are thin and cylindrical, topped by 2 to 5 oblong leathery leaves about 5 to 10 cm long. The inflorescences are up to 8 cm long and bear 2 to 15 crystalline white flowers about 1.5 cm across and drooping. The flowers do not open widely and the segments, which are thin and pointed, tend to reflex. This species has a habit of producing masses of aerial growths at the expense of flowers.

This species is easy to grow in intermediate to cool humid conditions. It can be grown in a pot with a coarse mix or mounted on a porous substrate such as tree fern. It should be grown in bright light and given a drier resting period in winter and early spring.

Dendrobium speciosum complex

This is the largest species in this section and is the best known and probably the most widely grown species of Australian native orchids. It is also the most widely distributed in nature. When in bloom, a large specimen is a magnificent sight. The species complex has formerly been divided into a number of forms of sub-specific rank which were recently elevated to the rank of species in their own right, although this classification has not been widely accepted. In the descriptions below the old, more familiar names are used, but the new names are given in brackets and readers can use whichever they please.

D. speciosum Sm. var. *speciosum* [*D. speciosum*]

This large robust epiphyte or lithophyte occurs from eastern Victoria to south-east Queensland, Australia, growing from sea level to about 500 m altitude. It grows mostly on rocks, but occasionally as an epiphyte in areas with a year-round rainfall. The pseudobulbs are up to 60 cm long, but commonly about 30 cm, and 2 to 6 cm thick, with 2 to 6 leathery leaves from to 4 to 25 cm long and 2 to 4 cm wide, at the apex. The inflorescence is up to 60 cm long, but usually shorter, with numerous fragrant flowers 2.5 to 5 cm in diameter. The flowers are white to cream or yellow and last about 2 to 3 weeks. Flowering is in late winter and spring.

This species grows in a wide range of habitats, from exposed rocky outcrops to high in the canopy of rainforest trees, and therefore its cultural requirements can be met in a number of ways. They make excellent rockery plants in suitable situations or can be grown in the garden on a suitable host tree. If grown in pots, plenty of room should be left for their development. Eventually they outgrow normal pots but then can be transferred to tubs where they make excellent and spectacular specimens. At all times a coarse mix must be used and regular watering over the summer months is essential. They can be grown either in full sun or in shade. Variety *speciosum* requires intermediate to cool conditions.

Dendrobium speciosum Sm. var. *curvicaule* F.M. Bailey [*D. curvicaule*]

Synonym: *Dendrobium curvicaule* (F.M. Bailey) M. Clem. & D.L. Jones
This large robust variety occurs in coastal north-eastern Queensland from sea level to about 1200 m altitude, growing on rocks and epiphytically in rainforests and adjacent open forests. In this area there is high rainfall, spread throughout the year, but with a drier winter and early spring. The pseudobulbs are from about 10 to 80 cm tall and 1.5 to 5 cm thick, prominently curved with 2 to 4 leathery leaves, 5 to 30 cm long and 2 to 10 cm wide, at the apex. The inflorescences are 15 to 40 cm long with numerous flowers 2 to 3.5 cm across, fragrant. Flowering is in late winter and spring and the cream-yellow flowers last about a week to 10 days.

Cultivation is as for var. *speciosum*. Warm to intermediate conditions with filtered light and a slightly drier period in winter are recommended.

D. speciosum Sm. var. *grandiflorum* F.M. Bailey [*D. rex*]

Synonyms: *Dendrobium rex* M.A. Clem. & D.L. Jones, *D. speciosum* Sm. var. *hillii* Masters forma *grandiflorum* (F.M. Bailey) F.M. Bailey, *D. speciosum* Sm. subsp. *grandiflorum* (F.M. Bailey) D. Banks & Clemesha
This large robust variety occurs in south-east Queensland, growing as an epiphyte or lithophyte in rainforests and adjacent open forests in areas with a distinctly drier season in winter. It occurs from sea level to about 1000 m altitude. The pseudobulbs are 30 to 90 cm long and up to 5 cm thick. There are 2 to 5 leathery leaves up to 30 cm long and 8 cm wide, at the apex of the pseudobulbs. The inflorescences are up to 60 cm long with numerous cream to yellow, fragrant flowers about 3 to 7 cm across. More than 100 flowers are commonly present in a single inflorescence. Flowering is late winter to spring and the flowers last about 7 to 10 days.

Cultivation is as for var. *speciosum*. Intermediate conditions with bright light and a drier period in winter and spring are recommended.

D. speciosum Sm. var. *pedunculatum* Clemesha [*D. pedunculatum*]

Synonym: *Dendrobium pedunculatum* (Clemesha) M.A. Clem. & D.L. Jones
This small to medium sized variety is normally a lithophyte, but occasionally grows epiphytically. It occurs on the north Queensland tablelands at altitudes of about 500 to 1000 m, in exposed positions often with full sun and a dry period in winter and spring. The pseudobulbs are 5 to 30 cm long and 1.5 to 4 cm thick, with 2 or 3 leathery leaves, 5 to 15 cm long and 2.5 to 5.5 cm wide, at the apex. There is usually only one inflorescence per pseudobulb, 25 to 50 cm long, erect with numerous flowers each about 2 cm across. Flowering is in winter and the flowers last about 7 to 10 days.

Cultivation is as for var. *curvicaule*, but the plants do best in intermediate conditions in a clay pot with coarse medium. They should be given full sun and a dry period in winter and early spring.

Dendrobium tetragonum complex

In this group are the Australian species with 4-angled stems and star-shaped flowers. There are two schools of thought concerning this complex – some regard all the plants with 4-angled stems (*D. cacatua, D. capitisyork* and *D. melaleucaphyllum*) as varieties of *D. tetragonum*, others as separate species. In Australia both sets of names are currently being used. In the descriptions below the older more familiar names are retained but the alternative names are given in brackets and readers can use whichever they please.

Dendrobium tetragonum A. Cunn. var. *tetragonum*

This small epiphyte occurs in coastal areas from about Sydney to south-east Queensland in Australia. It grows from sea level to about 1000 m altitude, growing in rainforest and in stream bank forests usually in shaded positions. The pseudobulbs are up to 40 cm long, initially erect then arching to pendulous, very slender at the base, with a prominently 4-angled, swollen part 1 to 1.5 cm wide at the apex. There are 2 to 5 dark green, thin but tough leaves, 3 to 8 cm long and 1.5 to 2.5 cm wide, at the apex. The inflorescence arises near the apex of the pseudobulb and comprises 2 to 5 flowers, each 3 to 5 cm long. The flowers are cream, green or bronze with dark edging and a white lip with some red stripes. The flowers last about 2 weeks and flowering is in winter and spring. Old pseudobulbs continue to flower each year and a large plant may be covered in flowers.

This species is relatively easy to grow if mounted on a slab of cork, tree fern or weathered wood. It should be grown in predominantly shady conditions in intermediate temperatures with high humidity and should be watered throughout the year, although watering may be reduced in winter and early spring.

D. tetragonum A. Cunn. var. *cacatua* [M.A. Clem. & D.L. Jones] H. Mohr [*D. cacatua*]

Synonyms: *Dendrobium cacatua* M.A. Clem. & D.L. Jones, *D. tetragonum* var. *hayesianum* Gilbert

This medium sized epiphyte occurs in north Queensland, Australia, where it grows in upland rainforests and stream bank forests above about 800 m, although plants are occasionally reported from lower altitudes. The pseudobulbs are similar to those described for *D. tetragonum*, but may be up to 60 cm long. The flowers are borne in groups of 2 to 5 and are up to 10 cm long. They are light green, occasionally with a small amount of red markings, and a white lip. Flowering is in winter and early spring and the flowers last for about 7 to 10 days. This variety is very similar to *D. tetragonum* var. *giganteum*, differing mainly in flower colour and altitude range.

Cultivation is as for *D. tetragonum*.

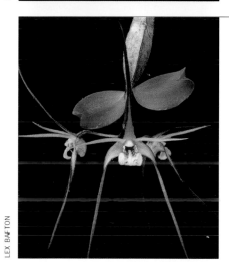

BILL LAVARAACK

LEX BAFTON

Dendrobium tetragonum var. giganteum Gilbert [D. capitisyork)]

Synonym: *Dendrobium capitisyork* M.A. Clem. & D.L. Jones
This medium sized epiphyte occurs in north Queensland and Cape York Peninsula, Australia. It grows in rainforests and stream bank forests, mostly in the lowlands, but also up to about 700 m altitude in the ranges. The stems and leaves are as described for *D. tetragonum*, but the stems are usually longer, up to about 50 cm. The flowers are the largest in the section, being recorded up to 17 cm long, although 10 cm is more common. They are usually yellowish, heavily spotted with dark red, and while usually produced at the apex, may also appear at lower nodes on the swollen part of the pseudobulb. Flowering is in late winter and early spring and the flowers last about 7 to 10 days.

Cultivation is as for *D. tetragonum*. The plants should be given warmer conditions than others in the complex.

Dendrobium tetragonum A. Cunn. var. melaleucaphyllum [M.A. Clem. & D.L. Jones] Dockr. [D. melaleucaphyllum]

Synonym: *Dendrobium melaleucaphilum* M.A. Clem. & D.L. Jones
This small epiphyte occurs from northern New South Wales to central Queensland, Australia, mostly at low altitude, but also up to about 600 m. It commonly grows on *Melaleuca styphelioides*, a species with papery bark, which grows in swampy areas usually near the coast. The stems are similar to those of *D. tetragonum*, up to about 30 cm long. The flowers are larger than those of *D. tetragonum*, up to 10 cm long, but usually around 7 cm long and greenish-yellow with red spots on the lip. They differ in having a more widely flared mid-lobe of the lip. Flowering is in late winter and spring and the flowers last for about 7 to 10 days.

Cultivation is as for *D. tetragonum*.

Section *Dichopus* (Blume) Schltr. (Genus *Dendrobium*)

Synonym: Genus *Dichopus* Blume
This section includes only one species, *Dendrobium insigne* (Blume) Rchb.f. ex Miq., which was recently transferred to the genus *Grastidium*, but is generally regarded as separate by most authorities. The status of this species has yet to be satisfactorily resolved. There are three names that could be used – *Dendrobium insigne*, *Grastidium insigne* and *Dichopus insignis*. Such decisions should be taken as part of an overall classification of the subtribe, not in isolation. In this book the familiar name *Dendrobium insigne* is used, but should not be taken as a statement of the authors' position on the matter. If *Grastidium* is regarded as a genus, then *Dichopus* should either be included in *Grastidium* or given the status of a genus in its own right. Details of the habitat, distribution, habit and flower are given below.

The section is distinguished by the large, moveable appendage which arises from the base of the stigma, and by the leaves, which are larger on the basal part of the stem and much smaller on the apical part. It also has a larger seed capsule and larger seed than members of the genus *Grastidium*.

GEOFF STOCKER

Dendrobium insigne (Blume) Rchb.f. ex Miq.

Synonyms: *Dichopus insignis* Blume, *Grastidium insigne* (Blume) M.A.Clem. & D.L.Jones

This is a long straggling epiphyte from lowland habitats in New Guinea and adjacent islands as far east as the Solomons and as far west as Ambon. It is recorded from Australia, but the record refers to Saibai Island, which is only a matter of kilometres from New Guinea. It grows in mangroves and adjacent rainforests and other coastal vegetation, including coconut plantations, in hot steamy conditions with bright or filtered sunlight and a dry season in some areas. The stems are slender and brittle, up to 70 cm long, erect, then pendulous. The leaves are ovate, about 6 or 7 cm long and 2 or 3 cm across, often with some purple colouring. The size of the leaves decreases towards the apex of the stem. The flowers last a day and are from 2.5 to 5 cm across, borne laterally in short inflorescences of 1 or 2 flowers, on short peduncles. The flowering is spasmodic throughout the year, with a peak in summer.

This species does well on a slab or in a pot of well-drained medium. In the tropics it is best tied securely to a tree. It needs consistently warm, humid conditions although it will tolerate night temperatures as low as 10°C for short periods. It requires bright light and year-round watering, but can withstand a drier period in winter.

Genus *Diplocaulobium* (Rchb.f.) Kraenzl.

This genus was formerly accorded only sectional status by Schlechter but is now widely regarded as a 'good' genus. It comprises probably more than 100 species distributed across South-East Asia from Malaysia through Indonesia and New Guinea to the western Pacific islands. One species occurs in Australia. The centre of diversity is New Guinea with about 90 per cent of the species endemic to that island.

This genus is characterised by pseudobulbs that are closely spaced together and of only one internode. The flowers are pedicellate, mostly single and arise from a conspicuous bract at the base of the single terminal leaf. Flowers are ephemeral, mostly lasting only a day but occasionally longer. The sepals and petals are mostly slender or filiform but in one group they are more lanceolate in shape. The bases of the sepals are broader and united with the column foot to form a distinct mentum. The labellum is attached to the apex of the column foot and is either entire or variously trilobed. The disc usually has distinct keels and may be pulvinate. The pseudobulbs are often distinctly angular in cross-section.

Two sections are recognised in this genus: section *Diplocaulobium* with pseudobulbs that are crowded and closely spaced together on a very short rhizome, and section *Goniobulbon* with pseudobulbs that are closely appressed against a rhizome that may be long and creeping. There are several species of *Diplocaulobium* which do not fit comfortably in either of the two sections that have been described. They differ principally in their growth habits and floral characters and are best left unassigned until the genus is revised.

WAYNE HARRIS

Diplocaulobium abbreviatum (Schltr.) A.D. Hawkes

Section *Diplocaulobium*
Synonym: *Dendrobium abbreviatum* Schltr.
This species is a New Guinea endemic and is restricted to altitudes above about 500 m where it grows in small colonies in exposed conditions on rainforest trees. Conditions there are wet for most of the year with moderate temperatures. This species is the smallest in this section and at first glance resembles many of the species in section *Goniobulbon*. The pseudobulbs are small, cylindrical and up to 2 cm long. The papery bracts at the base of the pseudobulbs are dark brown to purplish. The leaves are from 2 to 4 cm long and 5 mm broad. The single flower is produced at the top of the pseudobulb and is about 2 cm in diameter. Flowering is mostly late spring but can occur any time after pronounced temperature drop.

Culture for this species requires moist humid and intermediate temperatures for most of the year. Plants can either be mounted on a slab or grown in live sphagnum moss in bright light.

WAYNE HARRIS

Diplocaulobium arachnoideum (Schltr.) Carr

Section *Diplocaulobium*
Synonym: *Dendrobium arachnoideum* Schltr.
A number of species all closely similar are centred around this species, many of them exhibiting intergrading variations in leaf character, flower size, etc., so identification is often problematic. The plants are of moderate size with pseudobulbs to 20 cm or so long, typically flask-shaped, narrowing gradually towards the apex. The leaves are up to 12 cm long and 5 mm broad. The flowers are produced singly at various times throughout the spring, summer and into early winter and are widely spreading, up to 10 cm wide. The species in this complex are common elements in the rainforests throughout New Guinea at altitudes between about 800 and 1500 m.

Cultivation requires intermediate conditions with abundant water during the growing season and moisture and high humidity throughout the rest of the year. They can be grown either mounted with attention to watering and humidity, or potted in a suitable epiphyte medium. They respond well to culture in sphagnum moss.

GEOFF STOCKER

Diplocaulobium aureicolor (J.J.Sm.) A.D. Hawkes

Section *Diplocaulobium*
Synonym: *Dendrobium aureicolor* J.J. Sm.
This spectacular species is widespread in New Guinea from near sea level (about 100 m) to over 1200 m, forming clumps up to 60 cm high on rainforest trees. The pseudobulbs are swollen at the base, tapering to a long slender stalk, becoming broader at the base of the single leaf and inflorescence. The leaf is 11 to 15 cm long and 2 to 3 cm wide. One or 2 flowers, up to 5 cm in diameter, are borne at irregular intervals throughout the year.

As this species comes from high rainfall areas it should be given plenty of moisture and humidity for most of the year. It can be grown mounted if these requirements can be accommodated, or grown in a pot with sphagnum moss or chopped tree fern fibre. Intermediate to cool temperatures suit this species well.

DAVID BANKS

Diplocaulobium bicolor P.J. Cribb & B. Lewis

Section *Diplocaulobium*
This species occurs in Papua New Guinea, Bougainville and through to the Solomon Islands, growing in coastal and lowland montane forest up to about 200 m altitude. It is a slender species up to about 30 cm tall with pseudobulbs that are swollen at the base to about 1.5 cm and then tapering to about 2 mm above. The single leaf is 10 to 15 cm long and 1 to 2 cm wide. The single flower, 4 to 6 cm in diameter, arises from a lanceolate papery bract. Flowering can occur at any time, but late spring and summer flowerings are more common.

In cultivation this species requires warm conditions all year but can be grown in cooler climates where protection from temperatures of less than about 5°C can be provided. This species does well in sphagnum moss.

GEOFF STOCKER

Diplocaulobium centrale (J.J.Sm.) P.F. Hunt & Summerh.

Section *Diplocaulobium*
Synonym: *Dendrobium centrale* J.J. Sm.
This New Guinea endemic closely resembles both *D. aureicolor* and *D. regale* in its vegetative characteristics but clearly differs in colour and in the structure of the lip. It grows between about 1500 and 2000 m. Pseudobulbs are about 30 cm tall and are swollen at the base to about 1 cm in diameter and then taper to 2 to 3 mm. The single leaf is about 12 cm long and 2 cm broad. One or 2 flowers about 3 cm in diameter are produced sporadically, mostly from late spring through summer.

This species from wet montane forests requires cool to intermediate conditions with high humidity and plenty of water in the growing season. It grows well in sphagnum moss but can also be cultivated in an epiphyte mix.

WAYNE HARRIS

Diplocaulobium compressicolle (J.J. Sm.) P.F. Hunt & Summerh.

Section *Diplocaulobium*
Synonym: *Dendrobium compressicolle* J.J. Sm.
This species forms very large clumps up to 30 cm high and occurs between 80 and 450 m altitude throughout the New Guinea mainland. It is a species of the wet rainforest, monsoonal rainforest and also adjacent to savanna woodlands. The pseudobulbs of this species are distinctive in that they are bright green and fleshy and are up to 15 cm high, 8 to 10 mm wide at the base tapering to about 5 mm at the apex. The single leaf is erect, oblong to lanceolate, up to 15 cm long and 30 mm wide. The single flowers appear sporadically throughout the year and are up to 8 cm in diameter with a pedicel up to 15 cm long. Flowering is throughout the year.

This species will do well either in a pot of epiphyte mixture or mounted on a suitable host in warm to intermediate conditions. Water should be applied copiously during the growing season and the plant should have moisture and high humidity most of the year. It tolerates semi-shade to bright light.

Diplocaulobium cyclobulbon (Schltr.) A.D. Hawkes

Section *Goniobulbon*
Synonym: *Dendrobium cyclobulbon* Schltr.
This species is typically lowland and coastal in its distribution in New Guinea and the Solomon Islands. It is frequently found close to the ocean, often on coconut palms and on limbs of large trees such as *Barringtonia* overhanging the ocean water. It also extends further inland to the foot of montane ranges at altitudes up to 250 m. It is readily recognised by its flat almost circular pseudobulbs, which are appressed close to the bark of the host tree, and by its very compact growth. Pseudobulbs are about 1 cm long and a little less broad. The thick leathery leaf is up to 2.5 cm long and about 1 cm broad, oblong to elliptical in shape. The small flower is about 10 mm wide and is one of the smallest in this genus.

This species can be successfully cultivated under warm conditions. The mat-forming habit makes it particularly suited to mounting and cork is an appropriate medium. Humidity and moisture should be maintained throughout the year, along with moderate to bright light.

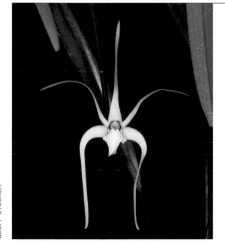

Diplocaulobium glabrum (J.J.Sm.) Kraenzl.

Section *Goniobulbon*
Synonym: *Dendrobium glabrum* J.J. Sm.
This is a widely distributed species on the southern coast of the island of New Guinea and extends into Queensland, Australia, as far south as Cairns. It extends from near sea level to about 500 m altitude and may occasionally occur lithophytically as well as epiphytically. It is a creeping species and is readily recognised by its erect cylindrical to ovoid pseudobulbs to about 3 cm high. The leaf is held erect and is elliptical up to 5.5 cm long and 2 cm broad. Both the leaf and pseudobulb are light green to yellow-green in colour. The flower opens widely and is up to 3 cm broad.

This species prefers high light conditions, a warm environment with abundant water and humidity during the growing season, with a slightly drier period in winter. Flowering can occur at any time between spring and late autumn.

Diplocaulobium hydrophilum (J.J.Sm.) Kraenzl.

Section *Diplocaulobium*
Synonym: *Dendrobium hydrophilum* J.J. Sm.
This is a widespread species throughout New Guinea, favouring the lowlands from sea level to about 400 m altitude. It forms tufted clumps up to 30 cm high. The pseudobulbs, up to 20 cm high, are spindle-shaped and are topped by a single narrow-lanceolate leaf up to 10 cm long and 10 mm broad. One, or occasionally 2, flowers arise from a bract in the leaf axil and are 3 to 4 cm in diameter. They turn pink in the late afternoon as the flower ages. It flowers frequently throughout the year.

In cultivation this species prefers warm conditions and will do equally well mounted or potted in a well-drained epiphyte mix or sphagnum moss.

Diplocaulobium jadunae (Schltr.) A.D. Hawkes

Section *Goniobulbon*
Synonym: *Dendrobium jadunae* Schltr.
Diplocaulobium jadunae is a lowland species from Papua New Guinea and is common in the savanna woodlands and drier forests from sea level to about 200 m in altitude. It is a creeping species forming large colonies to about 5 cm high. The rhizome is crowded with small rounded and compressed pseudobulbs up to about 1.5 cm tall. The single leaf is ligulate to lanceolate in shape and about 2.3 cm long. The flowers are produced singly and are about 2 cm wide. They appear sporadically between spring and early autumn.

This species enjoys warm conditions and bright light. It is best grown on a suitable mount with copious water being given during the summer and a drier resting period in winter and early spring.

Diplocaulobium kirchianum (A.D. Hawkes & Heller) P.F. Hunt & Summerh.

Section *Goniobulbon*
Synonyms: *Dendrobium kirchianum* A.D. Hawkes & Heller, *D. bulbophylloides* J.J.Sm.

This species was previously generally known as *Dendrobium bulbophylloides* J.J.Sm. It is another of the small creeping species in this section, which forms long branching strands crowded with pseudobulbs up to 1.5 m high, 3- to 5-angled and fusiform in shape. The leaf is stiff and leathery, up to 3.5 cm long and 10 mm broad. One or 2 flowers are produced from each pseudobulb and are about 2 cm wide. This species from the lowlands of Papua New Guinea is common in the mangroves and swamp forests of the south coast where the conditions are hot and humid throughout the year.

Successful culture is therefore dependent on emulating this environment. It requires a warm environment with high humidity and plenty of water in summer. It is best grown mounted on a suitable slab such as cork.

Diplocaulobium nitidissimum Rchb.f.

Section *Diplocaulobium*
Synonym: *Dendrobium nitidissimum* Rchb.f., *D. mettkeanum* Kraenzl.
This species is the type of the genus and occurs in the Solomon Islands, New Britain, New Ireland, Manus Island and New Guinea. It is a common epiphyte in coastal communities of these islands and may form clumps up to 30 cm wide and 40 cm tall, often on old dead rainforest trees in very exposed conditions. It is the only species in the genus with dimorphic leaves and is thus readily recognisable. The non-flowering pseudobulbs are ovoid fusiform to narrowly conical, up to 4.5 cm at the base, tapering to about 1 to 2 mm at the apex. The leaf on these pseudobulbs is about 12 cm long and 10 mm wide. The flowering stems arise from the base of a pseudobulb and are up to 40 cm long with a slightly swollen base. The leaf is smaller than the others and is up to 3 cm long and 8 mm wide. These flowering pseudobulbs stand several centimetres above the others. The inflorescence may carry up to 4 flowers about 6 cm in diameter and can appear at any time during the wet season.

This species is easily cultivated in an epiphyte mix or mounted, provided adequate moisture and humidity is provided during the growing period. It should be given a warm environment and bright light.

Diplocaulobium obyrnei W.K. Harris

Section *No section yet defined*
This recently described species is from lowland habitats near Rigo and on Misima Island in the eastern district of Milne Bay, Papua New Guinea. Its habitat is seasonally dry rainforests to about 300 m altitude. The species is distinctive in that although the pseudobulbs are initially clustered, they soon become pendent. These pseudobulbs are fusiform, 4 cm long and 5 mm in diameter. The leaf is stiff and erect, linear up to 10 cm long and 4 mm wide. The flowers are produced singly during spring and summer and are held erect on a 4 to 5 cm long pedicel. The flowers are up to 1.5 cm across and may last 2 to 3 days.

Like most lowland species in the genus, *D. obyrnei* requires humid warm to intermediate conditions with abundant moisture in summer. It is best grown on a suitable slab, but pot culture in a well-drained epiphyte mix or sphagnum moss is also successful.

BILL LAVARACK

Diplocaulobium pulvilliferum (Schltr.) A.D. Hawkes

Section *Diplocaulobium*
Synonym: *Dendrobium pulvilleriferum* Schltr.
This is one of the smaller species in this section, with pseudobulbs to about 10 cm high and very obviously bottle-shaped. The base of the pseudobulb is globular and 10 to 15 mm in diameter and is followed by a slender stalk to about 6 cm long and 2 mm in diameter. The leaf is erect and oblong, up to 10 cm long and 2 cm broad. The single flowers are 6 to 8 cm wide and occur spasmodically through late spring to autumn. This species is relatively common and widespread in Papua New Guinea and occurs in mossy rainforests from about 350 to 1200 m altitude.

This species should be kept moist all year round and watered heavily. It does very well in sphagnum moss but could be grown in a fine well-drained epiphyte mix or mounted, provided that high humidity and adequate moisture is maintained.

WAYNE HARRIS

BILL LAVARACK

Diplocaulobium regale (Schltr.) A.D. Hawkes

Section *Diplocaulobium*
Synonym: *Dendrobium regale* Schltr.
This species is probably the most spectacular in terms of colour and shape in the genus, although like others in the genus the flowers last only 1 day. However, plants produce many flowers at one time and will provide the grower with a spectacular display. Originally described from the Finisterre Range in Papua New Guinea, this species is common throughout most of the island at altitudes from 1500 to about 2500 m. Plants are up to 70 cm tall, with gradually tapering pseudobulbs. The leaves are oblong–lanceolate up to 20 cm long and 4 cm broad. Flowers are up to 8 cm wide and may be nearly white through to dark rose-red in colour. The type variety is light red and the variety *euanthum* Schltr. is pale pink.

This species can be readily cultivated in intermediate conditions. A well-drained epiphyte mix is suitable and moisture and humidity should be maintained year round with semi-shade to moderate light.

GEOFF STOCKER

Diplocaulobium stelliferum (J.J. Sm.) A.D. Hawkes

Section *Goniobulbon*
Synonym: *Dendrobium stelliferum* J.J. Sm.
As presently known, this taxon represents a complex of forms which may be recognised as separate entities in the future. They occur at moderate altitudes in Papua New Guinea up to about 800 m altitude where they may form extensive mats. The pseudobulbs are more or less cylindrical, becoming ribbed with age. They are about 2 cm tall and are topped by a lanceolate leaf to 3 cm long and about 10 mm wide. The single flower is erect and is about 2 cm wide.

Cultivation requires humid warm to intermediate conditions with abundant water during the growing season. The species is best accommodated on a suitable mount.

DAVID BANKS

Diplocaulobium tipuliferum (Rchb.f.) Kraenzl.

Section *Diplocaulobium*
Synonym: *Dendrobium tipuliferum* Rchb.f.
This species was described originally from the Fijian islands. When in flower, it is readily recognised by the fimbriate margin to the mid-lobe of the lip, the only species in the genus to possess this character. In Fiji this species occurs from sea level to about 900 m altitude and can be found growing on mangroves near the coast or on rainforest trees inland. The plants are not large, with pseudobulbs to about 20 cm long and 3 to 4 mm wide. The single leaf is about 10 cm long and 8 mm wide.

Intermediate to warm conditions suit this species and it can be grown either mounted or in a pot with a well-drained epiphytic medium with adequate year-round moisture and humidity.

GEOFF STOCKER

Diplocaulobium tropidophorum (Schltr.) A.D. Hawkes

Section *Goniobulbon*
This species is readily recognised by its characteristic growth. Initially the pseudobulbs adhere closely to the host but the rhizome soon becomes elongated and pendent. The pseudobulbs are up to 3 cm long, cylindrical and 4- to 6-angled. The leaf is elliptical to ligulate in shape and up to 7.5 cm long and 1 cm wide. Flowers occur singly at any time during late spring through to autumn and are up to 2 cm wide. This species is from the mountains of Papua New Guinea up to about 800 m altitude, where it grows in exposed sites as an epiphyte.

Because off its pendent nature this species can be difficult to establish and is best on a suitable host such as a tree fern slab. It requires moisture and humidity all year with intermediate temperatures.

Diplocaulobium sp. aff. *D. chrystropis* (Schltr.) A.D. Hawkes

Section *Goniobulbon*

This species occurs in Papua New Guinea at altitudes around 1000 m. It has a creeping rhizome with erect pseudobulbs 1 to 2 cm apart. They are 4- to 6-angled, 1 to 2.5 cm high and about 5 mm in diameter. Leaves are narrowly oblong, 3 to 5 cm long and 5 to 8 mm wide. Flowering is in spring through to autumn and can result in a mass display. The species is readily recognised by its relatively large flowers to 3 cm in diameter, the strongly falcate lateral sepals and the attractively marked labellum. It flowers at irregular intervals between late spring and early winter.

This species can be grown in a shallow pot using a well-drained epiphyte mix, but due to its rambling habit it is probably more suited to mounting on a moisture-retentive host. It requires high humidity, year-round watering, moderate light and intermediate conditions.

WAYNE HARRIS

Diplocaulobium sp. aff. *D. mekynosepalum* (Schltr.) Kraenzl.

Section *Goniobulbon*

It is believed that this medium sized species came from the Southern Highlands Province of Papua New Guinea. The plants are tufted and erect with pseudobulbs 20 to 30 cm long. The pseudobulbs are reddish-brown, terete, 3 to 4 mm in diameter, somewhat grooved and tapering slightly towards the apex. The single leaf is relatively thin, dark green on its upper surface, lighter below, lanceolate, 10 cm long and 3.5 cm wide. One to 5 flowers are borne from the apex of the leafy pseudobulbs. Although flowers last only 1 day, flowering occurs every month or so throughout the year.

The species is easily grown in bright, moist, intermediate conditions in a small pot of well-drained medium.

GEOFF STOCKER

Section *Distichophyllum* Hook.f. (Genus *Dendrobium*)

This is a section of around 35 species which occur from Myanmar (Burma) to New Caledonia. The centres of distribution are in mainland South-East Asia with about 13 species and, more particularly, Borneo with 20 species. The majority of species occur at low to moderate altitudes in areas where there is year-round rainfall. It is related to *Grastidium*.

The plants mostly have long, fairly slender stems with leaves in 2 ranks along the length of the stem. The flowers are rather small and are borne singly or in pairs (occasionally up to 3) from the leaf axils. They are mostly in shades of white, yellow, orange and green, some changing colour quite markedly as they age. There is a prominent mentum, the lip is usually 3-lobed and the petals and sepals are often reflexed. A few of the species are quite well known in cultivation.

Dendrobium austrocaledonicum Schltr.

Synonyms: *Dendrobium inequale* Finet non Rolfe, *D. cerinum* Schltr. non Rchb.f., *D. critaeurbrae* Guillaumin, *D. mendoncanum* A.D. Hawkes
This is a medium sized epiphyte found in New Guinea and the Pacific islands, including Bougainville, Gaudalcanal, New Georgia, Vanuatu and New Caledonia. It grows mostly at low altitudes, but is recorded up to 1000 m, in rainforest that is moist all year round, often in forest lining creeks or near the ocean. The stems are long and cylindrical, eventually becoming pendulous, up to 60 cm in length and about 5 mm in diameter. The leaves are oblong, 2 to 4.5 cm long and borne along the stem in 2 ranks. The flowers are solitary and lateral. They start as white or greenish-white and change to dark yellow or orange as they age. They last about 3 weeks and the flowering season is mostly winter and spring, although flowers may occur at any time. They are about 2 cm across and waxy in texture.

Regular year-round watering and warm conditions are best. The plants grow well on a slab or in a well-drained hanging pot to allow for the pendulous stems. Medium to bright light and regular fertilising with dilute fertiliser are recommended.

Dendrobium bifarium Lindl.

Synonym: *Dendrobium excisum* Lindl.
This small to medium sized epiphyte is fairly common in the lowland forests of Peninsular Malaysia and Singapore. It also occurs in Thailand, Borneo and Ambon, growing in the lowlands and up to about 1800 m in lower montane rainforest. The stems are up to 30 cm long and a little less than 1 cm wide, with leaves in 2 ranks along most of their length. The leaves are elliptic–oblong, about 5 cm long and 1.1 cm wide. The solitary flowers are about 1.2 cm across and are borne laterally on the leafless stems. Flowering is most common in spring and summer.

Warm to intermediate temperatures with year-round watering and high humidity are recommended. The plants should not be allowed to dry completely. Either a slab or pot of well-drained medium is satisfactory.

Dendrobium connatum (Blume) Lindl.

Synonym: *Dendrobium subarticulatum* Teijsm. & Binn.
This epiphytic species occurs in Sumatra, Java and Borneo. It grows at altitudes of 400 to 1000 m, often low down on tree trunks in fairly open situations. The stems, which are up to 50 cm long, with leaves along their entire length, form a dense clump. The leaves are about 2 cm long and 8 mm wide, with overlapping bases. The flowers are about 12 mm across and are borne singly from the nodes along the stem. While there may be many flowers along the stem, only a few are open at one time.

In cultivation, this species should be grown in warm temperatures with year-round watering and high humidity. The plants should be given bright light. They can be grown in a pot of well-drained medium or on a slab as long as they are kept moist.

Dendrobium ellipsophyllum T. Tang & F.T. Wang

This species occurs as an epiphyte in the hot, steamy lowlands of Myanmar (Burma), Thailand, Laos, Cambodia, Vietnam and possibly China. There is a complex of similar species involving *D. ellipsophyllum*, *D. uniflorum* Griff. and *D. revolutum* Lindl. *D. ellipsophyllum* is very similar to the widespread *D. uniflorum*, differing in the lip, which has small, broadly triangular lateral lobes, while *D. uniflorum* has large lateral lobes and *D. revolutum* has virtually no lateral lobes. The stems are 30 to 50 cm long and about 5 mm in diameter. The leaves are about 3 to 4 cm long and 1.5 to 2 cm wide, and are borne in 2 ranks along the length of the stem. The flowers are about 2 cm long and are borne singly from nodes on the apical part of the stem. They last about 1 week, changing colour from white to dull orange as they age. Flowering in cultivation occurs throughout most of the year with an emphasis on winter and spring.

In cultivation, this species does well if grown in a mixture that retains some moisture. It should be given bright filtered light, high humidity and year-round watering, although slightly reduced watering in cooler weather may be best. It has also been successfully grown on a slab.

Dendrobium hosei Ridl.

Synonym: *Dendrobium multicostatum* J.J. Sm.
This medium sized epiphyte occurs in Peninsular Malaysia and Borneo, growing in the lowlands, often in stream bank forests, from sea level to about 800 m altitude. The stems are up to 60 cm long and 1.2 to 2 cm in diameter, with leaves along most of their length. The leaves are linear–lanceolate, 6 to 10 cm long and 1 cm wide. The flowers are borne laterally, singly or in pairs and are about 1.5 cm across, initially greenish, turning pale yellow. Some flowers have 2 extra anthers and tend to self-pollinate.

In cultivation warm, humid conditions are required. The plants should be watered regularly throughout the year, but a slightly drier period in winter may not be a problem. A slab or a pot of well-drained medium are recommended.

Dendrobium lamrianum C.L. Chan

This large epiphyte occurs in montane rainforest on the slopes of Mt Kinabalu in Sabah, Borneo at about 1700 to 1800 m altitude. It is a large-flowered species discovered as recently as 1993. The stems are up to 120 cm long and 4 to 7 mm thick, leafy in the apical half. There are 12 to 15 leaves about 6 to 12 cm long and 1 to 2 cm wide. The single flowers are about 6.5 cm across, fleshy and fragrant. They emerge laterally through the leaf sheaths on the upper part of the leafy stem and are borne with the lip uppermost. Flowering is in October to December in the habitat and the flowers last about a week.

Little is known of the cultural requirements of this species, but it is presumed to require intermediate to cool moist conditions. It should be tried in a hanging pot or on a slab, but should be kept moist throughout the year.

DAVID TITMUSS

PHILLIP CRIBB

PHILLIP CRIBB

WAYNE HARRIS

Dendrobium oligophyllum Gagnep.

Synonym: *Dendrobium tixieri* Guillaumin

This is a miniature epiphytic species from Thailand and Vietnam where it grows at about 600 to 700 m altitude. The pseudobulbs are short and relatively thick, up to about 6 cm long and 7 mm wide. There are a few leaves on the apical half of the pseudobulb. The leaves are 3 to 5 cm long and 1 to 1.5 cm wide, with a bifid apex. The inflorescences are borne on the leafy stems opposite the leaves and consist of 1 to 4 flowers, each about 2.5 cm across. The flowers are long-lasting and are produced at several times a year, but the main flowering season is spring. Plants flower while very small.

Warm or intermediate conditions are required with year-round high humidity. The plants should be given a slightly drier resting period in winter, but if they dry out between waterings, this should not be for more than a day. A slab is best, but a pot with a well-drained medium is also suitable.

JIM COMBER

Dendrobium pandaneti Ridl.

Synonym: *Dendrobium mega* Kraenzl.

This medium sized epiphyte occurs in Peninsular Thailand and Malaysia, Sumatra, Java and Borneo. It grows at altitudes below 600 m, often on sago palms and *Pandanus* species in the hot, steamy lowlands where there is year-round rainfall and high humidity. The stems are up to 60 cm long, occasionally branched, with leaves along most of their length. The leaves are about 8 cm long and 1.75 cm wide on the lower part of the stem, becoming smaller towards the apex. The inflorescences consist of 2 or 3 flowers which are borne laterally along the apical half of the stem. The flowers are about 2.5 cm wide. The lip is initially white, turning a dull yellow with age. There are 2 small additional anthers on either side of the median anther and these are reported to cause self-pollination of most flowers.

Warm temperatures are required in cultivation, with year-round watering and constant high humidity. The plants should be given bright filtered sunlight. They may be grown in a pot of well-drained medium or mounted on a slab.

JIM COMBER

Dendrobium uniflorum Griff.

Synonyms: *Dendrobium quadrisulcatum* J.J. Sm., *D. tonkinense* Wildeman

This medium sized epiphytic species is widespread in South-East Asia, occurring in Vietnam, Thailand, Peninsular Malaysia, Sumatra, Borneo and the Philippines. It occurs from the lowlands to 1800 m, in montane rainforests where there is year-round rainfall and high humidity. The stems are 30 to 40 cm long, with leaves along most of the length. The leaves are about 3 cm long and a little less than 1 cm wide, and are arranged in a single plane. The flowers are borne singly from the nodes opposite the leaves. They are about 1.3 to 2.7 cm across, and last about 2 weeks. The flowers change to a dull orange as they age. Flowering can be at any time of the year. This species is closely related to *D. ellipsophyllum* T. Tang & F.T. Wang and *D. revolutum* Lindl. See the former for a discussion.

In nature the species is recorded from a range of altitudes, so intermediate to warm conditions may be successful in cultivation. The plants should be kept moist throughout the year and given bright filtered sunlight. A slab or a pot with well-drained medium can be used.

Genus *Dockrillia* Brieger

Synonym: *Dendrobium* section *Rhizobium* Lindl.

This recently recognised genus includes about 30 species and is centred in Australia with about 18 species and New Guinea with about 10 species. There are also species in New Caledonia and Vanuatu. They are typically species of low to moderate altitudes, growing epiphytically or lithophytically in rainforests and open forests, often in situations with bright light.

Brieger erected this genus to accommodate those Australasian species that are characterised by having more or less terete, or at least thick and fleshy, leaves that are formed along a thin and wiry stem. The name commemorates Alick Dockrill, a prominent Australian orchidologist. Most are pendulous epiphytes but one, *D. striolata*, is mostly lithophytic. The flowers are usually presented in the non-resupinate position and have slender, sometimes curled, segments, with a 3-lobed lip. The inflorescences consist of few to many flowers. This genus is related to section *Lichenastrum* and some, including Brieger, consider that the 2 groups should be united in one genus. Members of this section are popular subjects for cultivation in Australia.

GERALD McCRAITH

Dockrillia bowmanii (Benth.) M.A.Clem. & D.L. Jones

Synonym: *Dendrobium bowmanii* Benth. This species was erroneously known as *D. mortii* for many years.

This medium sized to large species is widely distributed in Australia, from the Atherton Tableland in northern Queensland to the Clarence River in northern New South Wales, and in New Caledonia. It grows either epiphytically or lithophytically and is common in coastal scrubs and dry rainforest and extends well inland onto the Great Dividing Range. It has a straggly, mainly pendulous habit with scattered small green to pale brown flowers with a white conspicuous labellum. Leaves are terete and up to 15 cm long. Flowers are mostly in pairs and are about 2.5 cm in diameter. Plants flower mostly in spring and autumn but with occasional flowers appearing throughout the year.

This species is easily grown and is best cultivated on a suitable slab and given good light and humidity. Plants can also be established in suitable garden settings.

DAVID TITMUSS

Dockrillia brevicauda (D.L. Jones & M.A. Clem.) D.L. Jones & M.A. Clem.

Synonym: *Dendrobium brevicaudum* D.L. Jones & M.A. Clem.

This medium to large pendulous epiphyte or lithophyte is restricted to the slopes of mountains in the vicinity of Mt. Finnigan in north-east Queensland, Australia. It grows in rainforest at altitudes of about 700 m in areas with a wet climate for most of the year, but a slightly drier period in winter and early spring. The stems are slender and wiry, up to 20 cm long and 2 to 2.5 mm in diameter and lack aerial roots. The pendulous leaves are linear-terete, 15 to 60 cm long and about 3.5 to 5 mm in diameter. The short inflorescences arise from the base of the leaf and consist of up to 8 fragrant flowers each about 4.5 cm across. It may be distinguished from other Australia members of the genus by the short hairs on the labellum, column and column foot. Flowering is in summer and the flowers last about a week.

This species does best in an intermediate climate with a drier period in winter, although it should not be allowed to dry out for more than a day or two. It should be grown in semi shade and humid conditions. It is best tied to a slab of cork or hardwood.

Dockrillia calamiformis (Lodd.) M.A.Clem. & D.L. Jones

Synonyms: *Dendrobium calamiforme* Lodd., *D. teretifolium* R. Br. var.
fasciculatum Rupp
This large epiphytic species occurs from the wet tropics to Cape York
Peninsula in north-east Queensland, Australia, forming pendulous clumps up
to 2 m long. It is epiphytic or occasionally lithophytic and grows in, or near,
rainforest in the lowlands and up to 1300 m altitude in the ranges. The
pendulous terete leaves are robust and may be up to 40 cm long and 1.5 cm
in diameter. Aerial roots are lacking. Two racemes are present on the stem
and may be up to 8 cm long, bearing up to 15 crowded fragrant flowers
which are creamy white to yellow, about 1 cm in diameter. The perianth
segments do not spread widely. Some authorities prefer to unite this species,
along with *D. dolichophylla*, *D. fairfaxii* and *D. teretifolia*, in 1 variable
species with 4 varieties. The flowering period is spring.
  This species is easily grown on a suitable slab and can be grown in a
garden setting in intermediate conditions with a slightly drier period in winter.

Dockrillia casuarinae (Schltr.) M.A.Clem. & D.L. Jones

Synonym: *Dendrobium casuarinae* Schltr.
This species is endemic to New Caledonia and closely resembles the
Australian species *Dockrillia racemosa*. It is sometimes cultivated under the
name '*D. sylvanum*'. It grows both epiphytically and lithophytically
throughout most of the islands of New Caledonia. It prefers high light
intensities and will grow on exposed rocks as well as in open forest, favouring
Casuarina trees in particular. The slender terete leaves become pendulous
with age and the inflorescence carries 5 to 20 flowers. Flowering is mostly
late autumn through to spring.
  In cultivation this species requires high light intensities and warm to
intermediate conditions. It is best mounted on a suitable host. Watering
should be year round with a slightly drier period in winter.

Dockrillia cucumerina (MacLeay ex Lindl.) Brieger

Synonym: *Dendrobium cucumerinum* MacLeay ex Lindl.
Commonly called the cucumber or gherkin orchid because of the unusual
shape of its leaves, this species is readily recognised by this feature. It
occurs in south-east Queensland through to central eastern New South Wales
in Australia, where it is most commonly found growing on river oaks
(*Casuarina cunninghamiana*), from sea level to about 800 m. The gherkin-
like leaves are up to 4 cm long and are thick and fleshy. Plants may form
large dense clumps or form strands. Racemes are 2 to 4 cm long with 2 to
10 flowers 1.5 cm across, which do not open widely. The flower colour is
cream to greenish-white with purple striping. This species flowers from late
spring through summer.
  It can be difficult to maintain in cultivation and is difficult to re-establish.
The plants require intermediate conditions, bright light, high humidity and
less water in winter. Suitable mounts include cork or hardwood.

Dockrillia dolichophylla (D.L. Jones & M.A. Clem.) M.A.Clem. & D.L. Jones

Synonyms: *Dendrobium dolichophyllum* D.L. Jones & M.A. Clem., *D. teretifolium* R. Br. var. *aureum* F.M. Bailey, *D. teretifolium* R. Br. var. *album* C.T. White

This large epiphyte forms long slender clumps up to 3 m or more long. It grows on rocks and trees in moist shady forests mostly at moderate altitudes in south-east Queensland and northern New South Wales in Australia. Leaves are slender, terete and up to 1 m long. The inflorescences are up to 8 cm long with 1 to 5 fragrant flowers up to 5 cm in diameter. The flowers are yellow with prominent dark purple stripes near the centre. The flowering season is spring.

This species is easily cultivated on a suitable mount either in a shadehouse with adequate moisture, humidity and some shade, or in a suitable garden setting in intermediate to cool conditions.

Dockrillia fairfaxii (F. Muell. & Fitzg.) Rauschert

Synonyms: *Dendrobium fairfaxii* F. Muell. & Fitzg., *D. teretifolium* R. Br. var. *fairfaxii* (F. Muell. & Fitzg.) F.M. Bailey

This species is both a lithophyte and an epiphyte growing in mostly shady conditions up to 1000 m in the ranges and tablelands of south-east Queensland to the Blue Mountains of central eastern New South Wales, Australia. It forms large pendulous clumps up to 3 m long. Leaves are up to 80 cm long and terete. Aerial roots are present and the stems are straight. Racemes are up to 3 cm long with 1 to 4 flowers up to 5 cm across. Perianth segments are not recurved and are cream to pale yellow with prominent red stripes at their base. The flowering season is from late winter to early spring.

This species is easy to cultivate if mounted on a suitable slab or grown on a suitable host in the garden. It requires cool humid conditions with some shade and plenty of air movement.

Dockrillia fuliginosa M.A. Clem. & D.L. Jones

This medium sized species is presently known only from the type locality at Kaisipi swamp, Central Province, in Papua New Guinea, where it grows on *Casuarina* trees. It is a pendulous species forming sparse clumps to about 50 cm long. The leaves are terete and up to 20 cm long. The inflorescences are 3 to 5 cm long and bear 3 to 6 flowers, which do not open widely. They are about 2 cm wide with a musty fragrance and an attractive colour. Flowering is in spring with the flowers lasting up to 10 days.

It is easily cultivated under intermediate conditions and can be either mounted or grown in a pot of well-drained coarse epiphyte mix. It should be watered throughout the year. This species was previously known as *Dendrobium teretifolium* 'Black Pam' and has been widely used in hybridising.

WAYNE HARRIS

Dockrillia linguiformis (Sw.) Brieger

Synonym: *Dendrobium linguiforme* Sw.
Commonly called the tongue or thumbnail orchid, this characteristic species forms large mat-like colonies on either rocks or trees from sea level to over 1000 m altitude in north-east Queensland to south-east New South Wales in Australia. The leaf arises from very short stems and is oblong to obovate, up to 4 cm long and 1.5 cm wide, prostrate and borne alternatively along the stem. Leaves are fleshy and dark green and usually furrowed. The racemes are 5 to 15 cm long and bear 6 to 20 flowers up to 2 cm across. The segments are slender, cream or crystalline white and sharp pointed, in contrast to the closely related *Dockrillia nugentii*. The flowering period is winter and spring.

   Culture of this species is very easy if mounted on a suitable host in either the garden or shadehouse. The plants appreciate good light, high humidity and air movement and intermediate to warm conditions, with a slightly drier resting period in winter.

DAVID BANKS

Dockrillia mortii (F. Muell.) Rauschert

Synonyms: *Dendrobium mortii* F. Muell., *D. tenuissimum* Rupp, *D. robertsii* F. Muell ex Rupp, *Dockrillia tenuissima* (Rupp) Rauschert
This is a slender pendulous epiphyte occurring in rainforest on the upper branches of trees in south-east Queensland and northern New South Wales, Australia. This orchid is most abundant at altitudes above 1000 m, although it occurs occasionally in the lowlands. The plants are never very large and are usually less than 40 cm long. Leaves are pendulous and up to 10 cm long and about 4 mm in diameter. The inflorescence usually has 1 flower, but occasionally 2 or 3. The flowers are up to 2 cm across and pale to dark green with a white labellum with purple markings. The flowering period is spring.

   It is easily grown in temperate regions using slab culture. It requires intermediate to cool conditions with high humidity, year-round watering and semi shade.

WAYNE HARRIS

Dockrillia nugentii (F.M. Bailey) M.A. Clem. & D.L. Jones

Synonyms: *Dendrobium linguiforme* Sw. var. *nugentii* F.M. Bailey, *D. nugentii* (F.M. Bailey) M.A. Clem. & D.L. Jones
This miniature mat-forming species occurs in north Queensland to the base of Cape York Peninsula in Australia. It grows at low to moderate altitudes, from about 400 to 1000 m in open forests, usually near rainforest boundaries on trees or, more commonly, on rocks. In this area the climate is very wet in summer and autumn, with a distinct dry season in winter and early spring. This species is very closely related to *Dockrillia linguiformis* and many authorities consider it worthy of varietal status only. It differs in having more rounded and broader leaves, which are rough to the touch, and has smaller cream flowers with blunt segments.

   Cultivation is easy if the plants are attached firmly to a suitable slab and grown in warm to intermediate conditions in semi-shade to bright light. They should be given a drier resting period in winter and early spring.

but will grow on a wide variety of trees, from mangroves to open forest in the mountains. It is also occasionally lithophytic. The flowering period is from winter into spring.

In does well in cultivation, grown on a slab of hardwood or on a suitable host tree. It does best in intermediate conditions with bright light and a drier resting period in winter.

WAYNE HARRIS

Dockrillia vagans (Schltr.) Rauschert

Synonyms: *Dendrobium vagans* Schltr., *D. seemannii* L.O. Williams
This large pendulous epiphyte, up to 2 m long, is found in a number of western Pacific islands including Vanuatu, Samoa, Fiji and the New Hebrides. It occurs mainly as an epiphyte, less frequently lithophytically, from sea level near the beach or inland to about 800 m altitude. It favours a habitat with high light intensity and a seasonally dry climate. The leaves are terete, 14 to 20 cm long and about 2 mm wide. The inflorescence arises from the base of a leaf with a raceme 10 to 15 cm long carrying 7 to 15 flowers, widely opening and about 4 to 5 cm wide. This species flowers in the spring.

In cultivation, this species prefers to be mounted on a slab and given warm humid conditions with abundant water in summer and less in the dry season.

BILL LAVARACK

Dockrillia wassellii (S.T. Blake) Brieger

Synonym. *Dendrobium wassellii* S.T. Blake
This species is endemic to the Iron Range and McIlwraith Range on Cape York Peninsula, Australia, where it occurs in monsoonal rainforests, along creek margins on emergent trees, commonly on hoop pines (*Araucaria cunninghamii*) and occasionally on boulders. It is a lowland species extending to about 600 m altitude. The plant forms slender strands or spreading clumps and has upright leaves to 9 cm long and 1 cm in diameter. These are held stiffly erect and bear 5 longitudinal furrows. The inflorescence emerges from near the base of the leaves, is erect, and up to 20 cm long with up to 60 densely crowded flowers. These are about 2.5 cm across and are crystalline white with a pale yellow lip. The perianth segments are narrow and widely spreading. Flowering is throughout the year, but concentrated in late spring and early summer.

This species is easily cultivated on a slab or in a wide, shallow pot in warm to intermediate conditions. Plants should be grown in high light with good humidity and air movement and watered throughout the year, but with a slightly drier period in winter.

GEOFF STOCKER

Dockrillia sp. aff. *D. chordiformis* (Kraenzl.) Rauschert

This species was found as a pendulous epiphyte to 60 cm long on trees in open forest in the Ramu Valley, Madang Province, Papua New Guinea, at an altitude of about 400 m. The thin wiry rhizome bears terete leaves 13 to 15 cm long and 4 mm wide, which are spaced about 5 to 7 cm apart. One or 2 inflorescences arise from near the base of each leaf. They are about 8 cm long and bear 10 to 12 flowers. Each flower is about 2 cm across and lasts for a week.

This species grows well on a cork slab allowed to dry out between waterings. Warm, bright conditions appear optimal.

Dockrillia sp. ex Snake River

This species was found on scattered trees along the road which follows the Snake River to its source in Morobe Province, Papua New Guinea. It has also been reported from the *Araucaria* forests of the Bulolo Valley a little further to the south. It has shorter rhizomes and fewer leaves than most of the other pencil orchids. Plants are pendulous but rarely hang down more than 40 cm. The terete leaves are 10 to 15 cm long and 4 mm wide and are spaced at about 3 to 5 cm intervals along the rhizome. The inflorescences arise from near the base of the leaves and carry about 6 flowers that last a week. Each of the flowers is about 2 cm across.

Seedlings have proved easy to grow in peat/perlite medium. It is suggested that adult plants be attached to a cork slab, hung in a bright position and given intermediate to warm temperatures.

Section *Dolichocentrum* Schltr. (Genus *Dendrobium*)

This is a section comprised one species only – *D. furcatum* from Sulawesi. It grows in montane rainforests in an area with year-round rainfall. It sometimes colonises coffee plantations. According to Schlechter, it is not closely related to any other sections, but it may be related to *Conostalix*.

The flowers are fairly large and white. The feature that distinguishes this section is the spur formed from the sepals.

Dendrobium furcatum Reinw. ex Lindl.

Synonyms: *Dendrobium amabile* Schltr., *D. sarasinorum Kraenzl., D. dolichocentrum* Koorders

This is a medium sized, pendulous epiphyte from the Minahassa Peninsula of north-eastern Sulawesi, where it grows in montane rainforests at altitudes of about 900 to 1700 m. It is also quite common on older trees in coffee plantations. The pseudobulbs are up to 45 cm long, occasionally branching, with leaves in 2 ranks along most of their length. The leaves are narrow, 2 to 5 cm long, with 2 unequal teeth at the apex. The short inflorescences are borne laterally or near the apex of the stem, with 2 or 3 flowers. The flowers are 3 to 4 cm in diameter, white, but with a small amount of rose colouring on the reverse side. There are records of flowering from October to May in the habitat.

This species is not well known in cultivation, but is an attractive species worthy of more attention. The habitat suggests it should be grown attached to a slab and kept evenly moist throughout the year. Intermediate to warm temperatures and bright filtered light are suggested.

Section *Eleutheroglossum* Schltr. (*Genus Dendrobium*)

This small group of 4 species occurs in New Caledonia and north-eastern Australia. New Caledonia, with 3 species, is the centre of distribution. These are plants of low to moderate elevations, growing epiphytically or lithophytically in open forest or less dense rainforest. Schlechter considered this section closest to *Phalaenanthe* and *Spatulata*.

The plants are mostly small to medium sized with club-shaped pseudobulbs. The leaves, which are grouped near the apex of the stem, have a distinct sheath. The inflorescences arise from near the apex of the stem and have a few small flowers that are usually in shades of yellow with maroon or purple markings. The lip is 3-lobed with a cleft at the apex and there is a prominent incurved mentum. A typical feature of the flowers is the arrangement of the lateral sepals which are prominent and held at an angle of about 45° to the vertical, like the ears on a dog.

DAVID BANKS

Dendrobium closterium Rchb.f.

Synonyms: *Dendrobium eleutheroglossum* Schltr., *D. jocosum* Rchb.f., *D. myrticola* Kraenzl.

This small epiphyte or lithophyte is restricted to New Caledonia. It grows at a range of altitudes from sea level to 1000 m on small trees such as *Casuarina* and *Melaleuca* species in open situations where there is bright light and year-round rainfall. The pseudobulbs are 4 to 15 cm long and about 8 mm wide, with 3 to 5 leathery leaves at the apex. The elliptic leaves are unequally bilobed, 3 to 8 cm long. The inflorescences arise from the apical nodes and bear 2 to 20 flowers, each 2 to 3 cm across. The flowering season is late spring and summer.

This species has proved relatively easy to cultivate. It is best tied to a slab or in a small, very well-drained pot. It requires year-round watering, with the plants being allowed to dry out between waterings. The conditions should be humid with bright light and warm to intermediate temperatures.

GERALD McCRAITH

Dendrobium fellowsii F. Muell.

Synonyms: *Dendrobium bairdianum* F.M. Bailey, *D. giddinsii* T.E. Hunt

This is a small epiphyte from the tropical highlands of north-east Australia. It grows in moist open forests on the eastern margin of the ranges where rain and misty conditions are common, usually at altitudes from 500 to 1000 m. It usually occurs high up on bloodwoods (*Corymbia* spp.) and she-oaks (*Casuarina* spp.), all of which have rough or fibrous barks. It is the only member of the section *Eleutheroglossm* outside New Caledonia. The pseudobulbs vary in length up to about 20 cm, but are commonly about 10 to 15 cm long and less than 1 cm in diameter, with 3 to 5 linear–lanceolate leaves, 3 to 9 cm long, clustered at the end of the pseudobulb. The flowers are about 2 cm across and there are from 2 to 7 on each short inflorescence. The flowering period is during the beginning of the wet season in late spring and summer, with the flowers lasting a week or two. Frequently there are 2 bursts of flowering a month apart.

This species has proved difficult to cultivate and is certainly intolerant of disturbance, so care is necessary if repotting. It should be given intermediate to cool conditions and should not be allowed to dry out completely. Good light and air movement are important. A slab or small pot is recommended.

S. SPRUNGER/RGB, KEW

Dendrobium ngoyense Schltr.

This miniature species is restricted to New Caledonia where it occurs as an epiphyte throughout the island at altitudes up to 800 m, often in scrubland in bright light situations and year-round rainfall. The pseudobulbs are short, 2 to 4 cm long and 1 cm wide, with 2 or 3 fleshy leaves at the apex. The leaves are oblong, 2 to 4 cm long and 1 cm or less in width. The inflorescences arise from the apical nodes and are short, with 2 to 6 flowers each about 12 mm across. The flowering season is summer and autumn.

This species has proved relatively easy to grow in cultivation. It requires good light, intermediate temperatures, high humidity and year-round watering. It is best on a slab of tree fern, cork or other suitable material.

PHILLIP CRIBB/RGB, KEW

Dendrobium poissonianum Schltr.

This small epiphytic species is restricted to New Caledonia. It occurs in open low forests where there is bright light and high humidity, at altitudes from sea level to 900 m, often growing on *Casuarina* trees and occasionally in rainforests. The pseudobulbs are club-shaped, 4 to 27 cm long, with 2 to 4 leaves at the apex. The leaves are leathery and 3.5 to 6 cm long and 1 cm, or slightly less, in width. The inflorescences are borne from the apical nodes and are erect, with 2 to 10 flowers, each about 2 cm across. The flowers start yellow and turn orange as they age. The flowering season is late spring and summer.

This species has proved relatively easy to grow in cultivation. It is best grown on a slab, but should be kept in humid conditions. A small pot with a well-drained medium may also be used. Watering should be maintained throughout the year, with the plants being allowed to dry between waterings. Bright light and warm to intermediate temperature conditions are recommended.

Genus *Epigeneium* Gagnep.

Synonyms: *Sarcopodium* Lindl., *Dendrobium* section *Sarcopodium* Hook.f., *Katherinea* A.D. Hawkes

This genus has often been treated as *Dendrobium* section *Sarcopodium* or as the genus *Sarcopodium*. There are about 35 species distributed from India, Thailand, China and Taiwan to Borneo, Indonesia and the Philippines. Most species occur in eastern Malaysia and Indonesia. They are mostly epiphytes of montane rainforests, preferring to grow high up in trees in bright light. The flowers are long lasting.

The lip is prominently 3-lobed and there is a short mentum. The pseudobulbs are usually short and often angular on elongated rhizomes, which are shortly erect, creeping or sometimes hanging. There are 1 or 2, occasionally 3, leathery leaves at the apex of the pseudobulb. Inflorescences consist of one or more showy, long-lasting, large flowers appearing between the leaves. While the genus is certainly correctly placed in the Dendrobiinae, it shares some features with the Bulbophyllinae and may represent a link between the two subtribes. Some authorities believe that the genus should be split into two – *Epigeneium* with a single leaf and *Katherinea* with 2 or 3 leaves.

WAYNE HARRIS

Epigeneium coelogyne (Rchb.f.) Summerh.

Synonyms: *Dendrobium coelogyne* Rchb.f., *Sarcopodium coelogyne* (Rchb.f.) Rolfe, *Katherinea coelogyne* (Rchb.f.) A.D. Hawkes
This species from Myanmar (Burma) and Thailand is a rambling epiphyte. There is some confusion with the closely related *E. amplum* (Lindl.) Summerh. from India, Nepal and Bhutan, but it appears that *E. coelogyne* grows at about 1400 m altitude. The elongated rhizome is clothed in scales and the pseudobulbs, which are 4-angled, are borne at considerable distances from each other. They are about 6.5 cm tall and are topped by 2 glossy leathery leaves to about 10 cm long. The single-flowered inflorescence arises between these leaves. The large flowers are about 7.5 cm in diameter. The heavily textured and fragrant flowers are short-lived and are produced in late autumn and early winter.

The widely spaced pseudobulbs and rambling habit make it difficult to confine this species to a conventional pot. Cultivation is best in baskets or shallow pans with an open epiphyte mix. They should be kept moist all year in a humid warm environment. Care should be taken to avoid stale compost through poor drainage.

WAYNE HARRIS

Epigeneium cymbidioides (Blume) Summerh.

Synonyms: *Desmotrichum cymbidioides* Blume, *Dendrobium cymbidioides* (Blume) Lindl., *Sarcopodium cymbidioides* (Blume) Rolfe
This miniature species occurs on the islands of Java and Sumatra and through to the Philippines, at altitudes from 1500 to 2800 m, where it is found as epiphytes in moss forests in high light conditions. Unlike the previous species, the pseudobulbs are placed close together and are more or less ovoid with blunt angles and are about 4 cm high. The 2 oblong leaves at the apex of the pseudobulbs are about 15 cm long and 2.5 cm wide. The inflorescence in this species is multi-flowered with up to 10 flowers on a rachis about 25 cm long. The flowers open widely to about 4 cm in diameter. The flowers of this species are fragrant, and long-lasting and are produced in spring.

This species grows well in cool to intermediate conditions provided that moisture and humidity is provided year round. A pot of well-drained medium is best.

WAYNE HARRIS

Epigeneium nakaharai (Schltr.) Summerh.

Synonym: *Dendrobium nakaharai* Schltr.
This miniature species is found in the central mountain range of Taiwan at altitudes between 800 and 2400 m. The species is epiphytic and grows in moist semi-shaded conditions on large trees. The pseudobulbs are borne on a creeping rhizome, spaced closely together, and are many-angled. They are about 2.5 cm tall and have a single terminal leaf at the apex. The leaf is about 3.5 cm long and 1 cm broad. The solitary flowers are borne at the apex of the pseudobulb and are about 2.5 cm across. Flowering time is autumn and the flowers are relatively short-lived.

Successful cultivation of this species requires intermediate conditions. The plants should be kept moist and humid all year round with heavy watering during the warmer months. The species can be grown mounted or in a shallow tray or basket with well-drained epiphyte mix.

Epigeneium stella-silvae (Loher & Kraenzl.) Summerh.

Synonyms: *Sarcopodium stella-silvae* Loher & Kraenzl.,
Dendrobium stella-silvae (Loher & Kraenzl.) Ames, *Katherinea stella-silvae*
(Loher & Kraenzl.) A.D. Hawkes
This miniature epiphytic species is recorded from Luzon in the Philippines
where it occurs on the slopes of mountains in Abra, Bontoc, Ifugao, Rizal,
Surigao and Zambales provinces at about 1000 m altitude. The short squat
pseudobulbs are ovoid in shape, up to about 3 cm tall and 2 cm wide. There
are 2 thick, leathery leaves about 5 to 7 cm long and 2 cm wide. The
terminal raceme is up to 25 cm long, erect, and carries about 4 flowers on a
2.5 cm long pedicel. The flowers open widely to about 4 cm in diameter.
Flowering is in January to May in the habitat.

Not much is known of this species in cultivation, but intermediate to
cool conditions and year-round watering is recommended.

Epigeneium treacherianum (Rchb.f. ex Hook. F.) Summerh.

Synonyms: *Dendrobium treacherianum* Rchb.f. ex Hook.f., *Sarcopodium*
treacherianum (Rchb.f. ex Hook.f.) Rolfe, *Katherinea treacheriana* (Rchb.f. ex
Hook.f.) A.D. Hawkes
This colourful species is found in Borneo and the Philippines at altitudes of
100 to 400 m, in the crowns of large trees in dipterocarp forests where
moisture and humidity are in abundance. Plants are epiphytic with stout
creeping rhizomes bearing crowded pseudobulbs that are prominently 4- to
6-angled and about 3 to 8 cm long. The 2 stiff leathery leaves at the apex of
the pseudobulbs are up to 10 cm long and 3 cm broad. The 10 to 15 cm
long inflorescence is terminal at the apex of the pseudobulb and carries up to
7 flowers, each 3 to 4 cm in diameter. Flowers are produced in summer and
have a fragrance of desiccated coconut.

Because of the creeping habit of this species, it is best grown in a
hanging basket or shallow pan filled with a free-draining epiphyte mixture.
Copious water should be applied during the warmer months. Moisture and
high humidity should be retained all year round.

Epigeneium triflorum (Blume) Summerh. var. *orientale* (J.J. Sm.) J.B. Comber

Synonyms: *Desmotrichum triflorum* Blume, *Dendrobium triflorum* (Blume)
Lindl., *D. elongatum* Lindl. var. *orientale* J.J. Sm.
The species and its varieties are restricted to Java. Variety *orientale* is
common on mountains in East and Central Java from 1000 to 1680 m
altitude. It forms large clumps on branches where there is strong light. The
pseudobulbs are about 4 cm long and 1.5 cm wide and are spaced about 6
to 8 cm apart. The leaves are grouped at the apex and are about 20 to 30
cm long and about 2 cm wide. The inflorescence is pendulous with 6 to 17
flowers, each 2 to 3 cm across.

Cool to intermediate conditions with year-round humidity and regular
watering are required. The plants should be given bright filtered light and
good air movement. They are best grown in a broad shallow pot or basket
of well-drained medium or on a slab to allow for the creeping habit.

Genus *Eriopexis* (Schltr.) Brieger

Synonym: Genus *Dendrobium*, section *Eriopexis* Schltr.

This small group of about 6 erect or pendulous epiphytic species is restricted to New Guinea. They grow at moderate altitudes in cloud forests on moss-covered branches. These are areas of year-round high rainfall. The section is closely related to *Grastidium*, differing in the plant habit and in the extended column foot. Like *Grastidium*, this section has only recently been elevated to the status of a genus and it remains to be seen if this move gains wide acceptance.

The stems are broad and leaf-like. The leaves are in 2 ranks along the stem with prominent flattened leaf-like sheaths. The flowers are large and fleshy, often white, but like *Grastidium*, last only a day. They are borne in pairs laterally. The column foot is elongated, forming a sac-like chin or mentum. The lip is 3-lobed.

GEOFF STOCKER

Eriopexis quinquelobata (Schltr.) Rauschert

Synonym: *Dendrobium quinquelobatum* Schltr.

This robust species has been recorded from several areas on the island of New Guinea, including upper montane forests on Mt Gahavesuka in Eastern Highlands Province, and on the Maboro Range in the Waria District in Morobe Province of Papua New Guinea at altitudes of 1200 to 2200 m. It often grows low down on tree trunks in cloud forest. It has short rhizomes with semi-pendulous pseudobulbs about 60 cm long. The leaves are large, up to 17 cm long and 2.5 cm wide, very numerous and densely arranged on either side of the pseudobulbs for almost all their length. The flowers are borne in pairs in the leaf axils. They are about 3 cm across and appear to last for 1 or 2 days.

Nothing is known of its requirements in cultivation. Its habit and environment suggest that a large hanging basket filled with a free-draining medium and cool to intermediate conditions may be a useful starting point. The potting medium should be kept moist and the light at moderate to low levels.

Section *Euphlebium* Schltr. (Genus *Dendrobium*)

This section of about 4 species occurs from Peninsular Malaysia, the Philippines and Borneo to New Guinea, which is probably the centre of distribution. They occur in habitats with year-round rainfall at low to moderate altitudes. They grow as epiphytes, often low down on mossy tree trunks.

The club-shaped pseudobulbs have angled stems, sometimes square in cross-section, with a few, usually 2, leaves at the apex. The flowers last only a day and are borne at the apex or in short inflorescences laterally on the stem.

Dendrobium lacteum Kraenzl.

Synonym: *Dendrobium inaequale* Rolfe
This small epiphytic species is quite abundant from sea level to about 1000 m in New Guinea and the islands as far west as the Aru Islands. It grows in rainforests, often low down on smooth-barked trees overhanging rivers and swamps, in areas with a year-round high rainfall. The pseudobulbs are club-shaped, up to 35 cm long and over 10 mm wide at the swollen apical part, which is conspicuously 4-angled. There are usually 2, but up to 5, leaves at the apex of the pseudobulb, 5 to 12 cm long and 2 to 3 cm wide. The inflorescences consist of 1 or 2 flowers each about 3 to 5 cm across and are borne from the upper nodes. The flowers last only a few hours and the flowering season is throughout the year, possibly following a sudden drop in temperature.

This species requires intermediate to warm conditions and perfect drainage. It is best grown on a slab, but it must be watered regularly and must not be permitted to dry out. Care must be taken to avoid rotting of the new growths. It does best in semi-shade.

Dendrobium spurium (Blume) J.J. Sm.

Synonym: *Dendrobium euphlebium* Rchb.f. ex Lindl.
This medium sized epiphyte or lithophyte occurs in Peninsular Malaysia, Sumatra, Java, Bali, Borneo and the Philippines. It grows at altitudes of sea level to 1100 m in rainforests on low mountain ridges near the coast, on limestone rocks in some areas and on mangroves in other areas. The climate in all these areas features year-round rainfall and constant high humidity. The pseudobulbs are club-shaped, to 30 cm long, about 2 or 3 mm wide in the lower half, gradually widening to 1 cm near the apex. There are 2 or 3 leaves near the apex of the pseudobulb, about 14 cm long and 2.5 cm wide. The flowers, borne singly near the apex of the pseudobulb or lower, are about 3 to 4 cm across and last only a day.

Warm temperatures and year-round watering are recommended, although the watering should be decreased slightly in winter without allowing the plants to dry out for long periods. The plants tend to be pendulous with age and a slab or hanging pot with well-drained medium is recommended. Bright filtered light is recommended.

Genus *Flickingeria* A.D. Hawkes

Synonyms: *Ephemeranthera* P. Hunt & Summerh., *Desmotrichum* Blume. (Schlechter regarded *Desmotrichum* as a section of *Dendrobium*.)
This is a genus of about 65 to 70 species, widely distributed from mainland Asia and Indonesia to the Philippines, New Guinea, Australia and the islands of the Pacific. These are creeping epiphytes with a rhizome from which branching erect or pendulous stems arise. These stems have several internodes with sheathing scale leaves. The last internode is swollen to form a pseudobulb. There is a solitary leaf at the apex and the inflorescence is terminal to sub-terminal and consists of 1 or occasionally 2 flowers, which last less than a day.

The genus has been divided into 3 sections, based on the shape of the mid-lobe of the labellum. Section *Flickingeria* has a mid-lobe with numerous long hairs arising on each side. Section *Plicatiles* has a plicate mid-lobe with undulate edges, while section *Bilobulatae* has a bilobed mid-lobe.

Flickingeria angustifolia (Blume) A.D. Hawkes

Section *Bilobulatae*
Synonyms: *Desmotrichum angustifolium* Blume, *Flickingeria anamensis* (A.D. Hawkes) A.D. Hawkes, *Flickingeria poilanei* (Gagnep.) A.D. Hawkes, *Dendrobium kelsallii* Ridl.
This small, branched epiphyte occurs in South-East Asia in Thailand, Peninsular Malaysia, Vietnam, Sumatra, Java and Bali. It grows as an epiphyte in the lower layers of the foothill forests. The stems are much branched, slender and wiry at the base, with the apical part swollen into a pseudobulb about 15 mm long and 3 mm thick. There is a single leaf 4 to 5 cm long and 7 mm wide. The flowers are about 1 cm across and are borne singly from the apex of the pseudobulb.

This species is best grown on a slab or in a hanging pot of well-drained medium. Warm to intermediate temperatures and year-round watering and semi-shade are recommended.

Flickingeria aureiloba (J.J. Sm.) J.J. Wood

Section *Plicatiles*
Synonym: *Dendrobium aurieloba* J.J. Sm.
This is a medium sized, branched lithophytic species that occurs in Java and Sumatra. It grows on lava rocks from about 640 to 1000 m altitude. The bases of the stems are slender, about 5 mm wide, with a flattened apical pseudobulb about 7 cm long by 1 cm wide. The single leaf is lanceolate, up to 15 cm long and 6 cm wide. There are 1 to several flowers per pseudobulb. The flowers are about 3.5 cm across and fragrant.

This species should be grown on a slab or hanging pot of well-drained medium. The plants should be watered throughout the year and kept in warm, humid conditions with bright filtered light.

Flickingeria bancana (J.J. Sm.) A.D. Hawkes

Section *Bilobulatae*
Synonyms: *Dendrobium bancanum* J.J. Sm., *D. trilamellatum* Schltr.
This is a large, pendulous epiphytic species from Thailand, Peninsular Malaysia, Sumatra and Borneo. It grows at low altitudes below 500 m in montane rainforest and has also been reported in mangroves and sclerophyllous ridge forest. The branched stems form a bushy plant. The pseudobulbs are slightly flattened, about 3 cm long with a single leaf about 15 to 20 cm long and 2 cm or more wide. The flowers are borne singly from the apex of the stem and are about 1 cm across. They last a day. The apical part of the lip changes colour after a few hours from orange to red-purple.

Warm conditions with year-round watering and bright filtered light are recommended. A slab or hanging pot or basket filled with a well-drained medium is best to accommodate the pendulous habit.

Flickingeria bicostata (J.J. Sm.) A.D. Hawkes

Section *Bilobulatae*
Synonyms: *Dendrobium bicostatum* J.J. Sm., *D. mattangianum* Kraenzl., *Ephemeranthera bicostata* (J.J. Sm.) P.F. Hunt & Summerh.
This medium sized epiphytic species is restricted to the island of Borneo. Not much is known of the habitat, but it has been found growing in moist mossy forest above 700 m altitude. This species is unusual in that it lacks the usual aerial branched stems with pseudobulbs decreasing in size. A creeping rhizome gives rise to unbranched, erect, closely packed stems, consisting of an olive-green compressed pseudobulb about 12 cm long and 1 to 2 cm across with one edge rounded and the other edge quite sharp. There is a single very tough and leathery dark green oblong leaf at the apex, about 12 to 24 cm long and 3 to 6 cm wide. The flowers are about 3 cm across and are borne singly from a yellow bract at the apex of the pseudobulb, emerging behind the leaf axil. They are presented 'upside-down', with the lip uppermost, and have a faint cinnamon scent.

Little is known of cultivation, but it is likely that the species requires warm to intermediate, humid conditions with year-round watering. It is probably best grown on a slab with a little moss added to help retain moisture, or in a pot of well-drained medium in bright filtered light.

Flickingeria comata (Blume) A.D. Hawkes

Section *Flickingeria*
Synonyms: *Dendrobium comatum* (Blume) Lindl., *Desmotrichum comatum* Blume, *Dendrobium thysanochilum* Schltr.
This is a large, branched epiphyte of lowland hot, steamy rainforests from Peninsular Malaysia through Indonesia to New Guinea, Australia, New Caledonia, Fiji and Samoa. It grows predominantly as an epiphyte, but is also found on rocks, usually in shaded areas of high humidity and year-round rainfall. A short branching rhizome gives rise to slender stems that branch several times and end in a pseudobulb which is up to 10 cm long and 1.5 cm wide. The whole plant is up to 1 m long, initially erect, but becoming pendulous as it lengthens. The pseudobulbs have a single leathery leaf. The flowers are about 2 to 3 cm across with an elaborately fringed mid-lobe of the labellum. They are borne terminally from a group of bracts, one or more at a time. Occasional flowers are borne laterally from nodes below the pseudobulb. Flowers may be borne at any time of the year with an emphasis on the wetter part of the year, and last less than a day.

In cultivation, this species requires warm, humid, semi-shaded conditions and year-round watering. It should be mounted on a slab or, if in a pot, it must have good drainage.

BILL LAVARACK

Flickingeria convexa (Blume) A.D. Hawkes

Section *Bilobulatae*
Synonyms: *Desmotrichum convexum* Blume, *Ephemeranthera convexa* (Blume) P. Hunt & Summerh.
This is a small creeping epiphyte of lowland hot, steamy rainforests along river banks, in swamp forests and mangroves, from Peninsular Malaysia through Indonesia to southern New Guinea, Australia and the Solomon Islands. Unlike other members of the genus, the rhizomes of this species produce roots along the slender part of the stem and are attached to the substrate, forming a mat of rather brittle stems. The slender pseudobulbs are up to 5 cm long with a single leaf about as long as the pseudobulb. The flowers last a day and are produced apically. They are about 1 cm in diameter. Flowering may occur at any time of the year.

The sprawling form of this plant means it is not suited to a pot. It is best grown on a slab of weathered wood or cork. It should be watered daily and kept in a sheltered semi-shaded position in warm to hot conditions.

PETER O'BYRNE

Flickingeria fimbriata (Blume) A.D. Hawkes

Section *Plicatiles*
Synonyms: *Dendrobium fimbriatum* Blume, *D. flabellatum* Rchb.f., *D. plicatile* Lindl., *D. insulare* Steudl., *D. binnendijkii* Rchb.f., *D. kunstleri* Hook.f., *D. mentosum* Schltr., and several other names in the genera *Desmotrichum* and *Ephemeranthera*.
This medium sized to large vigorous species is widespread throughout South-East Asia including Hainan Province in China, Vietnam, Thailand, Peninsular Malaysia, Sumatra, Java, Sulawesi, Borneo, the Philippines, Sulawesi and several smaller islands in Malesia. It grows from sea level to about 1000 m in hot steamy conditions, forming dense bushy clumps, often overhanging the sea or streams. The stems are much branched, climbing or pendulous, the pseudobulbs at intervals of 4 to 15 cm, 4 to 8 cm long and 2 to 4 cm wide. The single leaf is 12 to 19 cm long and 4 to 5 cm wide. The flowers are fragrant, variable in size to about 3.5 cm across, borne singly or in a cluster from the apex of the pseudobulbs.

This species can grow into a large plant and requires plenty of room. It is best grown on a tree in the tropics. If grown in an orchid house it should be attached to a slab and kept evenly moist throughout the year. It should be given warm conditions and bright light.

JIM COMBER

Flickingeria grandiflora (Blume) A.D. Hawkes

Section *Bilobulatae*
Synonym: *Dendrobium conspicuum* Bakh.f.
This large erect epiphyte has been recorded from Sumatra, Java, Flores Island and Timor. It grows at altitudes of 1000 to 2100 m in undisturbed montane forests, often growing low down on trees. The stems are much branched with a slender base and a swollen pseudobulb 3 cm long and 1 cm wide at the apex. The single leaf is 9 cm long and 2 cm wide. The flowers are up to 2 cm long and 2.2 cm wide, borne singly or in pairs from the apex of the pseudobulb. Flowering occurs throughout the year.

In cultivation, this species requires intermediate temperatures, high humidity and year-round watering. It should be grown in a pot of well-drained medium or on a slab. Semi-shade is recommended.

Flickingeria luxurians (J.J. Sm.) A.D. Hawkes

Section *Plicatiles*
Synonym: *Dendrobium plicatile* var. *convocarii* Ames and Quisumb.
This is a large, straggling epiphyte or lithophyte from Peninsular Malaysia,
Java, Borneo and the Philippines. It grows from sea level to 1000 m altitude,
in riverine forests, high up in the canopy and occasionally on roadside rocks.
The stems are much branched, up to 60 cm long with a slender basal part
and a pseudobulb 8 cm long and 1.5 cm wide. The single leaf is about 20 cm
long and 5 cm wide. There are several flowers per pseudobulb, arising laterally
from upper and lower nodes. They are fragrant and about 3 cm in diameter.
    In cultivation, this species should be grown on a slab or hanging pot of
well-drained medium. It should be watered throughout the year and kept in
warm, humid conditions with bright filtered light.

Flickingeria rhipidoloba (Schltr.) A.D. Hawkes

Section *Plicatiles*
Synonyms: *Dendrobium rhipidolobum* Schltr., *Desmotrichum fimbriatum*
Kraenzl.
This medium sized to large epiphytic species is widespread in Irian Jaya and
Papua New Guinea where it forms large clumps in gallery forests overhanging
water or on rocks in full sun at altitudes below 500 m. The stems creep
along the substrate attached by roots from the nodes. Branching stems up to
60 cm long grow upwards from the creeping rhizome, with terminal
pseudobulbs about 3 to 7 cm long and 5 to 12 mm wide, slightly
compressed. The single leaf is about 6 to 15 cm long and 2 to 3 cm wide.
The flowers are produced singly from the apex of the pseudobulbs and are
about 2 cm across. They last only 6 to 8 hours and flowering is probably
throughout the year.
    This species has proved difficult to grow. In the tropics it is best
attached to a tree. If grown in an orchid house it should be attached to a
slab and kept constantly moist. It needs warm humid conditions and bright
light and resents disturbance.

Flickingeria xantholeuca (Rchb.f.) A.D. Hawkes

Section *Bilobulatae*
Synonyms: *Dendrobium lonchophyllum* Hook.f., *D. pallidiflorum* Ridl.
This medium sized epiphyte occurs in Thailand, Peninsular Malaysia,
Sumatra, Java and Borneo. It grows in the hot steamy lowlands up to
1000 m altitude. The much branched stems arise from a creeping rhizome
and have a slender basal part, with a pseudobulb 2 to 5 cm long,
lengthening with age, and 6 to 12 mm wide. The single leaf is up to 13 cm
long and 2 cm wide, lanceolate with a small tooth at the apex of the leaf.
The flowers are about 1 cm across and are borne singly from below the leaf.
    This species should be grown on a slab or hanging pot of well-drained
medium. It should be watered throughout the year and kept in warm,
humid conditions with bright filtered light.

Section *Formosae* (Benth. and Hook.f.) Hook.f. (Genus *Dendrobium*)

This section is also known as *Nigrohirsutae*. It includes about 30 species, which are distributed from India through South-East Asia to Sumatra, the Philippines and Borneo. South-East Asia from India to Indochina and Thailand appears to be the centre of distribution with about 20 species, while Borneo and the Philippines have about 12 species. It does not occur further east than Borneo. The plants are epiphytic in areas with or without a defined dry season. The section is related to section *Dendrobium*.

The plants are made up of clumps of usually long, relatively robust pseudobulbs with leaves along their length. The leaf sheaths are covered in dark hairs and last for several years. The flowers are usually large and waxy or thin in texture, usually with white predominating, and are long-lasting. They are borne from the upper part of the stem in groups of 1 to 3. The lip is 3-lobed. Some species are among the most showy of all the orchids and the group is popular in cultivation.

WAYNE HARRIS

Dendrobium bellatulum Rolfe

This miniature epiphytic species is widespread in mountainous areas in South-East Asia, occurring in India, Myanmar (Burma), Thailand, Laos, Victnam and Yunnan Province of south-west China. It grows between 1000 and 2100 m altitude, in deciduous forests where there is bright light and a strongly seasonal climate. The pseudobulbs are covered with black hairs and are clustered, squat, about 5 to 8 cm long and up to 1.5 cm wide, with 2 to 4 leaves on the apical part. The leaves are grey-green and deciduous, 3 to 6 cm long and about 1.5 cm wide. The inflorescences arise laterally on the apical part of the leafless stem. They consist of 1 to 3 flowers, 4 to 4.5 cm across. They are long-lasting and faintly fragrant. Flowering can occur throughout the year, but is at its heaviest in spring. The flowers are large in relation to the plant and the brightly coloured labellum, which tends to increase in intensity of colour as the flower ages, is a feature.

Cool to intermediate conditions are recommended. The plants should be given a drier resting period in winter when they are allowed to dry between waterings, but should not be kept dry for more than a day or two. This species is sometimes regarded as difficult to cultivate, and slab culture is best as the conditions around the roots must not become soggy, even when watered regularly in summer. Bright light, even full sunlight, or light shade are recommended.

GEOFF STOCKER

Dendrobium cariniferum Rchb.f.

This is a small to medium sized epiphyte which occurs in the foothills of the Himalayas from north-east India to Myanmar (Burma), Thailand, Indochina, and southern China. It grows in seasonal forests at about 700 to 1500 m altitude in semi-shade. The pseudobulbs are up to 20 cm long and covered with hairs. There are 4 to 6 leaves about 5 to 8 cm long and 2 cm wide, covered with hairs on the underside and grouped near the apex of the stem. The flowers are borne singly or in an inflorescence of 2 or 3 flowers near the apex of the pseudobulb. They are 2 to 3 cm across and last about 2 or 3 weeks. Flowering is in late spring and early summer. This species is very similar to *D. williamsonii* Day & Rchb.f. and the species are often confused in cultivation and in herbaria. Some botanists consider they are conspecific. *D. cariniferum* has prominent keels on the back of the sepals, while *D. williamsonii* has only small keels.

Intermediate temperatures are required, although plants will grow in warm conditions. A drier resting period is required in winter to initiate flowering. It is suggested that conditions should be allowed to become progressively drier throughout winter and early spring with the plants drying out for several days between waterings in early spring. In summer and autumn, high humidity and regular watering with filtered sunlight are required. A slab or a pot of well-drained medium is suitable.

Dendrobium christyanum Rchb.f.

Synonym: *Dendrobium margaritaceum* Finet
This is a small epiphyte, which occurs in Thailand, Vietnam and south-west China. It grows at about 1200 m altitude in forests with a distinct dry season. The pseudobulbs are 5 to 8 cm long with 2 to 4 persistent leaves about 3 to 6 cm long, grouped near their apex. Both leaves and pseudobulbs are covered in fine black hairs. The single flowers are about 5 cm across, slightly fragrant and long-lasting. Flowering occurs in the rainy season in summer and early autumn. This species is closely related to *D. bellatulum* Rolfe, but differs in the lip, which is white with red or yellow in the centre only. The flower size is large in comparison to the size of the plant.

Intermediate temperatures with bright filtered light and good air movement are required. The plants require a dry resting period in winter when they should be allowed to dry out thoroughly between waterings. A pot of well-drained medium or a slab is suitable for this species.

Dendrobium cruentum Rchb.f.

This is a small to medium sized epiphyte from Thailand, where it occurs at low altitudes (below 1000 m) in open forests. In these situations there is a distinct dry season in winter and warm temperatures. The pseudobulbs are up to 30 cm long, swollen at the base, with black hairs on the leaf sheaths. The leaves are elliptic–oblong, deciduous, 5 to 13 cm long, in 2 rows on the upper part of the stem. The inflorescence consists of a single flower or a pair of flowers, occasionally 3, borne from the upper leaf axils. The flowers are up to 5 cm across, last for about a month or more and are fragrant. Flowering can occur at any time of the year.

In cultivation, this species is best placed in a pot of well-drained medium and kept in warm conditions. A drier resting period in winter and early spring is best, but the plants should not be kept dry for longer than 2 or 3 days. While growing, it should be watered regularly. Bright filtered sunlight is best.

Dendrobium dearei Rchb.f.

This medium sized epiphytic species is restricted to the Philippines where it has been recorded from southern Luzon, Mindoro, Samar, Dinagat and Mindanao Islands. It grows in hot, humid tropical forests at low altitudes. The pseudobulbs are up to 90 cm long, but usually shorter, and about 1 cm in diameter, with leaves in 2 ranks along the apical half of the stem. The leaves are glossy, leathery and up to 7 cm long and 1.5 cm wide. The inflorescences are borne from the apical part of the pseudobulb. They are arching, with up to 10 flowers each about 5 cm in diameter. The flowers last several weeks and the flowering season is late spring and early summer, although plants in the tropics flower several times a year.

Warm, humid conditions are required to grow this species successfully. It should be watered regularly throughout the year and grown in bright filtered sunlight. A pot of well-drained medium is recommended, but plants may be grown on slabs if they are not permitted to dry out for long periods.

WAYNE HARRIS

Dendrobium formosum Roxb. ex Lindl.

Synonym: *Dendrobium infundibulum* Rchb.f. non Lindl.
This medium sized epiphyte grows at low to moderate altitudes in the foothills of the Himalayas from India to Thailand and Indochina. The climate is moderately seasonal and the plants often grow in situations with strong light. The pseudobulbs are robust and grow to 45 cm long with persistent leaves about 9 to 15 cm long in 2 ranks along the apical two-thirds of the stem. The leaf sheaths are covered in dark hairs. The flowers are large and showy, up to 12 cm across, and are borne on short inflorescences of up to 5 flowers from the apex or the adjacent nodes. The flowering season is winter and spring and the flowers last several weeks. It is closely related to *D. infundibulum* Lindl., but has larger flowers and a shorter mentum. Some large flowered forms are known as 'var. *giganteum*'.

In cultivation, the plant should not be dried out entirely, although slightly less water can be applied in winter. It should be given regular applications of fertiliser after the new shoots appear. It needs strong light and can withstand full sun. Warm or intermediate conditions and a well-drained mixture are required.

GEOFF STOCKER

Dendrobium infundibulum Lindl.

Synonym: *Dendrobium jamesianum* Rchb.f.
This is a large, showy species which is widespread in South-East Asia, including north-east India, Myanmar (Burma), Thailand, Laos, Cambodia and Vietnam. It mostly grows above 1000 m, but has been reported from altitudes as low as 200 m. The habitat is hillside deciduous forests with a seasonal climate. This species is closely related to *D. formosum* Roxb. ex Lindl., but has slightly smaller flowers and usually occurs at higher altitudes. The pseudobulbs are long and slender, up to 1 m long and covered in dark hairs. The leaves are persistent, oblong–lanceolate, 8 to 13 long, in 2 ranks along the upper half of the pseudobulbs. The inflorescences are borne from the upper nodes and consist of 2 to 5 flowers up to 10 cm in diameter. Although the flowers have a thin, papery texture, they last from 1 to 3 months, and the flowering season is spring and early summer.

In cultivation, the plants do best in intermediate or even cool conditions. They require a reduction in watering in winter, but while they should dry out between waterings, they should not be kept dry for extended periods. A pot with a well-drained medium is required, along with filtered light and moist conditions during the growing season.

Dendrobium sanderae Rolfe

This species is restricted to the island of Luzon in the Philippines where it is recorded in the mountains of the provinces of Benguet, Bontoc and Rizal. It grows as an epiphyte at altitudes of 1100 to 1650 m. There are at least 4 different varieties of this species recorded, with larger-flowered plants being known as variety *major*. The pseudobulbs are 30 to 100 cm long and about 1 cm in diameter, with leaves in 2 ranks along the upper part of the stem. The leaves are leathery, up to 10 cm long and 3 cm wide. The inflorescence arises from near the apex of the stem and has up to 10 flowers each 6 to 10 cm in diameter. The variety major flowers in spring, but the variety *parviflorum* flowers in autumn.

This species should be grown in intermediate to cool temperatures with constant high humidity. A slightly drier resting period is recommended in winter when the plants are allowed to dry out completely between watering, but they should not be permitted to remain dry for long periods. Bright filtered sunlight is recommended. The plants should be grown in a pot of well-drained medium.

WAYNE HARRIS

Dendrobium schuetzei Rolfe

This is a small epiphyte from northern Mindanao Island in the Philippines, where it grows at altitudes of 300 to 1000 m in rainforests with a year-round high rainfall. The stout pseudobulbs are 15 to 40 cm long, with persistent leaves 6 to 10 cm long along most of their length. The leaves are glossy, elliptic–oblong and hairless, and the leaf sheaths are covered in dark hairs. The short inflorescences arise from near the apex of the pseudobulb and bear 3 to 5 showy, waxy flowers, each about 6 to 9 cm across. The flowers last several weeks and may be produced at any time of the year.

Intermediate conditions appear best with year-round high humidity and regular watering. The plants should not be given a dry resting period and should be kept evenly moist throughout the year. Bright filtered light is recommended and plants may be grown in a pot of well-drained medium or on a slab.

GEOFF STOCKER

Dendrobium spectatissimum Rchb.f.

Synonyms: *Dendrobium speciosissimum* Rolfe; *D. reticulatum* J.J. Sm.
This is a spectacular medium sized epiphyte restricted to Mt Kinabalu in Sabah, Borneo. It grows as an epiphyte close to the ground, often on *Leptospermum* trees in open scrub at 1600 to 1700 m altitude, although there are reports of plants occurring as low as 200 m altitude. The pseudobulbs are long and slender, 30 to 40 cm long and about 2.5 cm in diameter. The leaves are ovate–oblong, 4 to 6 cm long and 2 cm wide, markedly unequally bilobed at the apex and covered with dark hairs. They are borne along the length of the pseudobulbs. The inflorescences are borne near the apex and have 2 faintly fragrant flowers up to 10 cm across. The flowers last up to 6 weeks.

In cultivation, this species requires intermediate conditions with bright light and evenly moist conditions throughout the year. Watering can be reduced slightly in winter, but the plants should not be allowed to dry out completely. Pots with a well-drained medium or slabs are equally suitable.

GEOFF STOCKER

Grastidium baileyi (F. Muell.) Rauschert

Synonyms: *Dendrobium baileyi* F. Muell., *D. keffordii* F.M. Bailey
This medium sized epiphyte, or occasionally lithophyte, occurs on the north-east coast of Queensland, Australia, in areas with high rainfall and humid conditions throughout the year. It grows in the lowlands up to about 900 m altitude in rainforest areas such as stream bank forest and mangroves. The slender stems form dense clumps and are up to 120 cm long, but more commonly about 30 to 50 cm long, with leaves along most of their length. The leaves are grass-like, about 4 to 9 cm long and 4 to 8 mm wide. The flowers are borne in pairs along the stem and are about 5 cm across when first open. They last about 2 hours before curling up and becoming intertwined. They then last a further day or two in this curled state. Flowering occurs at any time of the year with an emphasis on the wet season in summer.

This species requires warm humid conditions year round. It should be grown in semi shade, watered regularly and not permitted to dry out for more than a day. It may be grown on a slab or in a hanging pot to accommodate the stems, which become pendulous as they age.

Grastidium branderhorstii (J.J. Sm.) Rauschert

Synonyms: *Dendrobium branderhorstii* J.J. Sm., *D. angraecifolium* Schltr.
The name *Grastidium branderhorstii* has been used here, but *Dendrobium angraecifolium* predates it and clearly has priority. It appears the transfer to *Grastidium* has not been made at the time of writing. It is widespread and common throughout Papua New Guinea and Irian Jaya at altitudes below 800 m. It grows in a variety of habitats including overhanging streams, in tree tops, in humus on the forest floor and in exposed conditions on rocks. It grows into large clumps, with slender stems about 1 to 1.2 m long and 6 to 7 mm wide. The leaves are grass-like, 11 to 25 cm long and 13 to 23 mm wide, mostly on the apical third of the stem. The flowers are thick and fleshy, borne in pairs just below the leaves and about 2.7 cm across. They last less than a day and appear 4 to 9 days after heavy rain, throughout the year.

This is a large species which requires plenty of room in an orchid house. It is best grown in the open in a rockery or on a tree in the tropics. If potted it should be given excellent drainage and may be allowed to dry slightly between waterings in winter. It should be given bright light, watered and fertilised frequently and kept warm throughout the year.

Grastidium cancroides (T.E. Hunt) Rauschert

Synonym: *Dendrobium cancroides* T.E. Hunt
This medium sized species is restricted to the wet tropics area of north-east Australia. It grows at altitudes below 500 m as an epiphyte usually overhanging creeks in dense rainforest. This is an area of year-round high humidity and high rainfall. The stems are slender, slightly flattened, up to 90 cm long, but usually shorter, and about 5 mm wide. There are leaves in 2 ranks along the apical half of the stem. The leaves are 5 to 10 cm long and 1 to 3 cm wide and dark green in colour. The flowers are usually borne in pairs, facing each other, opposite the leaves. They are about 3 to 4 cm across, last about 2 days and do not open widely. Flowering can occur at any time of the year, with an emphasis on summer and autumn. There are very similar species in New Guinea.

Warm temperatures are required and plants should be kept in high humidity and watered throughout the year. They should not be allowed to dry out completely. They should be grown in semi-shade or full shade. A slab is best to accommodate the semi-pendulous habit. If a pot is used it should have a very well-drained medium.

Grastidium cathcartii (Hook.f.) M.A. Clem. & D.L. Jones

Synonym: *Dendrobium cathcartii* Hook.f.
This is a small to medium sized species from Sikkim in north-east India where it has been recorded from tropical valleys at altitudes of 600 to 800 m in areas with a strongly seasonal climate. The stems are slender, swollen at the nodes, 45 to 75 cm long and 4 mm wide, with leaves 10 to 12 cm long and 12 to 16 mm wide along the apical two-thirds. The inflorescences arise from about halfway along the internode and consist of 2 flowers, each about 2 to 2.5 cm long. The flowers are short-lived and flowering occurs from spring through to autumn.

Warm to intermediate conditions with bright light are required. The plants should be given a dry resting period in winter when they are allowed to dry out for short periods between waterings. A slab or a pot of well-drained medium is suitable.

DAVID TITMUSS

BILL LAVARACK

Grastidium luteocilium (Rupp) Rauschert

Synonym: *Dendrobium luteocilium* Rupp
Grastidium luteocilium is a large robust epiphyte of the humid tropical lowlands of north-eastern Queensland, Australia, the islands of Torres Strait and New Guinea. The stems reach almost 2 m long, although about 1 m or less is more common, and are slender, with relatively broad leaves 4 to 13 cm long, arranged in 2 rows on either side. The plants form extremely large clumps in lowland riverside forests, mangroves, other coastal forests and on rock faces near the coast, where the humidity is high. There are two similar species – *Dendrobium densifolium* from New Guinea and *D. pruinosum* from Ambon. Both predate Rupp's description of *D. luteocilium* and would replace it if either were shown to be the same species. The flowers are about 2 cm across, fragrant, lasting only a day, but there are several bursts of flowering throughout the year. A large plant is spectacular when in flower, with numerous flowers produced in pairs along the length of the stem. Flowering may well be triggered by sudden bursts of rain, which reduce the temperature.

This species does well in full sun or partial shade. It requires warm temperatures throughout the year, but will tolerate brief periods of temperatures as low as 10°C. It should be watered throughout the year, but requires a very well-drained medium in a large pot or mounting on a tree in the tropics.

Grastidium luzonense (Lindl.) M.A. Clem. & D.L. Jones

Synonym: *Dendrobium luzonense* Lindl.
This is a medium sized epiphyte from the Philippines where it occurs on Luzon, Mindanao, Mindoro and Leyete islands from sea level to 1300 m in areas with year-round rainfall. The stems are about 60 cm long and slender, with leaves along most of their length. The leaves are grass-like and about 14 cm long and 1 cm wide. The flowers are borne in pairs opposite the leaves, along the apical half of the stem. They are about 2 cm across and last a day. Flowering is throughout the year.

The plants require warm conditions with year-round moisture, although watering may be decreased slightly in winter. Bright light and good air movement are recommended. A pot of well-drained medium or a slab is recommended.

Grastidium papyraceum (J.J. Sm.) Rauschert

Synonym: *Dendrobium papyraceum* J.J. Sm.
This medium sized epiphyte has been reported from Irian Jaya and Papua New Guinea at altitudes of sea level to 1000 m. The stems are slender and about 40 cm long with leaves along most of their length. The leaves are relatively broad and about 5 to 6 cm long. The flowers are borne in pairs and are about 15 mm across. They last less than a day. Flowering is in bursts throughout the year. The species illustrated here is very similar to J.J. Smith's original description, but there are several entities of similar appearance and the exact identity is open to a little doubt.

This species is not known in cultivation, and the temperature regime would depend on the altitude from which an individual plant came. Year-round watering and a pot with a well-drained medium are suggested.

Grastidium peekelii (Schltr.) Rauschert

Synonym: *Dendrobium peekelii* Schltr.
This medium sized to large clump-forming species is widespread in New Guinea, including in the island of New Britain. It is a lowland coastal species not occurring above 60 m altitude. It grows in *Calophyllum* and other trees overhanging beaches, in rainforest and swamp forests, in coconut plantations and on street trees in Lae, Madang and other coastal towns. The stems are slender and 60 to 130 cm long, with thin, grass-like leaves 8 to 16 cm long and about 1 cm wide, along most of their length. The flowers are 5 to 8 cm across, borne in pairs and last less than a day, but a large plant can be covered in flowers. Flowering occurs throughout the year.

This species can be grown on a slab or in a pot or attached to a tree in the tropics. It should be watered heavily throughout the year and grown in warm humid, semi-shaded conditions. If grown well, it rapidly becomes a large plant.

Grastidium polyschistum (Schltr.) Brieger

Synonym: *Dendrobium polyschistum* Schltr.
This large species occurs at several localities in Papua New Guinea at altitudes of around 1000 to 2200 m in rainforest. In these areas there are moist conditions throughout the year. This species forms large tangles of stems that branch and reach 50 cm or more in length. The leaves are borne along most of the length of the stem, are about 5 to 8 cm long and about 2 mm wide. The flowers are 3 cm across, borne in pairs, with a distinctive broad hairy lip. The flowers last a day and flowering is throughout the year.

This species requires intermediate to cool conditions, light shade and should be kept moist throughout the year. A pot or slab will suit the plants while small, but the plants may become large and hard to manage.

Grastidium salaccense Blume

Synonym: *Dendrobium salaccense* (Blume) Lindl., *D. intermedium* Teijsm. & Binn.
This is a medium sized species which is widely distributed in Myanmar (Burma), Peninsular Malaysia, Laos, Vietnam, southern China, Sumatra, Java, Bali and Borneo, although there is some confusion in the taxonomy and there may well prove to be several species within this complex. It occurs from sea level to about 1800 m, growing as an epiphyte or lithophyte in forests and more open areas, sometimes in almost full sun. The stems are slender, 30 to 60 cm long, erect or arching, with leaves along most of their length. The leaves are grass-like, 8 to 12 cm long. There are 1 to 4 flowers per inflorescence, varying in size from 5 mm to 2 cm across and in colour from white to green or dull yellow. The flowers last less than 2 days and flowering can occur at any time of the year.

This species occurs in a variety of habitats, but in general it should be given warm temperatures with year-round waterings, although a slightly drier period in winter is recommended. Bright light and good air movement are best and a slab or a pot of well-drained medium is equally suitable.

Grastidium sladei (J.J. Wood & P.J. Cribb) M.A.Clem. & D.L.Jones

Synonym: *Dendrobium sladei* J.J. Wood & P.J. Cribb
This is a large, slender, clump-forming epiphyte from Vanuatu, Samoa, Fiji and other Pacific islands. It grows from near sea level to about 600 m in montane forests with year-round hot and moist conditions. The stems are slender, up to 120 cm long, with leaves along their apical half. The leaves are 5 to 11 cm long and 1.5 to 2.8 cm wide, in 2 ranks. The flowers are 2 to 3 cm long, borne in pairs opposite the leaves and last less than a day. Flowering is probably throughout the year with an emphasis on summer.

The plants require warm, humid conditions throughout the year, with regular watering. They should not be permitted to dry out completely. Filtered light is best and the plants are probably best mounted on a slab, although a hanging pot of well-drained medium is also suitable.

GEOFF STOCKER

Grastidium summerhaysianum (A.D. Hawkes & A.H. Heller) Rauschert

Synonym: *Dendrobium summerhaysianum* A.D. Hawkes & A.H. Heller
This is a medium sized epiphyte reported from the Torricelli Range in Papua New Guinea and the Lorentz River in Irian Jaya, at altitudes of 600 to 700 m in montane rainforest where there is year-round high rainfall. The stems are slender, unbranched and up to 50 cm long, erect or arching. The elliptical leaves are 5 to 9 cm long and 2 to 3 cm wide and are borne along most of the length of the stem. The flowers are borne in pairs, claw-shaped and about 2 cm across. They last about a day and flowering is in bursts throughout the year.

The plants require warm conditions with year-round watering and light shade. A slightly drier period in winter may be beneficial, but the plants should not be permitted to dry out entirely. A pot of well-drained medium or a slab is suitable. In the tropics the plants may be tied to a tree or post.

BILL LAVARACK

Grastidium tozerense (Lavarack) M.A.Clem. & D.L.Jones

Synonym: *Dendrobium tozerensis* Lavarack
This small to medium sized species forms large clumps and grows as a lithophyte or, less commonly, as an epiphyte in the Iron Range–McIlwraith Range area of Cape York Peninsula in north-eastern Australia. It occurs at low altitudes on rocks in full or filtered sunlight in areas with a distinct dry season in winter and spring. Temperatures, even in winter, are consistently hot and humidity levels are usually high. The stems are slender and brittle, 20 to 60 cm long and about 2 mm in diameter. The leaves are up to 8 cm long and about 5 mm wide and are borne in 2 ranks on the upper half of the stem. The flowers are borne in pairs laterally, are about 3 cm across and last less than a day. It is common for 3 anthers to be present. The flowering season is spasmodic throughout the year.

This species requires warm conditions throughout the year. It must be given excellent drainage and slab culture is recommended. If a pot is used, it should be small with good drainage. Bright light or full sunlight is required and watering should be reduced in winter and spring.

WAYNE HARRIS

Grastidium sp.

This medium sized clumping epiphyte has been recorded from low to moderate altitudes in Papua New Guinea, where it grows in mountain rainforests in areas with a high year-round rainfall. The slender stems are erect, then pendulous as they lengthen, reaching a length of up to 100 cm. The leaves are 6 to 10 cm long and about 2 cm wide, arranged densely along the apical two-thirds of the stem. Flowering is throughout the year and the flowers last a day.

This species requires warm growing conditions with consistent year-round watering, so that the plant never dries out completely. Semi-shade and high humidity are recommended. A hanging pot or basket or a slab are recommended to accommodate the eventually pendent habit of the plants.

Grastidium vandoides (Schltr.) Brieger

Synonym: *Dendrobium vandoides* Schltr.

This is a large, clump-forming epiphyte from lowland areas of New Guinea where the climate is hot and humid with year-round rainfall. It frequently grows among dense ferns and mosses on branches overhanging streams below 800 m altitude. The erect stems grow to about 2 m, but commonly are about half that. They are covered at the apical part by overlapping strap-like leaves in 2 ranks, like species of the genus Vanda. The lower part of the stem is enclosed in the persistent leaf bases. The leaves are 10 to 20 cm long and 2 to 4 cm wide. The inflorescences are short, usually consisting of 2 flowers, but sometimes 1 or 3, and produced from the upper leaf axils with the flowers partly hidden by the leaf bases. The flowers are about 2 cm across and last only a day or less. Flowering is probably throughout the year, apparently several days after heavy rain.

This is a slow-growing species in cultivation. It should be potted in a rich medium such as fern peat and should be watered throughout the year. Warm, humid conditions with filtered light are best. It should be fertilised regularly with a dilute fertiliser.

Grastidium sp. aff. *D. angraecifolium* Schltr.

This tall species forms large clumps with stems to 1.5 m long. It has been seen as an epiphyte in lower montane forests in Papua New Guinea on several occasions and may well be a variant of *Dendrobium angraecifolium* (*Grastidium branderhorstii*). The rhizome is short and bears numerous stems with well spaced (about 2.5 cm apart) and narrowly ovate leaves 13 cm long and 2.2 cm wide. The species flowers several times each year. The white flowers are borne in pairs along the upper portions of the stems. Their segments are quite thick and almost fleshy in texture. Although the flowers are partially open for several days, they are only fully open for a few hours.

The species is easy grow as a potted plant given a free-draining, moist medium and moderate light. It may make an interesting garden plant for those who dwell in a warm temperate climate.

Grastidium sp. aff. *G. angustispathum* (J.J. Sm.) M.A. Clem. & D.L. Jones

This is a member of a small group of grastidiums that have thin grass-like leaves and wiry branched stems. A first glance they may not be recognised as orchids and, unless in flower, are very difficult to tell apart. They are mainly found in the montane forest zone of the island of New Guinea. They are either epiphytes or terrestrials. The stems are about 1 mm in diameter and they have a few well spaced thin, linear leaves 7 cm long and 5 mm wide, which taper gradually to a point. Offshoots from the stems are the primary means of further vegetative growth. In an open situation on high ridges, they have been observed to form large tangled masses that may be several square metres in area and as much as 2 m high. The flowers of this species are about 4 cm across and are only open for a day.

As far as is known it has not been cultivated. If attempted, potting in a relatively fine, but well- drained potting mix, intermediate temperatures, bright light and no resting period, are suggested.

Grastidium sp. aff. *G. cyrtosepalum* (Schltr.) Rauschert

This species occurs in lowland forest on the north-eastern coast of Papua New Guinea. It has a short rhizome and erect stems 30 to 45 cm long, with leaves spaced about every 12 mm along the upper two-thirds. The rather thick leaves are light green, ovate in shape, 6 cm long and 2 cm wide, with a slight constriction (sometimes more easily felt than seen) about one-third of the way back from the tip. This species flowers several times each year. The flowers are about 2.2 cm across and are borne in pairs along the stem, opposite the leaves. They last only a day.

This species is easily grown in a pot in warm to intermediate conditions. It should be watered regularly throughout the year and given a bright place in the greenhouse.

Grastidium sp. aff. *G. longissimum* (Schltr.) Rauschert 1

This very pendulous species is occasionally seen in tall lowland *Anisoptera* forest in Papua New Guinea, hanging from large branches like a curtain. The rhizomes are short. The stems are typically 2 m long, but may reach 4 m in sheltered habitats. They are leafy throughout most of their length. The leaves are in 2 ranks and are held at a downward angle of about 45 degrees to the stems. They are narrowly ovate, about 15 cm long and 3 cm wide. The flowers last only a day and are about 2 cm across.

The plant photographed was collected in low foothill forest to the south of Lae, Morobe Province, and re-established in the grounds of the University of Technology at Lae where it was tied to a large palm tree. Although it took some time to recommence growing, it eventually settled down and flowered every few months. Warm conditions with year-round watering and constant high humidity would be required.

Grastidium sp. aff. *G. longissimum* (Schltr.) Rauschert 2

This plant may only be a form of that described above. It was found at about 1800 m altitude in low montane forest on a high ridge to the north of Lae in northern Papua New Guinea. Although vegetatively very similar to the species described above, no plants were seen with stems longer than 2 m. The flowers were about 2 cm across and lasted for only a day.

As far as is known, it has not been grown in cultivation. If available, it is suggested that it could be grown out of the bottom of a hanging basket in a greenhouse maintained at intermediate temperatures.

Grastidium sp. aff. *G. vandoides* (Schltr.) Brieger

Several lowland grastidiums have a vegetative habit very reminiscent of some of the strap-leaf vandas such as *Vanda coerulea*. Most grow high on the branches of large forest trees in the lowlands of Papua New Guinea. Here the rainfall is heavy and dry periods longer than 2 weeks are rare. The night minimum temperatures rarely fall below 20°C and the day temperatures are consistently in the low 30s. This species was found near Lae. Several others from this group are also found in this area. The flowers are borne in pairs in the axils of the leaves. They are about 2 cm wide when fully open and last scarcely a day.

As far as is known this species is not in cultivation. The habitat and environment in which the plant was found suggests that it should be grown in a warm humid shady situation. An occasional short dry period might not do the plants any harm.

Section *Herpethophytum* Schltr. (Genus *Dendrobium*)

This section of about 14 species is restricted to the island of New Guinea. They are mostly epiphytes of moderate altitudes, growing in montane rainforests where there is year-round rainfall. They are small plants that grow in the dense moss on limbs of trees in cloud forests.

The plants have a creeping rhizome and small, branched, wiry stems with small leaves along their length. The leaves have a sheathing base. They are closely related to section *Monanthos*, being distinguished by the plant habit and by the flowers, which are extremely small with the lateral sepals fused to their tips to form a spur which surrounds the column. The flowers are borne laterally on the stem with the lip uppermost and last only a day.

Dendrobium herpethophytum Schltr.

This is a small to medium sized species from the Bismarck Mountains in Papua New Guinea, where it grows in the mist forests on mossy branches at about 1500 to 1800 m altitude. The pseudobulb size is uncertain, but probably about 10 to 25 cm long, and is much branched and pendulous. The leaves are small, about 1 cm long. The short flattened inflorescences bear 1 or 2 flowers, which are about 4 mm long and last only a day.

Intermediate to cool humid conditions are required. The plants should be kept moist with daily waterings and frequent misting if possible. They may be grown in a hanging pot or on a slab, with the additions of some moss around the roots. Heavily filtered light and good air movement are required.

Dendrobium scopula Schltr.

This medium sized epiphyte occurs in the Finisterre Range and other localities in northern Papua New Guinea at altitudes of 1800 to 2300 m in rainforests with year-round rainfall. The stems are up to 60 cm long and resemble a broom, as the upper part is much branched and densely covered in leaves and the lower part bare or with short bracts. The leaves are up to 3.5 cm long and 2 mm wide. The flowers are about 5 mm across and are borne singly from the upper leaf axils. They last about 5 days and flowering can occur at any time of the year.

In cultivation, this species should be given intermediate to cool conditions with year-round watering and semi-shaded humid conditions. A small pot of well-drained medium that retains a little moisture is recommended.

GEOFF STOCKER

Dendrobium sp. ex Lae

This small densely tufted species grows to about 15 to 18 cm tall. It occurs in the lowland forests near Lae, Papua New Guinea. The stems are thin, about 1 mm in diameter, and bear soft linear leaves 35 mm long and 3 mm wide on their upper two-thirds. Plants flower several times a year with the flowers lasting about a week. The flowers are usually borne singly on the upper third of the leafy stems.

This species is easily grown in a small pot, in a mix composed of medium sized pieces of pine bark. It should be watered regularly and placed in a moderately bright position and kept in warm conditions.

Genus *Inobulbum* (Schltr.) Schltr. & Kraenzl.

Synonym: *Dendrobium* Section *Inobulbum* Schltr.

This group was recently raised from sectional to generic status. It consists of 2 species both restricted to New Caledonia. They occur in rainforests at low to moderate altitude in areas of year-round high humidity. The genus is closely related to the genus *Tetrodon*.

The pseudobulbs are short, fusiform and the nodes are adorned with rings of rigid hairs. There are 2 leaves at the apex of the pseudobulb. There is a short leaf sheath. The roots are granulose. The flowers are borne in a long, many-flowered raceme or a sparsely branched panicle. The lip is 3-lobed and there is a very short mentum.

J.H.ODDY/RBG, KEW

Inobulbum layardii (F. Muell. & Kraenzl.) M.A. Clem. & D.L. Jones

Synonyms: *Cirrhopetalum layardii* F. Muell. & Kraenzl., *Dendrobium muricatum* Finet var. *munificum* Finet, *D. munificum* (Finet) Schltr., *Inobulbum munificum* (Finet) Kraenzl.

This medium sized epiphyte is restricted to the mountains in the southern part of New Caledonia. It occurs in rainforests, often along creek banks, in shady, humid conditions from 200 to 700 m altitude in areas with year-round rainfall. The pseudobulbs are up to 15 cm long and 7 cm wide, fusiform, with distinctive rings of erect bristles formed from the remains of the old leaf bases at each node. There are 2 or 3 fleshy leaves up to 30 cm long and 4 cm wide at the apex of the pseudobulb. The inflorescences are arching or pendulous, branched and up to 30 cm long with numerous (up to 200) densely packed flowers, each about 3 to 5 cm across. The flowers close at night and open in the morning. The flowering season is summer and autumn. The name '*layardii*' seems to have some question marks attached to it and it is possible that the name for this species may revert to *I. munificum* (Finet) Kraenzl.

Slab culture is recommended, although pots with a well-drained medium are also used. The plants should be kept moist year round and grown in intermediate temperatures in semi-shade. Year-round watering is suggested, but slightly less frequent in winter.

Inobulbum muricatum (Finet) Kraenzl.

Synonym: *Dendrobium muricatum* Finet

This small epiphyte is restricted to New Caledonia, where it occurs in the mountains at altitudes of 300 to 1000 m. It grows in semi-shade or exposed to full sunlight in areas with high humidity and year-round rainfall. The pseudobulbs are about 8 cm long and 4 cm wide, with distinctive rings of erect bristles formed from the remains of the old leaf bases at each node. There are 2, or occasionally 3, relatively broad leaves, 20 to 25 cm long and 3 cm wide, at the apex of the pseudobulb. The inflorescence is up to 30 cm long, branched, arching, with up to 80 densely packed flowers each about 2.5 cm in diameter. They close at night and open in the morning. The flowering season is spring.

In cultivation, this species does well on a slab of tree fern, cork or similar material or in a pot of well-drained material. It should be given intermediate to warm conditions with year-round watering and high humidity. A decrease in watering during winter may be useful, but the plants should not be allowed to dry out completely. Bright filtered light is recommended.

Section *Kinetochilus* Schltr. (Genus *Dendrobium*)

This section comprises 3 or 4 species, which are restricted to New Caledonia. They grow as epiphytes or lithophytes at moderate altitudes in rainforest where there is year-round high humidity and relatively low light. Related to *Cannaeorchis* (section *Macrocladium* of *Dendrobium*) and the *Grastidium* group.

The stems are long and slender, reaching 2 m in some species and producing numerous aerial growths in 1 or 2 species. The leaves are in 2 ranks along the length of the stem and have a leaf sheath and often an unequally lobed apex. The inflorescences are borne laterally with 1 to 3 small flowers. The lip is usually undivided and is moveable as in *Bulbophyllum*.

Dendrobium crassicaule Schltr.

This is a large species with stems to 2 m long. It occurs in the southern part of New Caledonia, growing as an epiphyte or lithophyte on small mossy trees in the maquis vegetation. It has been recorded growing in partial shade and in full sun at altitudes between 700 and 1500 m. Here the temperatures are mild, humidity is high for most of the year and there is rain throughout the year. The stems are quadrangular, with 9 to 11 leaves on the upper part. The leaves are 3 to 5 cm long and about 1 cm wide. The stems form numerous plantlets when in contact with the substrate. The inflorescences are more or less upright, arise opposite the leaves and comprise 3 to 9 flowers each about 1 cm across. Flowering is mainly in summer.

In cultivation, this species should be given intermediate to cool temperatures. Bright light and good air movement are required. The plants should be watered regularly throughout the year, but should be allowed to dry between waterings, particularly in winter. Slab culture has proved most successful.

Section *Latouria* (Blume) Miq. (Genus *Dendrobium*)

This section includes about 50 species distributed from the Philippines to Samoa, but without doubt the centre of distribution is Papua New Guinea, with about 45 species. They are epiphytes of rainforest trees from sea level to high altitudes, usually in areas of year-round rainfall. The plant size ranges from small to very large and the long-lasting flowers vary similarly in size. The section is closely related to the section *Dendrocoryne*, but is distinguished by the fleshy flowers and the firm attachment of the lip.

The pseudobulbs are close together and although mostly club-shaped, vary greatly in shape, some being stout and others long and slender. The leaves lack a sheathing base and are borne near the apex of the stem. The inflorescences arise from near the apex, often appearing terminal, and have a few, rather fleshy flowers. The lip is prominently 3-lobed, with a prominent raised callus. Some large-flowered species are among the most spectacular in the subtribe and members of the section are becoming popular in cultivation.

BILL LAVARACK

Dendrobium aberrans Schltr.

This is a small epiphyte, which occurs in the eastern part of Papua New Guinea including Fergusson, Goodenough and Normanby Islands. It grows in mossy forests at 300 to 1900 m altitude, in areas with year-round high rainfall and high humidity. The pseudobulbs are club shaped, up to 20 cm long and about 1 cm in diameter, with 2 or 3 leaves at the apex. The oval leaves are about 4 to 10 cm long and 1.5 to 3 cm across. The inflorescences are borne from the apical nodes and are erect, becoming pendulous, with 2 to 6 flowers each about 1 to 1.5 cm across. The flowers last about 3 weeks and flowering may occur at any time, with a concentration on winter. Flowers are often produced on very small plants.

A pot of any standard well-drained medium is suitable. The plants do best in intermediate to cool conditions, in semi-shade, and should not be allowed to dry out completely. Slabs are equally suitable provided the plants are kept moist.

BILL LAVARACK

Dendrobium alexandrae Schltr.

Named by Rudolf Schlechter after his wife Alexandra, this attractive species is known from only one or two areas in Papua New Guinea, where it occurs at low to moderate altitudes (900 to 1100 m) in rainforests in cool, shady conditions on moss-covered branches. It was 'lost' for many years and was at one time considered a possible hybrid involving *D. spectabile*. However, the recent discovery of large numbers in a few areas, and a more careful study, has refuted this theory. The pseudobulbs are narrowly club-shaped, 50 to 70 cm tall and about 1 cm wide. There are 3 or 4 elliptic leaves, glaucous underneath and about 11 to 16 cm long and 3 to 5 cm wide, at the apex of the pseudobulbs. The inflorescences are erect, from the apical nodes, about 25 cm long with 3 to 7 flowers, each 5 to 8 cm across. The main flowering season is autumn and spring and the flowers last several weeks.

In cultivation, this species requires intermediate to warm conditions with good air movement and year-round watering and high humidity. It should be given bright filtered light. A pot with good drainage is best, but slab culture is also suitable. It can quickly grow into a large plant.

Dendrobium amphigenium Ridl.

Synonym: *Dendrobium fantasticum* L.O. Williams
This medium sized epiphytic, or occasionally terrestrial, species has been recorded from several locations throughout the central ranges of the island of New Guinea, where it occurs at altitudes of 1600 to 2300 m. It grows in mossy montane rainforests where there is year-round rainfall. The pseudobulbs are up to 40 cm long and less than 1 cm wide with 2 or 3 leaves at the apex. The leaves are lanceolate, 5.5 to 12 cm long and 1 to 2.5 cm wide. The inflorescences arise from the upper nodes and are 6 to 8 cm long with few flowers. The flowers are small and fleshy, about 1.8 cm long. This species is closely related to *D. dendrocolloides*, but can be separated by the mid-lobe of the labellum (see under *D. dendrocolloides*).

In cultivation, this species requires intermediate to cool conditions with year-round watering, high humidity and good air movement. It is best potted in a small pot of a medium which retains a little moisture without becoming soggy. Slab culture can be used, but some moss or similar material which retains moisture should be added. Bright filtered light is recommended.

Dendrobium atroviolaceum Rolfe

D. atroviolaceum was first described by R.A. Rolfe in April 1890 from a plant imported from 'eastern New Guinea' by Messrs J. Veitch and Sons. For some years the exact origins of *D. atroviolaceum* were somewhat uncertain due to the reluctance of professional orchid collectors to disclose localitites, but it is known from D'Encrecastreaux Islands and the Louisiade Archipelago off the eastern tip of New Guinea. In its natural habitat it grows on rainforest trees at altitudes ranging rom about 200 to 800 metres in about 50 per cent shade and always where there is consistently good air movement. The pseudobulb is spindle-shaped and 10 to 30 cm long with up to 6 leaves at the apex. There are a few large flowers, 4 to 6 cm across and nodding. Flowering can be at any time with an emphasis on autumn to spring. The flowers are very long-lasting, remaining in good condition for three months or more. It has been used quite extensively in hybridising.

It does well in an open orchid house in the tropics and in warm temperate areas, flowering freely if potted in a well-drained mixture and not allowed to stay dry for too long. Night temperatures of 5°C or a little less seem to cause no problems as long as the days are warm. Filtered sunlight is best.

Dendrobium bifalce Lindl.

Synonyms: *Dendrobium chloropterum* Rchb.f. & S. Moore, *D. breviracemosum* F.M. Bailey
This is a medium sized to large epiphyte, or occasionally a lithophyte, which grows into large clumps. It occurs in New Guinea and adjacent islands, Timor, Cape York Peninsula in northern Australia and the Solomon Islands. It is a species of the hot steamy lowlands almost always below 1000 m, in areas of year-round rainfall and hot temperatures. It often grows in situations of high light intensity, even in baking sun on rocks. The pseudobulbs are fusiform up to 60 cm long and 1 to 1.5 cm in diameter. There are 2 to 4 leathery, oval leaves up to 10 cm long, clustered at the apex of the pseudobulb. The inflorescences are erect, up to 20 cm long, with 6 to 10 flowers, each about 2 cm across, waxy and lasting a few weeks. The flowering

season is throughout the year with an emphasis on autumn and winter.

In cultivation, this plant needs good drainage and often a slab of cork or similar material is best. If grown in a pot, excellent drainage is required and plants should not be watered if they are moist, particularly in cool weather. Care should be taken with the new shoots, which are susceptible to rot. They should be kept moist through summer and autumn, but a rather drier period in winter and early spring seems beneficial. Definitely a species requiring warm conditions, it may be difficult to get plants to flower in temperate climates. Strong light is recommended.

Dendrobium biloculare J.J. Sm.

Little is known about this rare species from Irian Jaya, which was not seen for a period of more than 90 years after its first discovery. It was recently rediscovered, but details of the locality are not yet available and it should be noted that there are still some questions remaining about the identification of the newly discovered plants. It was first reported from lowland areas where the climate is hot, with year-round rainfall and high humidity. The pseudobulbs are up to 30 cm long, club-shaped with a slender base and 2 or 3 leaves at the apex. The leaves are thin and about 14 cm long and 4.5 cm wide. The inflorescences arise from the upper nodes and are pendulous with about 8 flowers, each about 2 to 3 cm across. It is related to *D. convolutum*, but is distinguished by the large lateral lobes of the lip and the large bilobed white callus that is free at the apex.

This species has not been tried in cultivation recently, so little is known of its specific requirements, but it should be given year-round warm, humid conditions with regular watering. A pot of well-drained medium or a slab should be used.

Dendrobium convolutum Rolfe

This is a medium sized epiphytic species from Papua New Guinea where it has been reported from lowland areas from Karkar Island along the north coast to Milne Bay at altitudes below 650 m. It is locally abundant in some areas on the Huon Peninsula. The habitat is hot, steamy lowland rainforest, but little is known of the precise growing conditions. The pseudobulbs are clustered and up to 30 cm long and 1.3 cm wide at the thickest part, with 3 leaves at the apex. The leaves are up to 13 cm long and 5 cm wide. The inflorescence is up to 12 cm long with 2 to 7 flowers, each about 3 cm across and waxy in texture. The flowering season is mostly spring to autumn, but can be at any time, and the flowers last for 4 to 6 months.

This species requires warm, humid conditions and should be watered throughout the year. It is best grown in a pot of well-drained medium; if grown on a slab, care must be taken not to allow the plants to dry out. If fertiliser is used it should be dilute.

GEOFF STOCKER

Dendrobium crutwellii T.M. Reeve

Synonyms: *Sayeria paradoxa* Kraenzl., *Dendrobium sayeria* Schltr.
This small, erect or pendulous epiphyte remained something of a mystery until it was renamed by T.M. Reeve in 1980. It occurs in isolated pockets of the Central Range of Papua New Guinea, between 1800 and 2400 m altitude. It grows low down on small trees on ridge tops often in shade, although usually in areas with good air movement and high year-round humidity. The pseudobulbs are 3 to 13 cm long and about 1 cm thick with 2 or 3 leaves at the apex. The leaves are 5 to 16 cm long and 1.5 to 4 cm wide. The inflorescences arise from the apex of the pseudobulb and are pendulous, with 3 to 12 flowers, each about 3 to 5 cm across. The flowers last 3 or 4 weeks and the main flowering season is autumn.

This species may be grown in a well-drained pot, but slab culture may be more suitable for the semi-pendulous habit. The plants do best in intermediate to cool conditions with semi-shade and high humidity. They should be watered throughout the year.

GEOFF STOCKER

Dendrobium dendrocolloides J.J. Sm.

Synonym: *Dendrobium incurvilabium* Schltr.
This is a miniature species from Irian Jaya and Papua New Guinea. It grows as an epiphyte in montane forests or terrestrially on exposed banks at 1100 to 1800 m altitude. It is recorded as growing on clay embankments and in sphagnum moss on exposed hill tops and in dense moss on the underside of branches in the middle canopy. The pseudobulbs are club-shaped, from 5 to 34 cm long and a little less than 1 cm wide, with 2 or 3 leaves at the apex. The leaves are 5 to 10 cm long and about 2.5 cm wide. The inflorescences are produced from the apical nodes, and are more or less erect with up to 10 fleshy flowers, each about 1.5 cm long. The flowers last at least 2 months. This species is closely related to *D. amphigenyum*, but it lacks the prominently bifid mid-lobe of that species. The labellum of *D. dendrocolloides* is bilobed with the mid-lobe being almost absent.

Intermediate to cool temperatures are required for this species. It should be kept humid and watered daily throughout the year. The plants are best grown in a hanging pot with a well-drained medium and a light covering of moss on the top of the pot. The new growths tend to tunnel down into the potting medium and may rot.

BILL LAVARACK

Dendrobium engae T.M. Reeve

Sometimes known as 'Pike's special', this spectacular species occurs in the Enga Province and other highland areas of Papua New Guinea, where it grows epiphytically on *Nothofagus* trees in montane rainforests, or occasionally lithophytically, often on exposed ridges between 1800 and 2700 m altitude. In this area there are cool to intermediate temperatures, and year-round rainfall. The plants grow high in tall trees, usually on forest margins and other situations where there is strong light. The pseudobulbs are up to 50 cm long, although commonly shorter, and 2 to 3 cm in diameter, with 3 to 5 leaves at the apex. The leaves are oblong, 5 to 20 cm long and leathery. The inflorescences arise terminally or near the apex, are up to 25 cm long, with 3 to 15 fragrant, fleshy, attractive flowers each 5 to 6 cm across. The flowers last about 10 weeks and the main flowering is reported as October to April in the natural habitat.

In cultivation, this species is intolerant of continued hot weather. It should be given intermediate to cool temperatures and kept evenly moist throughout the year. It may be grown on a slab or in a well-drained pot of bark or a similar medium. It requires good air movement, high humidity and bright filtered sunlight. It has proved a difficult species to propagate from seed and is very slow growing.

Dendrobium euryanthum Schltr.

This is a small, pendulous or erect epiphyte from the mountains of north-east Papua New Guinea, where it grows in montane forests at altitudes of 800 to 1500 m. The pseudobulbs are slender, almost cylindrical, to 12 cm long and 5 mm wide, with 2 bluish-green leaves at the apex. The leaves are twisted at the base so that they lie in one plane and are about 10 cm long and 3.5 cm wide. The inflorescences are borne from the apical nodes and consist of 3 to 4 flowers, about 2 cm across and not opening widely. This species is closely related to *D. armeniacum* and *D. punamense*, from which it differs in that it has an orange labellum while that of *D. punamense* is white or pale green.

Warm to intermediate temperatures are required for this species. It requires year-round watering and high humidity. It is best grown in a pot of well-drained medium, with a small amount of moss on the top to help retain moisture. Bright filtered light is recommended.

Dendrobium eximium Schltr.

Synonyms: *Dendrobium bellum* J.J. Sm., *D. wollastonii* Ridl.
This medium sized epiphyte was originally described in 1905, but from 1913 it largely disappeared from view until rediscovered in the Torricelli Mountains in Papua New Guinea in 1981. It is now known to occur in West Irian and in Papua New Guinea in several locations at altitudes of 400 to 1300 m. It grows on rainforest trees in areas with year-round rainfall and high humidity. The pseudobulbs are club-shaped with a very slender base which extends for about half their length. They are up to 40 cm long and about 1 to 2 cm at their thickest. There are 2 shiny, leathery leaves 7 to 18 cm long and 3.5 to 7 cm wide, at the apex of the pseudobulb. The inflorescences are terminal with 2 to 7 large showy flowers up to 11 cm across. The backs of the sepals are densely covered with hairs. The flowers have a faint honey scent and last about 3 months. Flowering is from July to November in the habitat, probably winter and spring in cultivation.

Intermediate to warm conditions are required with year-round watering and high humidity. The plants should be grown in a pot of well-drained medium or mounted on a slab. If a slab is used, care must be taken to ensure that the plant does not dry out for long periods. Bright filtered light is best.

GEOFF STOCKER

GEOFF STOCKER

Dendrobium finisterrae Schltr.

This is a medium sized to large epiphyte from Papua New Guinea, where it occurs in montane rainforests at altitudes 1300 to 2100 m. It grows in exposed situations in the upper branches of rainforest trees. The pseudobulbs are robust, club-shaped, up to 50 cm long and 3 cm in diameter, with 2 leaves at the apex. The leaves are leathery, up to 23 cm long and 9 cm wide. The inflorescences are erect, up to 25 cm long, with about 10 flowers. The flowers do not open widely, are about 5 cm across and last several weeks. The backs of the sepals and the ovary are covered with dense hairs. There is a distinctive hook-like appendage on the column foot, which distinguishes this species from others with a hairy ovary.

In cultivation, this species does best in intermediate temperatures with year-round high humidity and constant watering. It needs strong filtered light. It may be grown in a pot of well-drained medium or on a slab. When grown on a slab, care should be taken to ensure that the plants do not dry out for long periods.

Dendrobium forbesii Ridl.

Synonyms: *Dendrobium ashworthiae* O'Brien, *D. forbesii* var. *praestans* Schltr. This is a large, robust epiphyte occurring at altitudes of 900 to 1700 m in the mountains of Papua New Guinea. It grows as an epiphyte in montane rainforest, usually high up in the trees. This is a climate of warm to hot days, cool nights and high year-round rainfall and humidity. The pseudobulbs are strongly club-shaped, up to 32 cm long and 2.5 cm in diameter. There are 2 large, leathery leaves at the apex of the pseudobulb, up to 19 cm long and 10 cm across. The inflorescences arise from between the leaves and are relatively short and erect, with about 8 to 15 fragrant flowers, each about 5 to 7 cm in diameter. The backs of the sepals are almost smooth, but the ovary is covered with dense hairs. The flowers last several weeks and can occur at almost any time in the natural habitat.

In cultivation, this species requires intermediate conditions, strong light and good air movement. It should be potted in a well-drained pot in a standard mixture. It should be kept evenly moist throughout the year and responds to regular fertilising with a dilute fertiliser.

Dendrobium johnsoniae F. Muell.

Synonyms: *Dendrobium macfarlanei* Rchb.f., *D. niveum* Rolfe, *D. monodon* Kraenzl.
This is one of the outstanding orchids of New Guinea, with large flowers often on a small plant. It occurs in Irian Jaya and Papua New Guinea, extending to Bougainville Island. Records from northern Australia appear to be in error. It grows epiphytically in montane forests at altitudes of 500 to 1200 m, often on *Casuarina* trees along watercourses or on *Araucaria* trees and in other situations where light levels are high. The pseudobulbs are slender, club-shaped up to 30 cm long, with 2 to 5 leaves at the apex, each leathery and about 10 cm long and 4 cm wide. The inflorescences arise from near the apex of the pseudobulb and are erect, with up to 12 flowers, each from 6 to 12 cm across. The flowers last about 2 months and may be produced at any time of the year in the natural habitat.

In cultivation, this species requires warm to intermediate conditions, bright filtered light, good air movement and year-round moist, humid conditions. The roots are susceptible to rot if the surrounding medium becomes soggy, but neither should they not allowed to remain dry for long periods. A very well-drained pot with an open mixture is best.

Dendrobium *kauldorumii* T.M. Reeve

This medium sized epiphyte is restricted to a relatively small area in the Chimbu and Eastern Highlands Provinces of Papua New Guinea, where it grows in rainforest at 1500 to 2200 m altitude. The pseudobulbs are up to 40 cm long and 1 to 1.5 cm in diameter, with 2 to 3 leaves at the apex. The leaves are about 3 to 10 cm long and 1.5 to 5 cm wide, leathery, often suffused with purple-red colouring. The inflorescences are borne from the apical nodes and are erect with 3 to 15 flowers each about 2 cm across. The flowers last 3 or 4 weeks and flowering occurs in bursts throughout the year.

This species is uncommon in cultivation, but success has been achieved with plants in a pot of well-drained medium kept moist throughout the year. Slab culture should also succeed provided the plants are kept moist. It does best in intermediate conditions.

Dendrobium 'Kip's Special'

Dendrobium rhodostictum F. Muell. & Kraenzl. x *D. ruginosum* Ames
This attractive small natural hybrid with large flowers is quite abundant on Bougainville Island where it commonly grows on roadside cuttings and trees on the road to the Panguna mine at about 1200 to 2000 m altitude. In this area the climate is wet throughout the year. The plants are variable, but commonly about 20 cm tall with 2 to 4 leaves at the apex. The inflorescences bear a few large flowers up to about 8 to 10 cm across. They last 3 to 4 months.

As is often the case with natural hybrids, this plant does well in cultivation. It should be given intermediate to cool conditions with high humidity and year-round watering. It is best grown in a pot of well drained medium in bright filtered light.

Dendrobium macrophyllum A. Rich.

Synonyms: *Dendrobium veitchianum* Lindl., *D. ferox* Hassk., *D. brachythecum* F. Muell. & Kraenzl., *D. ternatense* J.J. Sm., *D. psyche* Kraenzl., *D. musciferum* Schltr.
D. macrophyllum is the most widespread of the section *Latouria*, extending from the western end of Java and the Philippines to Samoa. It was described by Achille Richard in 1834, which makes it one of the earliest orchids recorded from the island of New Guinea. It is one of the larger epiphytes in the forest, forming large clumps with pseudobulbs up to 60 cm long, usually high up in the canopy. The habitat is hot steamy lowlands, from sea level to about 500 m.

There are 3 large leathery leaves up to 30 cm long and 4 cm wide at the apex of the stem. The flowers are 3 to 5 cm across, variable in colour, but with combinations of green, cream, yellow and purple. The back of the sepals, ovary and pedicel are covered with dense hairs. The racemes bear up to 25 flowers that last about 2 months and are borne throughout the year.

In cultivation, this species is relatively easy to grow in tropical areas on a tree or in an open orchid house. In cooler areas it requires heat during winter. It should be potted in bark or another well-drained mixture and kept evenly moist throughout the year. It requires bright light to do well. The new shoots are produced very prolifically but are susceptible to rot, which starts from water trapped in the bracts on the developing stem. Treatment with a suitable fungicide can control this problem, or care can be taken to keep water out of these bracts.

Dendrobium mayandyi T.M. Reeve & Renz

This species is often seen in the highlands of Papua New Guinea. It is found in montane rainforest between about 1500 and 2300 m altitude, generally as a semi-pendulous epiphyte on small trees or on the boles or lower branches of emergents. The rhizome is short; the pseudobulbs clavate, up to about 30 cm long and greenish-brown to dark brown in colour. Each pseudobulb has 2 or 3 leaves attached near the apex. The leaves are dark green, leathery, ovate and about 9 cm long and 2 cm wide. The inflorescences are subterminal, about 5 or 6 cm long. Each bears about 4 to 7 fleshy flowers, which are long-lasting but never fully open.

Although its growth in flask is unreliable and slow (due apparently to dark phenolic exudates from the protocorms and plantlets), surviving seedlings are relatively easy to manage once successfully transplanted into the greenhouse. Plants should be kept moist throughout the year, moderately bright and in intermediate to cool temperatures.

Dendrobium otaguroanum A.D. Hawkes

Synonym: *Dendrobium chloroleucum* Schltr.
This small epiphyte occurs in both Irian Jaya and Papua New Guinea. It is restricted to the main island of New Guinea where it occurs at 1500 to 2200 m in moist, misty montane rainforests in the upper branches of *Nothofagus*, *Podocarpus* and *Castanopsis* trees and occasionally on cliff faces and road cuttings. In this habitat, there is constant high humidity, cool night-time temperatures and high light intensity when it is not cloudy. The pseudobulbs are slender and about 10 to 25 cm long with 2 or 3 leaves at the apex. The leaves are 5 to 7 cm long and around 1.5 to 2 cm broad. The inflorescence is erect from the apical nodes, with 2 to several flowers each 3 to 4 cm across. Flowering can occur at any time of the year and the flowers last 4 to 6 weeks.

In cultivation, this species requires cool to intermediate temperatures with constant high humidity, bright light and year-round watering. It is best grown in a small pot in a medium which retains some moisture without becoming soggy. They may also be grown on a slab, but if so care must be taken that the plants do not dry out for more than a few hours.

GEOGG STOCKER

Dendrobium polysema Schltr.

Synonyms: *Dendrobium pulchrum* Schltr., *D. macrophyllum* var. *stenopterum* Rchb.f.

This medium sized to large epiphyte occurs in eastern Papua New Guinea at altitudes of 1200 to 1900 m and in the Solomons and Vanuatu, where it ranges from sea level to 1000 m. It grows in montane rainforest in areas with year-round high rainfall and intermediate to warm temperatures. It is closely related to *D. macrophyllum* A. Rich., being distinguished by the 2-leaved pseudobulbs, tapering side lobes of the labellum and the heavily spotted mid-lobe. The pseudobulbs are club-shaped, up to 50 cm long and 2 to 3 cm wide, with 2 leaves. The inflorescences are terminal, erect with up to 12 flowers each 4 to 6 cm across. They are long-lasting and the flowering season is year round in nature.

This species should be potted in a well-drained pot of bark or similar medium. It should be watered throughout the year, but kept a little drier during winter, while not allowed to dry out completely for long periods. It requires bright filtered sunlight, high humidity and good air movement.

GEOFF STOCKER

Dendrobium punamense Schltr.

Synonym: *Dendrobium walerhousei* Carr

This small to medium sized, erect or pendulous epiphytic species occurs in the hot steamy lowlands of New Guinea, Manus, New Britain, New Ireland, Bougainville and Guadalcanal Islands. It grows on shrubs and the lower trunks of rainforest trees in deep shade, at altitudes of about 100 to 1000 m. The pseudobulbs are cylindrical, 25 to 30 cm long and less than 1 cm wide, with 2 leaves at the apex. The leaves are 15 to 20 cm long and 3 to 4 cm wide. The inflorescences are borne from the apical nodes and are about 10 to 15 cm long, with few flowers, each about 2 cm across. The flowers last a few weeks. This species is related to *D. curyanthum*.

Warm conditions, with constant high humidity and year-round watering are recommended. The plants should be given semi-shade and grown on a slab or in a hanging pot of well-drained medium, to allow for the semi-pendulous habit.

WAYNE HARRIS

Dendrobium rhodostictum F. Muell. & Kraenzl.

Synonym: *Dendrobium madonnae* Rolfe

This is a small to medium sized epiphytic or terrestrial species from Papua New Guinea, New Britain, Bougainville and the Solomon Islands. It grows between 800 and 1200 m as an epiphyte in montane rainforests or as a terrestrial on steep, well-drained mossy slopes of limestone. The pseudobulbs are variable, with those from the island of New Guinea tapering gradually to the apex and those from Bougainville having a long, extremely slender basal part and a short bulbous part at the apex, from which the leaves arise. The pseudobulbs are up to 25 cm long with 2 to 4 leaves crowded at the apex. The leaves are persistent, leathery, 5 to 11 cm long and 1 to 2.5 cm wide. The inflorescences are formed at or near the apex and consist of 2 to 6 large flowers from 6 to 9 cm across. The fragrant flowers last about 6 weeks and are borne in winter and spring in cultivation.

In cultivation, this species requires intermediate conditions with year-round watering. It should not be allowed to dry out completely, but the medium must be very well drained. Pots or slabs are equally suitable. It should be given filtered sunlight with good air movement.

Dendrobium rigidifolium Rolfe

Synonyms: *Dendrobium guttatum* J.J. Sm., *D. helenae* Chadim, *D. giluwense* P. Royen, *D. alpinum* P. Royen

This is a small to medium sized epiphyte or lithophyte, which is restricted to the high mountains of Papua New Guinea and Irian Jaya. It is a widespread species at high altitudes (2000 to 3800 m) in montane forest of *Nothofagus*, etc., usually epiphytic, but occasionally growing as a terrestrial in deep moss. The pseudobulbs are cylindrical, 7 to 40 cm long and about 6 mm wide, with 3 to 6 leaves on the apical half of the stem. The leaves are well spaced on the stem, elliptical, up to 10 cm long and 2.5 to 5 cm wide. The inflorescences are borne from the apex or adjacent nodes. They consist of 4 to 15 flowers, each 2.5 to 5 cm across, and often not opening fully. The plants are quite variable in size and in size and shape of the leaves, depending on the habitat in which they grow. This has led to the list of synonyms given above.

This is a high altitude species requiring cool growing conditions. It should be watered throughout the year and kept in high humidity and partial shade. The plants may be grown in a pot of well-drained medium with some moss on top to keep moisture levels high.

Dendrobium shiraishii Yukawa Nishida

This spectacular species appears to occur in northern New Guinea from East Sepik in Papua New Guinea to around Manokwari in West Irian. Although described in 1992, it appears to be the species mentioned by van Bodegom (1973) as '*D. macrophyllum* variety 3'. He reports that it had been found by Stuber near Hollandia before 1942. A photograph of this species was also recently found in the colour slide collection of the late Andre Millar who collected widely throughout Papua New Guinea. Written on the slide was 'Maprik', which is a town near the Alexander Mountains in East Sepik Province. *D. shiraishii* appears to occur in foothill rainforests at elevations between 500 and 1000 m. Vegetatively it closely resembles *D. macrophyllum* except that the pseudobulbs are somewhat thicker and much darker in colour. The inflorescences are produced from the tops of the pseudobulbs. They are to 40 cm long and bear about 12 flowers. Individual flowers are about 6 cm across.

Van Bodegom reported that the species is not difficult to grow when potted in tree-fern pieces, loose humus and fern-peat. Potted plants should be kept in half shade and given warm humid conditions with year-round watering.

Dendrobium spectabile (Blume) Miq.

Synonym: *Dendrobium tigrinum* Rolfe ex Hemsley

This species is noted for its spectacular, unusual, twisted flowers. It is a large, robust epiphyte from the hot, steamy lowlands of the islands of New Guinea, Bougainville and the Solomons, as far south as Vanuatu. It grows in swampy lowland forest and lower montane forest up to about 1000 m, occasionally in coconut plantations and rarely on rocks. It commonly grows high up in the canopy where it is one of the largest epiphytes. The pseudobulbs are cylindrical, up to 60 cm long and 2 to 3 cm thick with up to 6 leathery leaves at the apex. The inflorescences arise from just below the leaves and are erect, with up to 20 flowers, each 4 to 8 cm across and distinctively twisted in all their parts, which last last several weeks. The flowering season in the natural habitat is in the dry season, usually in winter.

In cultivation, this is a relatively easy species to grow, although water lodging in the bracts on the developing new growths can cause rotting and loss of the growth. The plants should be grown in a well-drained pot of relatively coarse medium that allows the roots to be well aerated. Bright, filtered light is best. The plants grow well in full sunlight if slowly acclimatised to it. Warm, humid conditions with year-round watering are required. Regular fertilising with a dilute fertiliser is beneficial. The plants flower best when they have been established in a pot for several years.

Dendrobium tapiniense T.M. Reeve

This medium sized to large epiphyte was known from the Tapini area of Papua New Guinea for many years as *D*. 'Tapini' until it was formally described in 1980 by T.M. Reeve. It grows in a restricted area in the Central Province at altitudes of 1500 to 2000 m, where the plants grow high in the branches of rainforest trees, in an area with cool nights and warm days, constant rainfall and high humidity. The pseudobulbs are from 40 to 60 cm long and about 2 to 3.5 cm in diameter with 2 or 3 leathery leaves at the apex. The leaves are 8 to 20 cm long and 4 to 8 cm wide. The inflorescence is erect from the apical nodes with 3 to 15 fleshy flowers, each 3.5 to 4.5 cm across and lasting 3 to 4 months. The flowering season in the habitat is November to February.

In cultivation, this species requires intermediate temperatures, high humidity, and regular watering year round. It should be given bright light and good air movement. It may be grown in a pot of well-drained medium or on a slab if care is taken not to let the plants dry out for any length of time.

Dendrobium terrestre J.J. Sm.

Synonym: *Dendrobium magnificum* Schltr.
As the name implies, this large spectacular species often grows as a terrestrial, although it is also epiphytic, particularly in the lower part of the altitude range. It occurs throughout the central ranges of the island of New Guinea and on New Britain at altitudes of 1800 to 2600 m. It grows on well-drained mossy banks or low down on trees in areas of bright light, good air movement and high humidity throughout the year. The pseudobulbs are slender, up to 50 cm long and about 2 cm in width, with 3 to 7 leaves at the apical part. The leaves are 3 to 7 cm long and 3.5 to 5.5 cm in width. The inflorescences arise from the apical nodes and are erect with 6 to 20 flowers each 2.5 to 6 cm across. Flower size and colour is variable with orange, yellow, and occasionally white, flowers variously marked with red-purple on the lip and other segments.

A well-drained medium, but one which retains a little moisture without becoming soggy, is recommended. Cool to intermediate temperatures are best with bright, filtered light and constant year-round humidity and year-round watering.

Dendrobium woodsii P.J. Cribb

This medium sized epiphyte occurs in the south-eastern part of Papua New Guinea where it grows in montane rainforests at altitudes ranging from 500 to 2000 m. The pseudobulbs are club-shaped with a very slender base. They are up to 40 cm long and about 1 cm in diameter with 2 leaves at the apex. The leaves are leathery, 18 cm long and 3.5 cm wide and glossy green on the upper surface. The inflorescences are borne from the apical nodes and are pendulous, with 4 to 7 flowers each about 2 cm across and fragrant. The flowers last a few weeks.

The plants grow well in a small pot of well-drained medium or on a slab. Moist year-round conditions with intermediate to cool temperatures are recommended. The plants should be watered year round and kept in bright, filtered light.

Dendrobium sp. aff. D. subquadratum J.J. Sm.

This small species is reported to come from lowland forest near Kokoda, Papua New Guinea, at about 500 m altitude. The rhizome is very short. The erect pseudobulbs are club-shaped, 12 to15 cm long and 4 mm wide near the upper end, with two lanceolate leaves 12 cm long and 3.5 cm wide at the apex. The inflorescences are generally borne under the leaves. They are 5 to 7 cm long and carry 3 to 5 flowers, each widely opening and about 1.2 cm across. It appears to be close to *D. subquadratum* and, although somewhat smaller in all parts, may eventually be shown to be conspecific.

This species has proved easy to grow under either warm or intermediate conditions. It flowers freely if grown in a small pot containing a free-draining mix and given moderate light. The potting mix should not be allowed to dry out.

Section *Lichenastrum* (Brieger) Dockr. (Genus *Dendrobium*)

Note: Brieger considered *Lichenastrum* to be a section of his genus *Dockrillia*.

This group of 3 species is restricted to north-eastern Australia in the area known as the wet tropics. They occur at low to moderate altitudes in rainforest, growing epiphytically or occasionally lithophytically. Originally placed in the section *Rhizobium* (genus *Dockrillia*), they are now considered to be separate, although closely related to this group and to section *Microphytanthe* from the island of New Guinea. If *Dockrillia* is considered to be a genus, then probably the same should apply to *Lichenastrum*.

The plants are small, with a creeping rhizome which forms a mat over the branches. There are no pseudobulbs, only short stems each with a single fleshy leaf. The leaves are close together or well spaced. The small flowers are borne singly at the base of the leaf. The flowers are entire or with extremely small lobes.

Dendrobium lichenastrum (F. Muell.) Kraenzl.

Synonyms: *Bulbophyllum lichenastrum* F. Muell., *Dockrillia lichenastrum* (F. Muell.) Brieger
There is confusion concerning the correct name for this miniature creeping species, which grows on trees or rocks at altitudes between 200 and 1200 m in north-east Australia. Some authorities consider that this species and *D. prenticei* (see below) are the same, as the flowers are virtually identical

and the main difference lies in the shape of the leaves. The rhizome is creeping and branching and forms a mat over the substrate. The leaves are closely packed, appressed to the substrate, variable in shape, but generally ovoid and fleshy and up to about 1 cm long. The flowers are borne singly on a peduncle about 1 cm long. They are about 4 to 7 mm across, vary in colour from green to cream or pink with varying amounts of darker striations and last about a week. The main flowering season is spring, but plants can flower at any time.

A slab of cork, tree fern or weathered wood is best for this mat-forming species. It should be firmly attached and kept in a sheltered place until attached. This species does well in warm to intermediate conditions with a drier period in winter. It should be given filtered sunlight and kept in humid conditions.

Dendrobium prenticei (F. Muell.) Nicholls

Synonyms: *Bulbophyllum prenticei* F. Muell., *Dendrobium lichenastrum* (F. Muell.) Kraenzl. var. *prenticei* (F. Muell.) Dockr., *D. variable* Nicholls, *D. aurantiaco-purpureum* Nicholls

This miniature mat-forming species occurs in north-east Australia. It grows on rocks and tree branches in humid rainforest conditions with warm to intermediate temperatures, usually in shade or filtered sunlight at altitudes of about 200 to 1000 m. The plants consist of a creeping rhizome with elongate, terete leaves. The flowers are about 4 to 9 mm in diameter and are borne singly on a short peduncle that arises from the base of the leaves. They vary in colour from cream to pink and some have heavy purple striations. They last a few days to a week. The main flowering season is spring, but plants can flower at any time.

A slab of cork, tree fern or weathered wood is best for this mat-forming species. It should be firmly attached and kept in a sheltered place until attached. This species does well in warm to intermediate conditions with a drier period in winter. It should be given filtered sunlight and kept in humid conditions.

Dendrobium toressae (F.M. Bailey) Dockr.

Synonyms: *Bulbophyllum toressae* F.M. Bailey, *Dockrillia toressae* (F.M. Bailey) Brieger

This is one of the smallest members of the subtribe. It is a tiny mat-forming species from the north-east part of Australia where it occurs from near sea level to about 1000 m altitude in rainforests and nearby open forests. It grows as an epiphyte or a lithophyte, in semi-shade and usually in humid conditions. This species forms dense mats comprising short rhizomes that give rise to small succulent leaves 4 to 8 mm long and 2 to 4 mm wide, about the size and shape of a grain of wheat. The single flowers arise from the base of the leaf with virtually no peduncle, and are about 6 mm in diameter. They may appear at any time of the year and last a few days.

A slab of cork, tree fern or weathered wood is best for this mat-forming species, which is unsuited to a pot. It should be firmly attached and kept in a sheltered place until attached. This species does well in warm to intermediate conditions with a drier period in winter. It should be given filtered sunlight and kept in humid conditions.

Section *Microphytanthe* Schltr. (Genus *Dendrobium*)

This is a small section of only 3 or 4 species, all of which occur on the island of New Guinea at moderate to high altitudes. They are plants of montane rainforests, usually growing on the trunks or larger branches of *Castanopsis* and *Nothofagus* trees. The plants appear to be related to the Australian species *Dendrobium torressae*, *D. lichenastrum*, and *D. prenticei* which are placed in section *Lichenastrum* or in *Dockrillia* (section *Rhizobium*) by some authorities.

The plants are small and usually creeping, with the small pseudobulbs well spaced and with a single leaf, resembling a *Bulbophyllum* species. While the flowers are small, they are large for the size of the plant and a mature plant can be covered in flowers. They are borne singly, arising from the apex of the pseudobulb and are yellow, orange or maroon. The lip is entire. The flowers last 1 to 3 weeks.

GEOFF STOCKER

Dendrobium bulbophylloides Schltr.

This is a miniature species from altitudes between 1000 and 2500 m in the island of New Guinea. In these areas the climate is cool and moist year round. *D. bulbophylloides* forms dense mats on tree limbs in mossy montane rainforests. The pseudobulbs are spaced about 5 to 20 mm apart on a slender, branched rhizome. They are 4 to 10 mm high and 2 to 6 mm in diameter, with a single leaf 6 to 20 mm long and 3 to 11 mm wide. The flowers are borne singly from the apex of the pseudobulb. They are 9 to 14 mm across and last 2 or 3 weeks. Flowers can be borne at any time, with a concentration on summer.

In cultivation, cool to intermediate conditions with year-round watering and semi-shade are required. Because of the creeping habit, the plants are best tied to a slab, but care must be taken to keep them moist. Plants can be slow initially, but once established will grow quickly in favourable conditions.

GEOFF STOCKER

Dendrobium margaretae T.M. Reeve

This is a miniature species from altitudes between 1500 and 2500 m in the island of New Guinea. It forms large mats on trunks of trees in mossy montane forests where the climate is cool and moist year round. The pseudobulbs are spaced about 5 to 15 mm apart on the branched rhizomes. They are smaller than *D. bulbophylloides*, about 3 to 7 mm long and 3 to 5 mm wide, with a single leaf about 6 to 16 mm long and 4 to 7 mm wide. The leaves are sometimes tinged with purple. The flowers are borne singly from each pseudobulb, but a second flower invariably follows the first. The flowers are 7 to 11 mm across and last 7 to 11 days. Flowering can be at any time throughout the year. The plant shown here is either *D. margaretae* or a very closely related species.

In cultivation, cool to intermediate conditions with year-round watering and semi-shade are required. Because of the creeping habit, the plants are best tied to a slab, but care must be taken to keep them moist. Plants can be slow initially, but once established will grow quickly in favourable conditions.

Dendrobium brevicaule Rolfe

Synonyms: *Dendrobium cyatheicola* P. Royen, *D. calcarium* J.J. Sm., *D. montistellare* P. Royen, *D. quinquecristatum* P. Royen, *D. aurantivinosum* P. Royen

Although this beautiful alpine miniature species is very variable, it has the largest flowers of any in the section. Currently 3 subspecies based on plant habit and flower features are recognised. Two of these, subsp. *brevicaule* and subsp. *pentagonum*, are confined to the eastern part of Papua New Guinea, while the third, subsp. *calcarium*, is found on many of the island's high mountains. The species is typically an epiphyte in alpine shrubberies between 3000 and 4000 m, or on the tree ferns which are characteristic of the frost- and fire-induced savannas. The photograph is of subsp. *calcarium* and was taken *in situ* in alpine shrubberies at about 3200 m in the mountains above Porgora, Enga Province. The description below is of this subspecies. The plants are sub-erect to pendulous, tufted to loosely branched. The pseudobulbs are 0.5 to 5 cm long and 2 to 5 mm thick, more or less fusiform and bearing 1 to 5 linear to lanceolate leaves, 1 to 8 cm long and 2 to 7 mm wide, near the apex. There are 1 to 3 flowers, which are borne from near the apex of the leafy pseudobulbs. They are 2.8 to 4.5 cm long and appear to be long lasting.

At the present time this species is virtually unknown in cultivation. So far it has proved almost impossible to grow from seed and research is needed to determine whether this problem is one of unsuitable media or an extremely short period of seed viability. The next problem will be to determine the degree to which the species will need to have the temperatures of its natural habitats (nearly freezing at night to mid teens during the day) reproduced before it will grow and flower satisfactorily.

Dendrobium cyanocentrum Schltr.

Synonyms: *Dendrobium lapeyrouseoides* Schltr., *D. flavispiculum* J.J. Sm.

This small tufted species grows at lower elevations than any other of the oxyglossums and has been collected from the low branches of a tree overhanging a small tributary of the April River in northern Papua New Guinea at 40 m altitude. It is characteristic, however, of somewhat higher elevations to about 1600 m where it is often found as a twig epiphyte in low secondary forest. Although it has been recorded from many localities throughout New Guinea, most collections have been made in the eastern part. Plants are generally erect, about 3 cm high, and although tufted, do not often form large clumps. Pseudobulbs are 4 mm high. Each is topped with 2 or 3 more or less linear leaves about 3 cm long. The long-lasting flowers are generally borne in pairs (occasionally 1) from the apex of the pseudobulbs. The sepals and petals may be strongly reflexed. While the flowers are usually a shade of blue, sometimes plants with flowers that have white sepals and petals and yellow lips are seen. At first glance the latter appear more like the closely related *D. subuliferum*. However, the latter has much broader sepals and petals and each inflorescence generally contains only a single flower. Its petals and sepals are never reflexed.

Small plants are relatively easy to grow in pots with intermediate temperatures, moist conditions and strong light. While young plants are usually quite vigorous and flower well, they are not easy to grow into large clumps.

BILL LAVARACK

Dendrobium dekockii J. J. Sm.

Synonyms: *Dendrobium chrysornis* Ridl., *D. montigenum* Ridl.,
D. erythrocarpum J.J. Sm., *D. cedricola* P. Royen, *D. gaudens* P. Royen,
D. kerewense P. Royen

This beautiful miniature species is characteristic of the tree line and alpine shrubberies of the mountains of the island of New Guinea. It is a tufted epiphyte generally 2 or 3 cm high. The pseudobulbs are usually about 1 cm long but vary considerably in size and shape. They are often characterised by a constriction at about the middle. Each is topped by 1 to 4 dark green, linear to lanceolate leaves about 1 cm long (occasionally much longer). The very short inflorescences arise from the leafy stems and usually have 1 or 2 flowers. The flowers are 1.5 to 3 cm long and last for many weeks.

   Although experience in the cultivation of this species is limited, it appears that it is both difficult to establish and to flower. The best results to date have been by growing it in a small pot of tree-fern fibre. The medium should be kept moist and the plant placed in a bright position in the cool greenhouse.

GEOFF STOCKER

Dendrobium delicatulum Kraenzl.

Synonyms: *Dendrobium minutum* Schltr., *D. nanarauticola* Fukuyama, *D. parvulum* Rolfe

There are currently 3 subspecies recognised within this species. All are small creeping plants, 1 to 2 cm high, which often form large mats on the trunks and large branches of trees predominantly in cloud forests. The first is subsp. *delicatulum*. It has a very wide distribution throughout New Guinea and down through the eastern island chain to Vanuatu and possibly Fiji. It has also been recorded from the Caroline Islands in the northern Pacific. Its long-lived flowers are generally deep blue, although red and intermediate shades have been recorded. Subspecies *parvulum* (Rolfe) T.M. Reeve occurs in western New Guinea and Sulawesi. While plants have a similar appearance to subspecies *delicatulum*, they have longer flowers (larger than 1.2 to 1.5 cm). The third subspecies, *huliorum* T.M. Reeve & P. Woods, is fairly distinct and can usually be separated from the other two even when not in flower. Its leaves and pseudobulbs are much greener, lacking the purplish flush of the other two, and the flowers are cream coloured with a tendency to self-pollinate.

   Despite their creeping habit all 3 subspecies of this species have been easiest to grow in a pot with a medium of peat and perlite. Establishment on a slab or in bark-based mixes has often proved to be difficult, possibly because they dry out too quickly. Moist, intermediate, moderately bright greenhouse conditions appear to suit it well.

MARY MACLENNAN

Dendrobium habbemense P. Royen

Synonym: *Dendrobium spathulatilabratum* P. Royen

This is an unusual *Oxyglossum* with an elongated curved stem and pendulous habit and is reminiscent of some of the species in section *Calyptochilus*. It is confined to the mountains of the island of New Guinea. Although the stems may be branched, they are usually solitary at the point of attachment to the host. Its flowers are borne singly along the stems and appear to last for several months. Plants are often found in dense shade low down on trees near small mountain streams at about 2500 m. However, it has also been found in exposed alpine situations as high as 3500 m.

   Unfortunately this very desirable species has, like several other of the high-elevation oxyglossums, proved difficult to grow from seed or to re-establish in cultivation from wild collections. Suggested starting points are a cool environment with high humidity and moderately low light.

GEOFF STOCKER

Dendrobium hellwigianum Kraenzl.

Synonyms: *Dendrobium rhaphiotes* Schltr., *D. geluanum* Schltr., *D. cyananthum* L.O. Williams

This medium sized to small, tufted species, about 10 to 20 cm high, is usually a twig epiphyte on large Nothofagus and other trees in montane forest. It has been recorded from between 1400 and 2700 m elevation and appears to be widespread throughout Papua New Guinea. Plants are generally small, though occasionally clumps over 15 cm across are found. It tends to occur in colonies and from the numerous plants observed on fallen branches, the population in the crowns of some large trees must be in the thousands. Its terete to semi-terete leaves makes it relatively easy to identify. It is perhaps closest in appearance to *D. violaceum* var. *cyperifolium,* but has shorter and stouter leaves and smaller flowers. The terminal inflorescences from the tops of the old pseudobulbs contain from 1 to 3 flowers. While the flower colour within a population seems fairly consistent, it may vary among populations from light blue through purple to very pale pink.

This species is relatively easy to propagate by either division or standard *in vitro* techniques. It grows well in a small pot filled with free-draining mix and given intermediate temperatures, high humidity, good air movement and moderate to bright light.

GEOFF STOCKER

Dendrobium masarangense Schltr.

Synonyms: *Dendrobium pumilio* Schltr., *D. theionanthum* Schltr., *D. trigidum* Schltr., *D. caespitificum* Ridl., *D. gemma* Schltr., *D. pseudofrigidum* J.J. Sm., *D. monogrammoides* J.J. Sm., *D. chlorinum* Ridl.

This small, tufted epiphyte is usually about 2.5 to 3 cm high. It is usually found in small colonies, either as twig epiphytes in the crowns of montane forest trees or on the stems of small shrubs among tall grasses and sedges in secondary woodland. Occasionally this species extends to the lowlands but is generally found in wet humid environments above 1500 m. The species is widespread from Sulawesi in the west, through New Guinea to Fiji and New Caledonia in the South Pacific. Two subspecies are recognised. Subspecies *masangarense* is the more widespread and generally the one found at low elevations. It has small, white, relatively open flowers and leaves which are narrow, even terete. Subspecies *theionanthum* is confined to New Guinea. Its leaves are somewhat broader and its flowers larger and generally yellowish in colour. Superficially the plants appear close to several other small species in this section, e.g. *D. subacaule, D. cyanocentrum, D. subuliferum, D. nanoides* and *D. deckokii.* Fortunately these species are usually found in flower and may be readily distinguished by flower colour and shape.

D. masarangense has not been easy to grow. In flask it tends to proliferate strongly and the thin elongated explants readily succumb to dehydration and fungal attack. Observation from the natural habitat suggests that this species is most likely to grow best in an environment with intermediate temperatures, high humidity and moderate light levels.

Dendrobium nebularum Schltr.

Synonyms: *Dendrobium keysseri* Schltr., *D. tumidulum* Schltr., *D. murkelense* J.J. Sm., *D. palustre* L.O. Williams

This species occurs in the Moluccas, the Philippines and the island of New Guinea and, although widespread, does not appear to be common. It is usually found as an epiphyte in mid-montane forest in the crowns of smaller trees. If this very desirable section has to have a black sheep then it must be this species, for the flowers are usually of a nondescript greenish colour (although purple-red forms have been observed) and do not open widely. Vegetatively the plants are about 10 cm tall and resemble those of *D. pentapterum* and the taller forms of *D. vexillarius*. A cluster of 2 to 5 flowers arises from the top of each pseudobulb.

D. nebularum is easily grown in a small pot with free-draining mix, intermediate temperatures and moderate light.

Dendrobium pentapterum Schltr.

This species has mainly been found in Madang and Morobe Provinces of Papua New Guinea. Its habitat is the lower montane and secondary forests at about 1500 m altitude where it is an erect epiphyte 10 to 15 cm high in the branches of small trees. Vegatively it resembles *D. nebularum*, *D. violaceum* subsp. *violaceum* and some forms of *D. vexillarius*. *D. pentapterum* has greenish-white to cream coloured, very long-lasting flowers. One or 2 are borne on the top of each pseudobulb. A well-grown plant will rapidly form a large clump, which will be covered in flowers for most of the year. This species may be confused with the white-flowered form of *D. violaceum* subsp. *violaceum* in cultivation. In the field *D. violaceum* is usually found closer to 2000 m; its pseudobulbs are thicker at the base; the plants are taller and the white colour form is relatively rare (pink to violet is the dominant colour).

This species is one of the easiest of the section to grow, either on a slab or in a pot with well-drained mix, moderate temperatures and moderate to high light.

Dendrobium rupestre J.J. Sm.

This species appears to be widespread, though not particularly commonly encountered, throughout the island of New Guinea. It is essentially a species of the upper montane zone and is most abundant between 2000 and 3000 m altitude. Although usually epiphytic on large *Nothofagus* trees, it is occasionally found as a terrestrial or lithophyte, especially on road cuttings and other steep banks. In habit plants of *D. rupestre* are small, about 2 to 4 cm high. They are generally clumped or occasionally creeping. The leaves usually have a purplish tinge, especially on the underside. The flowers are about 2.5 cm long and, although lasting for several weeks, they are not as long-lived as those of many others in the section. However, this species is very desirable to specialist collectors.

Although wild-collected plants have been reported to be difficult to grow, seedlings, once successfully established, grow and flower relatively easily, at least for a time. They are, however, difficult to maintain in good condition for very long and, like many others in this section, appear susceptible to root-rot fungi, probably *Rhizoctonia*, which gradually seem to overwhelm larger plants. Perhaps with good sanitation, a sterile water supply and regular treatment with appropriate fungicides, plants of this species can be grown to the size of the large mats occasionally observed in the wild.

GEOFF STOCKER

Dendrobium subacaule Lindl.

Synonyms: *Dendrobium begoniicarpum* J.J. Sm., *D. tricostatum* Schltr., *D. oreocharis* Schltr., *D. junzaingense* J.J. Sm.

This tiny species was the first of this section to be recorded. It was found in the North Moluccas by C.G.C. Reinwardt in 1821. It is now know to range from the eastern Indonesian Islands through New Guinea to Gaudalcanal in the Solomon Islands. While it is generally a twig epiphyte on large montane forest trees between 1700 and 2500 m elevation, it is also found as a terrestrial on road cuttings. In the latter situation the plants observed are usually quite small and it is thought that they might not be able to survive in this environment for very long. In common with many of the oxyglossums, this species is usually found in colonies of 20 or more plants. Plants are generally tufted and about 2 to 3 cm high. The leaves tend to have a purplish tinge, especially to the underside. The flowers are about 1 to 1.5 cm long and usually in pairs. They are very long-lasting and vary in colour from light orange to reddish-orange.

The time from pollination to capsule dehiscence for this species is very short, about 6 weeks. *In vitro* culture is difficult due to proliferation and consequently losses on transplanting tend to be high. Plants are not easily grown in pots. Some seedlings are currently being tried tied on the stems of living shrubs (*Rhododendron* section *Vireya*). Results to date have been good.

WAYNE HARRIS

Dendrobium subuliferum J.J. Sm.

This small epiphyte appears to be widespread in the montane forests of the island of New Guinea from 300 to 2000 m altitude, but is not commonly encountered. It appears closely related to *D. cyanocentrum*, but has larger white flowers with much broader sepals and petals. Plants have very short rhizomes and tend to form small mats about 2 to 3 cm high. The leaves are green and terete. Generally 1, sometimes 2, flowers are borne from the top of leafy pseudobulbs. They open widely and are about 1.5 cm across, although larger forms with flowers 2.5 cm across have been reported.

This species is one of the easiest of the true miniatures to grow in cultivation and does well when potted in a peat moss/perlite mix with intermediate temperature and light conditions.

GEOFF STOCKER

Dendrobium sulphureum Schltr.

Synonym: *Dendrobium cellulosum* J.J. Sm.

This tufted species is occasionally found in large colonies on twigs and small branches in the crowns of trees in the montane forest of New Guinea, mostly between 1800 and 3000 m altitude, although there are some records from as low as 800 m. Most botanical collections have been from the eastern half of the island. Plants vary from 3 to about 12 cm high. Each stem bears about 3 to 6 leaves, each about 5 cm long and narrowly oblong. Several varieties based on stem length and shape, and flower size, are currently recognised. Some of the smaller forms of this species are occasionally difficult to distinguish from forms of *D. masarangense* subsp. *theionanthum*. However, both these species have been found in the same locality without any sign of intergradation. The flowers are generally borne from the apex of leafy stems. They vary from 1.5 to 2.5 cm long and from bright yellow to greenish-yellow in colour.

This species has not been particularly easy to grow, either in flask or as seedlings. In flask it has proliferated badly, making it difficult to obtain plantlets that are sturdy enough to make the transition from flask to pot. The variety *sulphureum* has been easiest to handle. Unfortunately it has the smallest and dullest flowers.

Dendrobium vexillarius J. J. Sm.

Synonyms: *Dendrobium semeion* P. Royen, *D. retroflexum* J.J. Sm., *D. caenosicallainum* P. Royen, *D. uncinatum* Schltr., *D. trialatum* Schltr., *D. trifolium* J.J. Sm., *D. bilamellatum* R.S. Rogers, *D. tenens* J.J. Sm., *D. xiphiphorum* P. Royen, *D. microblepharum* Schltr., *D. albiviride* P. Royen
This is probably the commonest of the oxyglossums in the island of New Guinea. It varies greatly in plant height and flower colour, but is readily distinguished from related species such as *D. pentapterum* and *D. nebularum* by its distinctively 3-winged ovary. It is usually found between 1000 and 3500 m altitude, growing on the twigs of shrubs and small trees on exposed ridges, but may occur terrestrially in grassland at higher parts of its elevation range. Plants are tufted and usually from 3 to 15 cm high. The plant size and flower colour is relatively constant in most populations, except in some where plants with cream coloured flowers may make up a significant proportion of a population which otherwise has flowers of either red, yellow, orange or bluish-grey colour. Seven varieties, based on plant habit and flower colour, have been recognised. The illustration shows var. *uncinatum*. The flowers usually open widely and are borne in clusters of 2 to 5 from the tips of both leafy and leafless pseudobulbs. They are from 2 to 4 cm long and very long-lasting.

Unfortunately this species has not proved easy to grow. Like some other species within this section, initial establishment from flask can be achieved and many brought into flower. However, irreversible decline in vigour often sets in. It is suspected that they may be very susceptible to root-rot fungi and/or fertiliser build-up in the media. Growers should attempt to minimise these problems by using sterile water and potting materials, regular heavy waterings to flush media and applying appropriate fungicides. Otherwise moist, bright, airy conditions and intermediate to cool temperatures are suggested.

Dendrobium violaceum Kraenzl.

Synonyms: *Dendrobium tenuicalcar* J.J. Sm., *D. quinquecostatum* Schltr., *D. dryadum* Schltr., *D. brachyacron* Schltr., *D. geminiflorum* Schltr., *D. pityphyllum* Schltr., *D. alloides* J.J. Sm., *D. cyperifolium* Schltr., *D. igneoviolaceum* J.J. Sm., *D. scottiferum* J.J. Sm.
This tufted epiphyte, usually 15 to 25 cm high, is found in New Guinea's montane forests on the branches of shrubs and small trees in exposed localities. Currently 2 subspecies are recognised. Subspecies *violaceum* is generally erect with leaves more than 2 mm wide and about 10 to 15 cm long. Subspecies *cyperifolium* (shown here) has slightly longer rhizomes, longer and narrower leaves (15 to 20 cm long and less than 2 mm broad) and is generally pendulous. Subspecies *violaceum* is the more widespread. Flower colour varies from white to pink, mauve, blue and grey. Some of the mauve forms have blue tips to the petals and sepals. The white forms are difficult to distinguish from *D. pentapterum* and some intergrades are suspected. The only colour observed for the flowers of subsp. *cyperifolium* has been mauve. The flowers are very long-lasting.

When cultivated in an open greenhouse on the Atherton Tableland in northern Australia, they are often visited, and apparently pollinated, early

Dendrobium pseudoglomeratum T.M. Reeve & J.J. Wood

For many years this common New Guinea species was confused with *D. glomeratum* Rolfe and *D. concavissimum* J.J. Sm. *D. pseudoglomeratum* is a semi-pendulous species from swamp forests and montane rainforests. It occurs throughout New Guinea from sea level to about 1800 m, often in slightly drier locations such as *Araucaria* forest. The stems are up to 70 cm long and slender, with rather thin leaves, which are deciduous after a year or two, along most of their length. The leaves are about 7 to 12 cm long and 1 cm wide. The inflorescences arise from the leafless or leafy stems, usually on the upper half. They consist of 6 to 15 densely packed flowers, each about 3 cm long and brightly coloured. The flowering season in nature is throughout the year, but in cultivation it is concentrated on spring. The flowers are fragrant and last about 2 to 5 weeks. The common highlands honeyeater has been recorded pollinating the flowers.

The range of altitude at which this species is found has made it relatively easily cultivated in a range of climates. It should be kept in intermediate to warm, moist humid conditions and watered throughout the year. A mixture that retains some moisture without becoming soggy is recommended. The eventually pendulous habit means that a hanging pot is best for this species.

Dendrobium purpureum Roxb. subsp. *candidulum* (Rchb.f.) Dauncey & P.J. Cribb

This medium sized to large epiphyte occurs in the North and South Moluccas and North Sulawesi. The subspecies *purpureum* has a separate distribution in the South Moluccas, Banda Island and the Aru Islands. Both subspecies grow in the hot steamy lowland rainforests below 800 m, in areas with year-round rainfall and high humidity. The pseudobulbs are variable in length, ranging from 20 cm to 150 cm, but mostly around 50 to 100 cm long. The leaves are about 9 to 13 cm long and 1.4 to 2.5 cm wide, deciduous, in 2 ranks along the apical half of the stem. The inflorescences arise from the leafless, or occasionally leafy, stems and consist of up to 60 flowers each 12 to 20 mm long. The flower colour varies with the following forms recorded: pink, pink and white, white or white with some green. The subspecies may be separated by the shape of the lip lamina, which is widest below the middle in subsp. *purpureum* and widest above the middle in subsp. *candidulum*. The flowers last a few weeks.

This species requires a warm climate with year-round watering and high humidity. It should be given semi-shade and is best on a slab or hanging pot to accommodate the pendulous habit.

Dendrobium rarum Schltr.

This species is occasionally found in the moist mid-montane forests at 1000 to 1500 m elevation in Papua New Guinea, growing on the trunks of small trees. It is a semi-pendulous species with a very short rhizome and slightly curved, narrowly fusiform pseudobulbs to 40 cm long and 0.5 cm diameter in the middle. The leaves are narrowly oblong, about 10 cm long and 0.5 cm wide at the widest part. The inflorescences are 3 cm long and hang from the undersides of the apical half of the pseudobulb. Each carries 10 to 12 flowers. Typically the flowers, which are each about 1 cm long, do not open widely and appear to be self-pollinating after about a week.

BILL LAVARACK

PETER O'BYRNE

GEOFF STOCKER

This species is easily grown in a pot or on a tree-fern slab. It should be kept moist and maintained at intermediate temperatures with low to moderate light levels.

BILL LAVARACK

Dendrobium secundum (Blume) Lindl.

Synonyms: *Dendrobium bursigerum* Lindl., *D. heterostigma* Rchb.f.
This is an epiphytic species which is often abundant and occurs over an extensive range from Myanmar (Burma) through Thailand, Peninsular Malaysia, Indochina, the Indonesian Islands west as far as Sulawesi, and north through Borneo to the Philippines. The plants grow at low, or occasionally moderate, altitudes usually in forests with a distinct dry season. The pseudobulbs are semi-erect or pendulous, up to 100 cm long but commonly 20 to 30 cm, and 1 to 1.5 cm in diameter. The leaves are up to 8 cm long and 3 cm wide, along most of the length of the pseudobulb, deciduous after 1 to 3 years. The inflorescences are borne from the upper nodes, usually on the leafless stems. They are up to 10 cm long with many densely crowded flowers each about 1.8 cm long. White flowered forms have been recorded. The flowers are usually arranged on one side of the inflorescence 'secund' giving rise to the name. The flowering season is spring and the length of time the flowers last is variable, usually about 1 to 2 weeks.

This species requires a dry resting period and generally warm conditions although it will tolerate intermediate temperatures. It should be given bright light, good air movement and copious water during the growing season. A small pot or slab is suitable.

Dendrobium smillieae F. Muell.

Synonym: *Dendrobium ophioglossum* Rchb.f., *D. hollrungii* Kraenzl.
Sometimes known as the bottlebrush orchid, this is an attractive large epiphyte of lowland areas of the island of New Guinea and north-eastern Australia. It grows in coastal rainforests and moist open forests up to 500 m altitude. It occasionally grows on rocks in open forests and can grow into large clumps with stems over 1 m long. The pseudobulbs are erect initially, but become pendulous when longer. The leaves are deciduous after about a year, thin-textured, lanceolate, 12 to 18 cm long and occur in 2 ranks along the length of the pseudobulb. The inflorescences are short, up to 12 cm long, with the numerous flowers extremely densely packed, and occur on the leafless pseudobulbs. Each flower is tubular and about 2 cm long and is thought to be bird-pollinated. There are 2 colour forms, one with prominent pink colour on the base of the floral segments and the other with white and green colouration. The flowering season is mostly in spring and early summer and the flowers last 2 to 6 weeks.

This species requires warm conditions and watering during the growing period and a drier resting period in winter and early spring, although the plants should not be kept dry for extended periods. Filtered sunlight and good air movement are required and the plants should be grown in a relatively small pot with well-drained medium or on a slab.

WAYNE HARRIS

Dendrobium sp. aff. *D. dichaeoides* Schltr.

This species differs from the type form of *D. dichaeoides* in that is generally more robust, is seldom branched and has pseudobulbs that are pendulous and not firmly appressed to the host. It appears to be widespread in the upper montane rainforests of Papua New Guinea above 1000 m altitude. The pseudobulbs grow to about 12 cm long, tend to be somewhat club-shaped, are oval in cross-section and from 2 to 5 mm thick. The leaves are broadly ovate, about 12 mm long and 7 mm wide. The flowers are borne on short inflorescences consisting of 5 to 8 flowers, borne near the ends of the pseudobulbs. Each flower is about 1.2 cm long.

   Plants may be grown in a small pot or on a tree fern slab, but must be kept moist. Intermediate to cool temperatures and low to moderate light levels are suggested.

Dendrobium sp. aff. *D. gnomus* Ames

The origins of this species are not known, although it is suspected to have come from moderate altitudes in Papua New Guinea. It resembles *D. gnomus* from the Solomon Islands in some respects, but differs mainly in details of the inflorescence. The species has a very short rhizome. It often grows from aerial growths produced along the lower third of the pseudobulbs. The pseudobulbs are about 25 cm long and 4 mm wide and are generally terete, becoming irregularly angular as they age. Each bears about 8 ovate leaves, which are 35 mm long and 7 mm wide. The younger leaves are sparsely clothed with brown scales that persist on the base part that sheaths the pseudobulbs. The flowers are borne in tight clusters of about 4 to 6 flowers on very short inflorescences borne along the older pseudobulbs. Each is about 8 mm long and lasts for several weeks.

   This species is easy to grow, either on a tree-fern slab or in a pot. The growing medium should be kept moist. Moderate light intensity and intermediate temperatures appear to be best for optimal flowering and growth.

Section *Phalaenanthe* Schltr. (Genus *Dendrobium*)

This is a small group of very showy species occurring from the Tanimbar Islands, Timor, southern New Guinea, the islands of Torres Strait and northern Australia. Three species occur in New Guinea and 2 to 4 in Australia. The species all occur in seasonally dry woodlands and savannas, in conditions that can be almost desert-like during the dry season. All are low altitude species occurring below 500 m. Most are epiphytes, but can occasionally grow as lithophytes.

   Some of the species are closely related and there is much debate about the limits of the individual species. Some authorities recognise 3 species in Cape York Peninsula, while others recognise only 1 variable species. The section is closely related to section *Spatulata* and natural hybrids occur quite commonly on the islands of Torres Strait and on Cape York Peninsula. The pseudobulbs may be long, or short and compact, with leaves at the apex. The flowers are large, showy, widely opening and long-lasting, in shades of pink, purple and white, and are borne on long arching racemes. The petals and sepals are larger than the lip. The mentum usually has two 'chins'. Two of the species are distinct, but the others are closely related and variable and there has been debate over the taxonomy, with some authorities recognising 6 species and some recognising 4 in the section. The species from this section are popular horticultural subjects.

BRUCE GRAY

Dendrobium affine (Decne.) Steud.

Synonyms: *Dendrobium dicuphum* F. Muell., *D. leucolophotum* Rchb.f., *D. urvillei* Finet

This species, although similar to *D. bigibbum* in many ways, is smaller in both plant and flowers. It occurs on the Tanimbar Islands, Timor, southern Irian Jaya and the Northern Territory in Australia. Plants from north-western Australia generally have shorter pseudobulbs (to 15 cm) and flowers with broader segments. It is possible that this provenance may be again recognised at species level in the future. It has been recorded on paperbarked *Melaleuca* trees, often overhanging creeks and lagoons, at low altitude or in dry vine thickets in areas with a very seasonal climate. The pseudobulbs are up to 1 m long, but usually much shorter, and about 2 cm in diameter. The leaves are ovate–lanceolate to oblong, 3 to 18 cm long, borne in 2 ranks along the apical half of the stems and deciduous after 1 or 2 years. The flowers vary from 2 to 5 cm across and are borne on long arching racemes, with up to 20 flowers, which arise from near the apex of the stem. The flowering season is autumn and winter and the flowers last about 4 to 6 weeks.

This species requires year-round warm conditions with a pronounced resting period in winter and spring. It should be kept moist and fertilised regularly while the new growths are developing. It does best in bright filtered light and excellent air movement. It may be grown on a slab or in a small pot of very well-drained mixture.

Dendrobium bigibbum complex

This complex includes many forms commonly known as the 'Cooktown orchid'. With its spectacular purple blooms, it is one of the finest horticultural subjects among the orchids. There is much debate and controversy about the taxonomic status of this orchid. Some authorities consider that there are 3 species on Cape York Peninsula — *D. bigibbum*, *D. phalaenopsis* and *D. lithocola*, but here they are considered as varieties of the one species.

BILL LAVARACK

Dendrobium bigibbum Lindl. var. *bigibbum*

Synonyms: *Dendrobium sumneri* F. Muell., *D. bigibbum* Lindl. var. *candidum* Rchb.f. Many other varieties have been described, but all of these represent either minor variants or, more commonly, hybrids and backcrosses with *Dendrobium discolor*.

The type variety occurs at low altitudes on the northern half of Cape York Peninsula, the islands of Torres Strait and southern New Guinea. It grows in hot conditions with an extremely dry winter, in open forests and on rocks. The pseudobulbs may reach 120 cm long, but are usually about 40 to 60 cm; they are about 1 cm thick, with 3 to 12 leaves in 2 ranks on the apical third of the stem. They are 8 to 15 cm long and about 2 cm wide, often with a purple tinge. There are one to several inflorescences per pseudobulb consisting of 2 to 20 flowers, each about 3 to 5 cm across, with slightly reflexed petals and sepals and usually a white spot on the lip. Flowering occurs in autumn and the flowers last about a month.

In cultivation, this species must be given warm conditions year round, and a dry resting period in winter and spring is essential. When the new growths appear, watering should be commenced and should be regular until the flowers have finished. The plants do best in a small pot with excellent drainage. A slab is also appropriate. Bright light conditions and

for this by producing large numbers of flowers several times each year. The flowering occurs in response to sudden drops in temperature, usually related to sudden tropical rainstorms. The dove orchid is a common sight on roadside trees in many parts of South-East Asia.

It is very amenable to cultivation, doing well in a basket, pot or on a slab or, best of all, on a tree, if the climate is suitable. A slightly drier period in winter seems not to be a problem for the plant, but it does best if watered regularly throughout the year and grown in partial shade. Plants in cultivation will tolerate temperatures as low as 5°C, provided this is for a short time only and the plants are dry at the time.

Dendrobium cymbulipes J.J. Sm.

This is a medium sized epiphyte from Borneo, where it occurs in the foothills of Mt Kinabalu, and other locations in Sabah, Sarawak and Kalimantan. It grows at altitudes of 900 to 2400 m in a range of forests including moss forests and lower montane forests. The stems are swollen above the base to form a short, many-angled pseudobulb, then are slender, branched and leafy to the apex. The leaves are 6 to 9 cm long, lanceolate in 2 ranks. The flowers are about 1.8 cm long and are borne laterally near the apex of the leafy part of the stem.

The plants are best grown on a slab or in a hanging pot with a well-drained medium. They should be given warm to intermediate temperatures, should be watered throughout the year and kept in humid conditions. Bright filtered sunlight is recommended.

Dendrobium equitans Kraenzl.

Synonym: *Dendrobium batanense* Ames & Quisumb.
This is a small epiphyte from the Batan Island group in the Philippines and from Orchid Island off the south-east coast of Taiwan. It grows at altitudes of about 600 m in thickets on forest slopes, in areas with year-round rainfall. The stems are from 9 to 40 cm long, with a short swollen pseudobulbous base and long slender apical part that bears the leaves and a leafless extension that bears the flowers. The leaves overlap at the base and are succulent, pointed at the apex, about 4 to 6.5 cm long and 3 to 6 mm wide. The single flowers are fragrant, about 2.5 cm long and last about a week. Flowering is throughout the year.

Warm to intermediate conditions with high humidity and bright filtered light are recommended. The plants should be watered regularly throughout the year. A slab or pot of well-drained medium is suitable.

Dendrobium gracile (Blume) Lindl.

Synonym: *Dendrobium gedeanum* J.J. Sm.
This is a large tangled epiphyte which occurs in Sumatra and Java. It grows in moss forests from 1600 to 2600 m. The stems are up to 60 cm long with a globose, pseudobulbous base and a slender straggling apical part. The leaves are borne along the slender apical part of the stem. They are terete, about 5 cm long and 1 mm in diameter. The inflorescences consist of several flowers, only 1 of which is open at a time. They are borne near the apex and are about 8 to 18 mm across. They last only a day, with flowering occurring 7 to 10 days after a sudden daytime drop in temperatures. All plants in an area flower at the

same time and there are several bursts of flowering throughout the year.

The plants may be grown on a slab or in a hanging pot of well-drained medium to allow for the pendulous habit. They should be watered throughout the year, although some reduction in winter seems acceptable. Intermediate conditions are required with constant humidity. Bright filtered light is recommended.

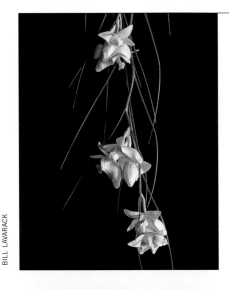

Dendrobium junceum Lindl.

This is a moderate sized, rather untidy epiphytic species from Borneo and the Philippines where it is recorded from Luzon and Mindanao Islands. It is a lowland species of hot steamy climates with rain for most of the year, but with a drier period in winter. The stems are slender and pendulous, up to 1 m long, branching, with a stout base up to 4 cm long and 2 cm wide, the apical part elongated, with slender, almost terete leaves, channelled above and up to 16 cm long. The fragrant flowers are borne on single-flowered inflorescences from small groups of bracts on the old leafless stems or from the upper leaf axils. The flowers last about a week and are borne during summer.

An easily grown species if given a warm humid climate, with watering for all the year but with a slightly drier period during winter. A small hanging pot is best to allow for the pendulous habit. Filtered sunlight is recommended.

Dendrobium litorale Schltr.

Synonyms: *Dendrobium eboracense* Kraenzl., *D. hymenocentrum* Schltr.
This is a branching, clump-forming epiphyte from New Guinea and nearby islands. It grows at low altitudes, usually below 600 m, on rainforest trees, in open forests, coastal forests or occasionally on rocks. It has adapted well to coconut plantations where it is often abundant. It grows into a large straggly clump up to 1 m across. The stems are erect, then pendulous up to 1 m long, branching by means of numerous aerial growths which may become attached to the host tree and eventually start a new plant. The basal internodes are swollen and angular and the ends of the stems are slender and without leaves when mature. The leaves are thick and leathery with a sharp point, in 2 ranks along the length of the stem and are deciduous after 2 or 3 years. The flowers are about 1.5 cm across and are borne singly on the slender apical part of the stem or on older leafless stems. The flowers last for a few days and are produced throughout the year. It is often mistakenly known as *D. acerosum* Lindl. or *D. macfarlanei* F. Muell.

This species requires year-round warm conditions and should be kept moist all year. It grows well in a well-drained medium in a pot or on a slab, or tied to a tree in the tropics. It requires good air movement and bright light and does well in full sun. It can be propagated by the numerous aerial growths, which should not be removed until there are at least 2 stems and roots are present.

Dendrobium peculiare J.J. Sm.

This is a long, slender, straggling epiphyte, which occurs in west Sumatra and Peninsular Malaysia. It grows in montane forests at altitudes of about 1300 to 1700 m. The stems are up to 30 cm long with a swollen basal part consisting of 1 node about 1 cm in diameter, with a very long, slender, slightly zigzag apical part that is leafy throughout. Older stems tend to be leafless in the apical part. The leaves are almost terete, with a groove on the upper surface, and are up to 9 cm long. The flowers are borne laterally from the leafless apical part of the stem. They are about 1.5 cm across and last only for a day, but there are several bursts of flowering throughout the year. Flowering occurs 7 to 14 days after a sudden daytime drop in temperatures, such as often occurs with a rainstorm.

The plants are best grown on a slab or in a hanging pot to accommodate the straggling growth habit. They should be watered throughout the year and kept in humid intermediate conditions. Semi-shade or heavily filtered sunlight is recommended.

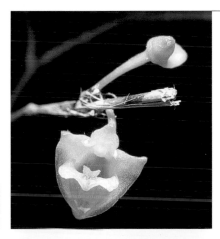

Dendrobium philippinense Ames

This is a medium sized epiphyte or lithophyte from the Philippines, where it occurs on several islands, and on Guam in the Mariana Islands. It grows at low altitudes in areas of warm temperatures and year-round rainfall. The stems are slender and up to 40 cm long, with needle-shaped leaves about 10 cm long. The flowers are about 1 cm across and are borne singly on a slender leafless extension of the stem. They are fragrant in the early morning and last a few days. Flowering occurs throughout the year, related to sudden drops in temperature during the day, about 7 to 14 days previously.

Warm temperatures, bright filtered light and high humidity are required for successful cultivation. The plants may be given a slightly drier period in winter, but should not be allowed to dry out for extended periods. A slab or a pot of well-drained medium is recommended.

Dendrobium puberilingue J.J. Sm.

This is a small epiphyte from western Kalimantan on Borneo. It grows on lower mountain ridges at altitudes of 1250 to 1800 m. The stems are about 10 cm long. They are slender at the base, then abruptly swollen for 2 nodes, then there is a very slender, slightly zigzag, leafy part. The leaves are linear–terete in 2 ranks and about 2.5 to 4 cm long. There are several flowers in each inflorescence, opening in succession. They are borne near the apex of the slender part of the leafy stems and are about 4 mm long.

This species should be given intermediate to cool temperatures and should be watered throughout the year. The plants may be tied firmly to a slab, provided they are not permitted to dry out, or placed in a pot with a well-drained medium. High humidity and bright filtered light are both recommended.

Dendrobium tenellum (Blume) Lindl.

This medium sized epiphyte occurs in Java and Lombok. It is a common species in East Java in humid and dry forests at altitudes of 1500 to 2200 m. The pseudobulbs have a swollen, almost globose base 2 to 3 cm long and 1.5 cm wide, red or dark brown in colour. The apical part of the stem is slender to 60 cm long with 10 to 12 almost-terete leaves, which are channelled above and up to 6 cm long. The leaves decrease in size towards the apex. The solitary flower is 1 to 1.25 cm across, not opening widely, and rises from near the apex. There is much variation in flower colour, with the base colour ranging from white to pale yellow, and variable striping. The flowers last only a few hours. Flowering is throughout the year.

This species requires intermediate temperatures with high humidity for most of the year. Watering may be reduced in winter, but the plants should not be allowed to dry out for long periods. A pot of well-drained medium or a slab are equally successful.

Dendrobium truncatum Lindl.

Synonym: *Dendrobium clavipes* Hook.f.
This is a small epiphytic species which occurs in Thailand, Peninsular Malaysia, Sumatra, Java and Borneo. It grows at altitudes from sea level to 1000 m, in lowland forests, lower montane forests, rubber plantations and roadside trees, in areas of bright light. The stems are 15 to 30 cm long, with a swollen, globular, pseudobulbous base which becomes warty with age. The slender apical part is often branched and is leafy throughout. The leaves are narrow–linear, 4.5 cm long and 4 mm wide. The flowers are borne singly on the apical part of the stem. They are about 1 cm long, fragrant and last a few days. Flowering is in several bursts throughout the year, 7 to 14 days after a sudden drop in daytime temperatures.

The plants may be grown on a slab or in a pot of well-drained medium. They should be watered throughout the year, although some reduction in winter seems acceptable. Warm conditions are required with constant humidity. Bright filtered light is recommended.

Dendrobium ventricosum Kraenzl.

This is a medium sized species from Luzon and Mindanao Islands in the Philippines and from Taiwan. It grows at low altitudes from sea level to about 300 m in rainforests in areas with a high year-round rainfall. The stems are 30 to 60 cm long with a swollen pseudobulbous base, a long slender part bearing the leaves and a slender, almost leafless apical part bearing the flowers. The leaves are sharp-pointed, succulent, about 4 to 5 cm long and 5 mm wide. The flowers are borne singly, are fragrant and about 2 cm long. The colour varies from white to yellow or light green. Flowering is at intervals of about 4 months throughout the year.

The plants require a warm climate with year-round high humidity and year-round regular watering. They should be given bright filtered light. A slab or pot of well-drained medium is recommended.

PHILLIP CRIBB

JIM COMBER

WAYNE HARRIS

BILL LAVARACK

Dendrobium sp. ex Mt Kinabalu

This is a branching, clump-forming epiphyte from Mt Kinabalu on Borneo. It has been recorded growing on rainforest trees at about 1800 m altitude. The stems are erect, up to 1 m long, branching by means of numerous aerial growths that may become attached to the host tree and eventually start a new plant. The basal internodes are somewhat swollen and the ends of the stems are slender and without leaves when mature. The leaves are succulent, overlapping and about 6 to 9 cm long and 1 cm wide, with a sharp point. They are in 2 ranks along the length of the stem and are deciduous after 2 or 3 years. The flowers are about 1.5 cm across and are borne singly on the slender leafless apical part of the stem. The flowers last for few days and are produced throughout the year.

This species should be given intermediate to cool temperatures and should be watered throughout the year. The plants may be tied firmly to a slab, provided they are not permitted to dry out, or placed in a pot with a well-drained medium. High humidity and bright filtered light are both recommended.

Section *Spatulata* Lindl. (Genus *Dendrobium*)

Synonym: *Ceratobium* Lindl.

The section *Spatulata* includes about 50 species distributed from the Philippines and Java to north Australia and the islands of the Pacific, as far to the east as Samoa. New Guinea and its nearby islands have about 30 species and are clearly the centre of distribution. The numbers attenuate to the west, south and east from New Guinea, with the Philippines having 1 species, Sulawesi 3, the Moluccas 9, Australia 8, Vanuatu 3 and Samoa 1. This is a section predominantly of the humid tropical lowlands in year-round high rainfall conditions, mostly near the coast and often growing in trees overhanging the water. Exceptions to this occur in northern Australia and southern New Guinea, where a related group of 4 species has adapted to the strongly seasonal conditions and thrives in climates with a pronounced dry season. Another group of about 6 species has adapted to the cooler conditions of the New Guinea highlands, occurring at altitudes up to 1800 m.

This section is closely related to sections *Trachyrhizum* and *Phalaenanthe*, but is quite distinctive. The pseudobulbs are usually long, with 2 ranks of leaves along most of the stem. The dry season adapted species mostly have shorter, more compact pseudobulbs. The flowers are produced on 1 or more long, multi-flowered racemes from the apical nodes. They are widely opening, long-lasting, and most have twisted petals and sepals and a 3-lobed lip with 3 or more keels along the mid-lobe. There is usually a prominent mentum. This section contains several popular horticultural subjects.

Dendrobium antennatum Lindl.

Synonym: *Dendrobium d'albertisii* Rchb.f.

John Lindley described *D. antennatum* in 1843 from a specimen from the northern coast of New Guinea. The name 'antennatum' comes from the resemblance to the horns of an antelope and the species is often known as the antelope orchid. It occurs from sea level to 1200 m altitude in coastal and subcoastal parts of the islands of New Guinea, New Britain, New Ireland, the Solomon Islands and on eastern Cape York Peninsula. The usual habitat is humid and semi-exposed and it is often abundant in coastal situations on *Calophyllum* trees overhanging the water or on mangroves. It often occurs in association with ant plants and other epiphytes. The pseudobulbs are yellow,

with a roughly 4-angled, swollen base and a slender apical part with succulent lanceolate leaves, which are variable in size. The inflorescences, which may be up to 50 cm long, bear 3 to 15 flowers varying from about 2 to 4 cm in length. They last about 6 weeks, and remain attached to the seedpods for months, turning green in colour. Flowering is throughout the year.

This species will grow in a garden situation on a suitable host tree in the tropics or in a sheltered bush-house in subtropical areas, but is sensitive to cool conditions. It does well in cultivation if given strong light and an exceptionally well-drained mixture and a small pot. In some regards slab culture is best, as the plant tends to spread rapidly and will quickly outgrow most pots.

Dendrobium bicaudatum Reinw. ex Lindl.

Synonyms: *Dendrobium rumphianum* Teijsm & Binn., *D. minax* Rchb.f., *D. burbidgei* Rchb.f., *D. antelope* Rchb.f., *D. demmenii* J.J. Sm.
This is a relatively small species for the section. It occurs on the northern arm of Sulawesi, the Sulu Archipelago, Ambon and Ceram, growing on trees or rocks at sea level to about 1000 m in areas with year-round rainfall, high temperatures and high humidity. The pseudobulbs are up to 40 cm long and 1.2 cm wide with 4 to 10 leaves along the narrower apical part of the stem. The leaves are up to 9 cm long and 2.4 cm wide. The few-flowered inflorescences are borne from the apical part of the stem amongst the leaves. The flowers are 3.5 to 5 cm in diameter and last for several weeks. *D. bicaudatum* is closely related to *D. antennatum*, replacing that species in the islands to the west of New Guinea. It differs in the smaller flowers, which are largely brown or purple-tinged, and in the broader mid-lobe of the lip. Flowering is throughout the year.

A slab of cork or tree fern or similar material may be best as plants can quickly outgrow a pot. If potted, a coarse well-drained medium should be used. The plants should be kept in warm humid conditions with regular watering throughout the year. Bright light and good air movement are recommended.

Dendrobium canaliculatum R. Br.
Synonym: *Dendrobium tattonianum* Bateman
This miniature species is known in Australia as the tea-tree or onion orchid. It occurs in northern Australia, the islands of Torres Strait and southern New Guinea. It grows in melaleuca woodlands and open forests below 500 m, where the climate has a very pronounced dry season in winter and spring. The common host tree is *Melaleuca viridiflora*. It is a small plant with ovoid or fusiform pseudobulbs from about 3 to 12 cm long and up to 4 cm in diameter. There are about 4 or 5 leaves at the end of the pseudobulb. These are almost cylindrical in cross-section, but with a deep groove on the upper surface. They are up to 20 cm long and usually less than 1 cm in diameter.

Flowers are often produced on extremely small plants. The flowers are about 2 to 3 cm across and are borne on a long, slender raceme with anything from 3 to 40 flowers. The colour of the flowers varies, with lighter forms from the southern part of the range being regarded by some authorities as a separate species, *D. tattonianum*, and the darker form from the north considered to be the typical form of *D. canaliculatum*. However, these differences appear superficial and worthy of differentiation at the level of the variety only. The flowering period is early spring and the flowers last several weeks.

This species can be grown in a small pot of very well-drained medium or on a slab. It requires warm to intermediate conditions and must have a dry period through winter and spring. It requires bright light and good air movement and will grow in full sun. It is intolerant of soggy conditions around the roots.

Dendrobium carronii Lavarack & P.J. Cribb

This miniature species is closely related to *D. canaliculatum*, and grows in much the same area, but in slightly moister habitats. It occurs on the northern part of Cape York Peninsula, the islands of Torres Strait and southern New Guinea. It grows in moist open forests, often on the margin of rainforests, usually low down on small trees at altitudes below 500 m. The pseudobulbs are globular to fusiform, from about 2 to 5 or 6 cm long. There are 3 or 4 leaves at the end of the pseudobulb, almost cylindrical in cross section, but with a deep groove on the upper surface. They are up to 15 cm long and usually less than 1 cm in diameter and often purple in colour. The flowers, which may be produced on extremely small plants, are about 2 cm across and are borne on racemes up to 20 cm long with 2 to many flowers. They last about 2 or 3 weeks and are borne in late winter or early spring.

Plants taken from the wild have proved extremely difficult to grow in cultivation and for this reason none should be removed. Plants raised from seed may prove easier to grow. Warm growing conditions are required with a dry resting period in winter and spring and a small pot with a well-drained medium, or on a slab. Light levels should be high, but not full sun, with good air movement.

Dendrobium cochlioides Schltr.

Synonym: *Dendrobium ruidilobum* J.J. Sm.
This is a medium to large species from the mountains of Irian Jaya and Papua New Guinea occurring at altitudes of 800 to 2000 m. It grows as an epiphyte, often on *Cordyline* or *Casuarina* trees overhanging or near water. In these areas the temperatures are cool to intermediate and there is year-round rainfall. The pseudobulbs are 60 cm to 2.6 m long, slender and about 1 cm in diameter. The leaves are 5 to 8 cm long and 2 to 3 cm wide and occur in 2 ranks along most of the length of the pseudobulbs. The inflorescences arise from the apical part of the stem and are erect or arching with 6 to 30 flowers, each about 4 to 5 cm across. Flowering is throughout the year and the flowers last several weeks.

The plants are best placed in a pot with a well-drained medium. The base of the pseudobulbs should be kept above the surface of the medium. Intermediate temperatures are best with watering carried out regularly throughout the year. Bright light and good air movement with high humidity are recommended.

Dendrobium conanthum Schltr.

Synonym: *Dendrobium kajewskii* Ames

This is a large, robust, epiphytic species from lowland areas of New Guinea, the Bismarck Archipelago, Bougainville, the Solomons and Vanuatu. It grows in the hot, steamy lowlands below about 800 m, in rainforest situations, but where there is bright light. The pseudobulbs vary from 50 cm to 3 m long and 1 to 3 cm diameter. The upper third has leaves in 2 ranks, each leaf 8 to 10 cm long and 3 to 5 cm wide. The inflorescences are borne from the upper part of the stem, are erect and 30 to 50 cm long with rather sparsely arranged flowers, each 3 to 4 cm across. The flowers last several weeks and are borne throughout the year in the habitat, but are more likely to appear in spring in cultivation. They vary in colour from dark brown to yellow or yellow-green, sometimes with streaks of red. It is quite similar to *D. discolor*, differing in the extremely large side-lobes of the lip.

In cultivation, this species requires room, as it grows into a large plant. It is best tied to a tree in the tropics, but if placed in a pot it should have a coarse, well-drained medium. The base of the pseudobulbs should be kept above the surface of the medium. It should be given strong light, even full sunlight, warm conditions and should be watered regularly throughout the year.

Dendrobium crispilinguum P.J. Cribb

This is a moderate sized epiphyte from mountainous areas of Papua New Guinea where it grows at altitudes of 1000 to 2000 m. It occurs in montane rainforests, often on *Gymnostoma papuana* trees along streams and on *Castanopsis* and *Ficus* trees, where there is year-round rainfall and high humidity. The pseudobulbs are long and slender, up to 2 m, but usually about 1 m. The leaves are in 2 ranks along the upper part of the pseudobulb. They are ovate–lanceolate, 8 to 13 cm long. The inflorescences are more or less erect, up to 40 cm long, but often shorter, with few to many flowers each about 4 cm long. The flowering season is late spring in cultivation and the flowers last about 6 weeks.

This is one of the few species in the section *Spatulata* which tolerates cool conditions, however it can be grown in warmer climates as long as it is kept evenly moist, but not soggy, throughout the year. It should be placed where it gets good air movement and remains humid, in partial shade. Pot and slab culture are both suitable. This species and the closely related *D. magistratus* are being used to develop cold-tolerant spatulatas for cultivation in temperate climates.

Dendrobium discolor Lindl.

Synonyms: *Dendrobium undulatum* R. Br., *D. elobatum* Rupp, *D. fuscum* Fitzg. Commonly known in Australia as the golden orchid, it is also known as Rigo twist, Moresby gold and Bensbach yellow in Papua New Guinea. This is a variable species from the east coast of Australia, the islands of Torres Strait and southern New Guinea. It grows at low altitudes from sea level to about 700 m. In northern Australia is quite common on coastal rocks in full sun, often in places where it receives salt spray, or in coastal vine forests on trees. The pseudobulbs are robust and can grow up to more than 5 m long and 8 cm in diameter, making this one of the largest orchids. The leathery ovate leaves are 5 to 20 cm long and are in 2 ranks along most of the length of the pseudobulb. The flowers are borne on long, many-flowered inflorescences arising from a few nodes near the apex of the pseudobulbs. The flowers are up to 5 cm in diameter and the colour ranges from dark chocolate brown to light yellow. The yellow form is usually known as var. *broomfieldii*. The flowering period is late winter to early spring with the flowers lasting up to 2 months.

This is a large plant that can take up a great deal of room in an orchid house. It requires warm conditions, but may grow in intermediate conditions if kept out of cool winds and kept dry at night. It should be given a well-drained medium in a large pot, or mounted on a slab or on a tree in subtropical or tropical climates. A drier resting period is required during winter and spring and it grows best in bright light, even full sun. It is particularly susceptible to attacks by the dendrobium beetle.

Dendrobium gouldii Rchb.f.

Synonyms: *Dendrobium imthurnii* Rolfe, *D. woodfordianum* (Maid.) Schltr. This large robust species occurs in New Ireland and the Solomons from Bougainville to Malaita and Guadalcanal. It grows abundantly on rocks or on trees in coastal and semi-coastal situations such as coconut plantations, but has been recorded up to 700 m altitude. In the Solomon Islands it grows on limestone cliffs overhanging the sea and, on many islands it is a feature on *Calophyllum* trees that line the beaches. The pseudobulbs are up to 2 m tall with leathery oblong–elliptic leaves 13 to 18 cm long along most of their length. The flowers are up to 5 cm across, last for about 6 weeks, and are borne on long arching inflorescences that arise from the apical nodes. This species has several common names such as Bougainville white and Gaudalcanal gold, the diversity in common names reflecting the variable nature of the flowers, which range in colour with white, blue, brown and gold colours predominating. Often the form from an individual island is unique.

It is an easy species to grow in the tropics, doing well in a large pot of bark or other free-draining mixture or on a suitable host tree. The addition of some moisture-retaining material, such as sphagnum moss, to the upper parts of the mix can be useful, depending on watering frequency. It needs good light to flower well and is intolerant of frosts or exposure to cold winds. It should be watered consistently throughout the year, but is best kept dry if the weather turns cold. The base of the pseudobulbs should be kept above the potting mixture to avoid problems of rot due to moist conditions.

Dendrobium hamiferum P.J. Cribb

This is a medium sized epiphyte or lithophyte from Papua New Guinea and Irian Jaya. It occurs in mountainous areas from 1100 to 1800 m altitude. It has been reported growing low down on shrubs in limestone areas and in montane rainforest. The pseudobulbs are slender, 30 to 110 cm long and about 5 mm wide, with about 6 to 10 leaves on the apical third of the stem. The leaves are leathery, 6 to 8 cm long and 1.5 to 2.5 cm wide. The inflorescences are borne from the apical nodes, more or less erect, up to 20 cm long, with about 10 to 30 flowers which are about 4 cm long. The flowers last a few weeks.

Of all the species of the section, this grows at the highest altitudes and requires intermediate to cool temperatures. It should be watered throughout the year and kept in constantly humid conditions. It is best grown in a pot of well-drained medium and kept in filtered sunlight.

Dendrobium helix P.J. Cribb

This is a large epiphyte occurring in the coastal lowlands of the east and south coasts of the island of New Britain. It grows on *Calophyllum* and other large trees near the coast and in rainforests up to about 150 m altitude where there is extremely high rainfall throughout the year. The pseudobulbs are robust, growing to more than 2 m long and up to 7 cm diameter. The ovate–elliptic leaves are up to 16 cm long and are borne in 2 ranks along the upper part of the stem. The inflorescences are borne from the upper axils and are up to 14 cm long with up to 20 flowers. The flowers have typically corkscrewed petals and sepals and are 5 to 10 cm across. They last for about 3 months. The flowering season varies for the different forms, but is mostly late winter and spring in cultivation. The variety of flower colours have resulted in several common names including Pomio brown, mushroom pink, Talasea lime-yellow.

This large-growing species requires room and is best in a large, but very well-drained, pot of coarse medium when mature, or on a tree. The base of the pseudobulbs should be kept above the surface of the medium. It needs warm conditions and watering throughout the year, but will tolerate minimum temperatures as low as 5 or 6°C if dry at the time. It should be grown in partial shade and watered and kept humid throughout the year.

Dendrobium johannis Rchb.f.

Synonym: *Dendrobium undulatum* R.Br. var. *johannis* (Rchb.f.) F.M. Bailey
This is a small to medium sized epiphyte from the north-eastern part of Australia, the islands of Torres Strait and southern New Guinea. Some authorities consider this to be conspecific with *D. trilamellatum* J.J.Sm. It occurs in areas with a pronounced dry season, in moist open forests, on the margins of rainforest and in gallery forests along creeks from sea level to about 300 m. Preferred host trees include *Welchiodendron longivalve*, *Lophostemon suaveolens* and *Dillenia alata*. The pseudobulbs are up to 30 cm long and 1 cm in diameter, often yellow with purple striations. There are about 3 to 8 leaves arranged in 2 ranks at the upper third of the pseudobulbs. The lanceolate leaves are leathery and 10 to 15 cm long. The inflorescences are borne from the upper nodes and are about 20 cm long, with anything from 2 to 20 flowers each about 3 to 5 cm diameter. The flowers last about 3 weeks and the flowering season is mostly in autumn in the southern part of the range, but may be in spring further north.

This is a warm-growing species that is best grown in a small pot with a well-drained mixture or on a slab. It should be watered copiously during summer and autumn, but less so during winter and spring. Moderate to high light and good air movement are required.

WAYNE HARRIS

Dendrobium lasianthera J.J. Sm.

Synonym: *Dendrobium ostrinoglossum* Rupp, *D. steuberi* Hort.
This is a large robust epiphyte, perhaps the most spectacular species of the section. It has several local names, such as Sepik River blue. It occurs along the north coast of New Guinea on either side of the Irian Jaya–Papua New Guinea border, growing near sea level in trees along rivers and in swamps. The climate is hot and extremely humid with year-round rainfall. The plant grows into large clumps with pseudobulbs up to 3 m long. The leaves are scattered along most of the length of the pseudobulbs in 2 ranks. They are ovate to elliptic, 4 to 14 cm long. The inflorescences are 20 to 50 cm long with up to 30 flowers and are borne from the apical nodes. The flowers are very attractive with various colour combinations of red, purple, pink, maroon and white and are 5 to 7 cm across. Flowering occurs at any time and the flowers last 6 to 12 weeks.

This large plant requires plenty of room in the orchid house. It has not proved an easy species to cultivate outside New Guinea. It is best grown in a pot with extremely well-drained medium. It should be watered throughout the year and grown in bright light, even full sunlight, although the roots should be shaded. It requires hot conditions and will not grow without heat outside the tropics.

WAYNE HARRIS

Dendrobium lineale Rolfe

Synonyms: *Dendrobium veratrifolium* Lindl., *D. cogniauxianum* Kraenzl., *D. augustae-victoriae* Kraenzl., *D. imperatrix* Kraenzl., *D. grantii* C.T. White
This handsome species is known as Morobe shower, Kui blue and by several other names pertaining to the form from a particular area. It has often been confused with the white forms of *D. gouldii,* a similar species from New Ireland and the Solomons. *D. lineale* occurs naturally along the north-eastern coast of New Guinea from inside the Irian Jaya border to Milne Bay, from sea level to about 800 m. The pseudobulbs grow to about 2 m long and 2 to 3 cm diameter, with leathery oblong or lanceolate leaves 8 to 15 cm long in 2 ranks along the upper two-thirds of the stem. The inflorescences are up to 75 cm long, arching, with numerous flowers up to 5 cm across that are variable in colour, with white or pale yellow and blue veining predominating. The flowers last 2 to 3 months. Flowering is throughout the year in its natural habitat, but is more common in late winter and spring in cultivation.

Warm conditions are required with strong light, even full sun, and good air movement. This species may be grown in a pot of coarse well drained mixture, or on a tree in tropical climates. It produces aerial growths that may be used for propagation. These should be removed when there are at least 2 pseudobulbs and roots present. It should be watered regularly throughout the year.

Dendrobium macranthum A. Rich.

Synonyms: *Dendrobium tokai* Rchb.f. var. *crassinerve* Finet, *D. pseudotokai* Kraenzl., *D. arachnostachyum* Rchb.f.
A medium sized to large epiphyte occurring in the Santa Cruz Islands, Vanuatu and New Caledonia. It grows at sea level in hot steamy conditions, often on trees overhanging the beach or occasionally on rocks. The pseudobulbs are up to 1 m long and 2 cm wide with leaves in 2 ranks along the upper half. The leaves are leathery, elliptic, 7 to 12 cm long and 2.5 to 4.5 cm wide, becoming progressively smaller towards the apex. The inflorescences arise from the upper part of the pseudobulbs and are erect, 20 to 30 cm long, with about 8 to 20 flowers, each 5 to 8 cm across. The flowers last several weeks and the flowering season is mostly summer.

In cultivation, this species requires warm, humid conditions with year-round watering. It can be grown in bright light, even full sunlight. It does well on a tree in tropical conditions or in a pot of coarse well-drained material. It should be fertilised regularly with a dilute fertiliser during the growing season.

Dendrobium magistratus P.J. Cribb

This medium sized to large species has been recorded from the Western Highlands of Papua New Guinea and from New Georgia in the Solomons. It grows at altitudes of 1300 to 1500 m in the Western Highlands and in lowland rainforest in New Georgia. The pseudobulbs are up to 60 cm tall and 1 cm wide, erect, with leaves along the upper half. The leaves are 10 cm long and 3.5 cm wide. The inflorescences arise from the upper part of the pseudobulb and are erect or arching, with few to many flowers, each about 3.3 cm long, often not opening widely. The flowers last several weeks. The plants from New Georgia lack any red markings on the lip. They seem out of place with respect to the habitat and further study may be required.

For the highland plants intermediate conditions with year-round high humidity and regular year-round watering are required. A pot of well-drained medium is best and filtered sunlight is recommended. Presumably the plants from the Solomons require warmer conditions.

Dendrobium mirbelianum Gaudich.

Synonyms: *Dendrobium wilkianum* Rupp, *D. buluense* Schltr., *D. rosenbergii* Teijsm. & Binn., *D. polycarpum* Rchb.f., *D. giulianettii* F.M. Bailey, *D. aruanum* Kraenzl.
This is a large, robust epiphyte growing on trees or exposed rocks from sea level to about 600 m. It often grows in mangroves, on trees overhanging beaches and in coastal forests. It occurs from the Moluccas through lowland New Guinea to the Solomons and south to north-eastern Australia, in areas with year-round high humidity and high rainfall. The pseudobulbs are up to 3 m long, although often much shorter, up to 3 cm thick, with a somewhat swollen lower third and with leaves along most of their length. The leaves are ovate, up to 15 cm long. The inflorescences are borne on the apical third of the pseudobulb and are up to 45 cm long with 4 to 30 flowers, each 3.5 to 5.5 cm across. In Australia and some southern New Guinea forms the flowers are self-pollinating and do not open fully, while the northern forms (described

by Schlechter as *D. buluense*) open widely and are larger. The flowering season is throughout the year in the habitat and the flowers last about 4 weeks.

This species should be given bright light, even full sunlight, and requires hot, humid conditions throughout the year. It should be grown on a tree in the tropics or in a pot of very well-drained medium and watered and fertilised with a dilute fertiliser throughout the year.

WAYNE HARRIS

Dendrobium mussauense Ormerod

This large robust epiphyte or lithophyte has been reported from the St Matthias Group in the Bismarck Archipelago, where it occurs on a small island 2 km off the shore of Massau. It grows close to the ocean at sea level. As it is very similar to *Dendrobium lineale* and easily confused with that species, it may well prove to be more widespread when more detailed collections are made. The pseudobulbs are cane-like, up to 1.5 m long and 1.5 cm in diameter with leathery leaves in 2 ranks along most of the length. The leaves are up to 14 cm long and 6 cm wide. The inflorescences are erect with up to 15 long-lasting flowers, each about 5 to 6 cm long. It is closely related to *D. lineale*, but has a broader lip (2 cm wide compared with 1.6 cm) and 5 distinct keels on the lip rather than 3.

Being a large species, *D. mussauense* requires plenty of room and may be too large when adult for many orchid houses. It is best grown out of doors on a suitable tree in tropical or subtropical climates. If grown outside the tropics, it should be protected from cold winds and kept dry during any cool temperatures. If grown in a pot, it should be given a very coarse, well-drained medium. It requires watering throughout the year and should be given bright light, even full sunlight.

BRUCE GRAY

Dendrobium nindii W. Hill

Synonyms: *Dendrobium toftii* F.M. Bailey, *D. ionoglossum* Schltr.
This is a large, spectacular epiphyte from north-eastern Australia and lowland areas of New Guinea from sea level to about 200 m. In New Guinea it appears to be widespread, but localised. In Australia it occurs from about Innisfail north, near the coast in high rainfall areas, often growing in swamps, in mangroves or in gallery forest along streams. The pseudobulbs are robust, usually dark, almost black in colour and up to 2 m long and 4 cm in diameter. The leaves are ovate elliptic, 5 to 15 cm long, in 2 ranks along the upper half of the stem. The flowers are large and colourful, from 5 to 7 cm in diameter, on long inflorescences with up to 20 flowers which arise from the upper leaf axils. The flowers last a few weeks and can be borne at any time of the year, with an emphasis on spring.

This is a spectacular species, well worth growing, but it has proved difficult to cultivate. It is intolerant of repotting and care must be taken not to disturb the roots. Many bush-collected plants do not survive, and this lovely species should not be removed from its natural habitat. It requires warm, humid conditions year-round with regular watering, but the medium must be well-drained. It responds to frequent applications of dilute fertiliser. In Australia it is classified as an endangered species due to the clearing of the habitat and the collection of plants from the wild.

WAYNE HARRIS

Dendrobium stratiotes Rchb.f.

This spectacular epiphyte from the eastern part of the Indonesian Islands occurs in the Moluccas, the Sunda Islands and possibly Sulawesi and Irian Jaya. It is a reasonably large plant, which grows epiphytically at low altitudes, and is related to *D. antennatum*, but with larger flowers. The pseudobulbs are up to 1 m long with a swollen base about 2 to 3 cm in diameter and a slender apex. There are leathery ovate leaves, 8 to 14 cm long, in 2 ranks along the apical half of the pseudobulbs. The inflorescences arise from the upper leaf axils and are up to 40 cm long, although usually shorter, with 3 to 10 flowers. The flowers are large, up to 10 cm in length, but more commonly about 5 cm long. They last up to 6 weeks and, while the main flowering season is spring, flowers may occur at any time of the year.

It is best grown in a large shallow pot with a well-drained mixture. It requires year-round warm and moist conditions. Watering should be kept up all year, perhaps a little less in cool weather. It responds well to regular application of a dilute fertiliser and should be grown in bright light with good air movement.

GEOFF STOCKER

Dendrobium strebloceras Rchb.f.

Synonym: *Dendrobium dammerboeri* J.J. Sm.
This large epiphytic species occurs in the Moluccas, on Halmahera Island, presumably at low altitudes. The pseudobulbs are up to 1.5 m long and 1.5 cm in diameter, with leaves along the upper half. The leaves are fleshy, ovate–oblong to lanceolate, up to 16 cm long and 5 cm wide, but mostly smaller. The inflorescence is up to 40 cm long with 6 to 8 flowers, each up to 5 cm long, fragrant. The petals and sepals are much twisted, pale yellow or green suffused with brown to dark brown, often becoming darker with age. Flowering is throughout the year and the flowers last up to 2 months.

Warm conditions with year-round watering and high humidity are recommended. A slightly drier period in autumn may be beneficial, but the plants should not be allowed to dry out for long periods. Bright filtered light and a pot of well-drained medium or a slab are recommended.

BILL LAVARACK

Dendrobium strepsiceros J.J.Sm.

This medium sized epiphyte is still poorly known, but is closely related to the well-known *D. antennatum*. For many years plants now known to be *D. tangerinum* were labelled as *D. strepsiceros*. It has been recorded from the Moluccas, West Irian, the north coast of Papua New Guinea and New Britain on rainforest trees at low altitudes, often on trees overhanging the sea. The pseudobulbs have a swollen base, tapering towards the apex. They grow to about 50 cm tall and 2 cm at the widest, with up to 6 leaves, 8 to 13 cm long, on the slender part of the pseudobulb. The flowers are 3 to 5 cm in diameter and are borne on inflorescences of up to 10 flowers from the upper, slender part of the stem. There may be 1 to 3 inflorescences per pseudobulb. The flowers are borne throughout the year with an emphasis on winter and spring. They last about 4 to 6 weeks.

If grown in a pot excellent drainage is required, but slab culture may be best as the plants have a rather rambling habit and tend to outgrow pots. Bright light, excellent air movement and year-round warm conditions are required. Watering all year is required and the plants respond well to fertilising with a dilute fertiliser.

Dendrobium sylvanum Rchb.f.

Synonyms: *Dendrobium warianum* Schltr., *D. cogniauxianum* Kraenzl. (in part), *D. prionochilum* F. Muell., *D. robustum* Rolfe, *D. validum* Schltr.
This is a large, robust epiphytic species from the lowlands of the north-east coast of Papua New Guinea and the islands of the Bismarck Archipelago to Bougainville and the Solomons. It grows in swamps and lowland coastal forests below 80 m altitude, often in full sunlight and in areas where there is year-round high rainfall, high humidity and high temperatures. The pseudobulbs are up to 120 cm tall and 2 to 3.5 cm in diameter, with leathery leaves 6 to 12 cm long and 3 to 5 cm wide in 2 rows along the apical part. There are 1 or more inflorescences up to 40 cm long, each with numerous flowers, arising from the apical part of the pseudobulb. The flowers are 3 to 5 cm across and range in colour from greenish-yellow to bright yellow, gold and brown. They last several weeks and the flowering season may be any time in the natural habitat, but usually spring in cultivation.

These plants do best if grown in bright conditions, even full sunlight. They require year-round high temperatures, high humidity, good air movement and regular watering. They are best tied to a tree in the tropics or placed securely in a large, well-drained pot with a standard, coarse medium. Regular fertilising is beneficial.

Dendrobium tangerinum P.J. Cribb

This handsome epiphyte occurs in coastal and subcoastal areas of Papua New Guinea between Madang and Milne Bay in two separate populations, one up to 400 m and the other at about 1600 m altitude. It grows on the upper limbs of rainforest trees, occasionally on rocks or sometimes overhanging the water. For many years this handsome species was known as *Dendrobium* 'Tangerine' or '*D. strepsiceros*' until formally described by Dr Phillip Cribb in 1980. The pseudobulbs are up to 75 cm long and about 3 cm in diameter, with leaves in 2 ranks along the upper half of the stem. The leaves are 7 to 9 cm long, oblong to elliptical. The flowers are borne on racemes up to 30 cm long with up to 15 flowers, each about 4 to 5 cm long. The flowers are long-lasting (up to 2 months) and flowering is year-round in the natural habitat, but usually restricted to winter and spring in other climates. This species has suffered from habitat-clearing and from collecting in recent years.

This species requires warm conditions, bright light, even full sun, and regular watering through most of the year. A slightly drier period in winter is of some benefit. It does well in a well-drained mixture or on a slab or tied to a tree in tropical climates. The plants frequently produce aerial growths from the stems and these can be used to produce new plants. These should not be removed until there are at least 2 pseudobulbs and roots present.

Dendrobium taurinum Lindl.

This large, robust, attractive epiphyte is restricted to the Philippines, where it occurs on Luzon, Palawan and Dinagat Islands, growing on mangroves and on trees in nearby open forests, in areas with a hot, wet, humid climate year round. The pseudobulbs may be as long as 3 m, but are usually about 1 m long, and 1.5 to 2 cm in diameter. The leaves are elliptical, 8 to 20 cm long, in 2 ranks along most of the stem. The inflorescences are borne from the upper axils and are up to 60 cm long with up to 30 well-spaced flowers, each large and waxy, 5 to 6 cm across. The flowering season is autumn and winter and the flowers last about 6 weeks.

In cultivation, this species needs plenty of space and may be a problem in a small glasshouse. It is best grown in a well-drained pot of bark or similar material. In the tropics it may be attached firmly to a tree. It should be grown in bright filtered light in a humid atmosphere with hot conditions year round. Watering should be maintained throughout the year.

Dendrobium trilamellatum J.J.Sm.

Synonyms: *Dendrobium semifuscum* (Rchb.f.) Lavarack & P.J. Cribb, *D. johannis* Rchb.f. var. *semifuscum* Rchb.f.
This medium sized epiphyte occurs on Cape York Peninsula, the islands of Torres Strait, Melville and Bathurst Islands, in the Northern Territory and in southern New Guinea. The preferred habitat is melaleuca woodlands on *Melaleuca viridiflora* and other species in harsh, seasonally dry habitats, often in full sun, at close to sea level. Some of the Cape York Peninsula habitats are desert-like during the dry season, yet the plants thrive in these difficult conditions. The pseudobulbs are spindle-shaped and about 20 to 30 cm long and 1.5 cm in diameter with several leathery leaves at the apical nodes. The flowers are fragrant, varying in size from 2 to 5 cm across, and are borne on long arching inflorescences, with three to many flowers, which arise from the upper leaf axils. There is some debate concerning the distinctness of this species from the closely related *D. johannis*. The separation in habitat, colour, scent and flower structure is considered sufficient to separate these species. The flowering period is late winter and spring and the flowers last a few weeks.

This species requires a warm climate and is intolerant of cold or damp conditions. It should be given strong light and a dry period during winter and spring when watering is only occasional and never in the evening. It requires a small pot with well-drained medium, or a slab.

Dendrobium wulaiense Howcroft

This recently discovered species is known as the Wulai Island white. It is closely related to *D. lineale* and was previously considered to be a variety of that species. It is restricted to Wulai Island off West New Britain where it grows at sea level on trees overhanging the beach. In this area the climate is hot and humid throughout the year with regular rainfall. The pseudobulbs are commonly 1 m or less, but can reach 1.5 m, and about 2 cm wide with leaves in 2 ranks along the upper half. The leaves are leathery, 5 to 15 cm long and 2 to 10 cm wide. The inflorescences are produced from the upper part of the pseudobulbs. They are erect, up to 45 cm long, with numerous flowers each 4 to 6 cm across. The flowers last several weeks and flowering is mostly in winter and spring. The densely packed flowers provide a method of separating the plants from those of *D. lineale*, which has well-spaced flowers.

In cultivation, this species does best in the tropics tied to a tree, but if grown in a pot it should be well drained with coarse medium. The conditions should be hot and humid with year-round watering and fertilising. Bright light, even full sunlight is required. It will not tolerate cool conditions.

Dendrobium sp. aff. *D. magistratus* P.J. Cribb

This appears to be an undescribed species related to a small group (including *D. crispilinguum*, *D. magistratus* and *D. hamiferum*) within the section. All are confined to the highlands of New Guinea. This species was brought to Lae by a collector from Chimbu, which is one of the highland provinces of Papua New Guinea. No details of its original habitat were obtained. The plant has a creeping rhizome bearing cane-like stems about 1 m long. They are about 1 cm thick at the middle and gradually taper towards the apex. The upper halves of the stems are leafy with about 20 leathery, elliptic–lanceolate leaves in 2 ranks, up to 7 cm long and 1.5 cm wide, spaced 5 cm apart. The leaves become smaller towards the apex. The inflorescences arise from the upper nodes. They are about 25 cm long with 8 to 10 flowers. The flowers are about 3.5 cm across and last for several weeks.

The original plant did not survive in the warm lowland environment of Lae. However, seedlings have survived and grown, albeit slowly, in pots filled with peat/perlite medium. They are kept moist, in a bright environment and at intermediate temperatures.

Section *Stachyobium* Lindl. (Genus *Dendrobium*)

This section of about 35 species occurs from India through South-East Asia with 1 species on Java. They grow epiphytically at low to moderate altitudes in areas with a distinct dry season. Thailand, with 20 species, appears to be the centre of distribution, but they are also present is significant numbers in Myanmar (Burma) and India. *Stachyobium* appears related to section *Dendrobium*.

The pseudobulbs are close together and are short and thick, almost globular in some species, to elongate. The leaves are borne along the length of the stem, except in those with a very short stem, and have a leaf sheath. They are deciduous after a year. The inflorescences have few to many flowers and are produced from near the apex of the stem, or from lower nodes, often on leafless stems. The lip is entire or obscurely 3-lobed and usually convoluted near the apex. There is a small mentum. A few of the species are popular in cultivation.

Dendrobium delacourii Guillaumin

Synonym: *Dendrobium ciliatum* Parish ex Hook.f. var. *breve* Rchb.f.
This is a miniature species from Myanmar (Burma), Thailand, Laos, Cambodia and Vietnam. It grows at low to moderate altitudes (250 to 1300 m). The climate is hot and seasonal, with a distinct dry season, and the plants often grow in deciduous forests exposed to full sun. The pseudobulbs are elliptical and about 2 to 6 cm long, occasionally reaching 9 cm in cultivation, and 1 to 2 cm wide. There are 2 to 4 deciduous leaves 2 to 3 cm long and about 1 cm wide, at the apex of the pseudobulb. The inflorescences, which consist of up to 10 flowers, arise from near the apex of the newly developed pseudobulbs. There may be several inflorescences per pseudobulb. The flowers are about 1.5 to 2.5 cm across. The prominent

fringe on the labellum is a feature of the flowers. This fringe is variable in colour, ranging from white to yellow or orange. The flowering season is summer and the flowers last for about a month.

In cultivation, this plant seems best suited to a slab of tree fern or similar material, but a small pot of well-drained medium is also successful. The plants should be given intermediate to warm conditions with cool winter nights and bright filtered sunlight.

Dendrobium denudans D. Don

This is a small epiphyte or lithophyte from north-east India and Nepal where it grows at altitudes of 1000 to 2000 m in the foothills of the Himalayas. They are reported as growing at the base of trees or on rocks, in areas with a distinct dry season. The pseudobulbs are 8 to 25 cm long, erect or pendent, with a few leaves, each 5 to 10 cm long and 1 to 1.5 cm wide. The inflorescences are pendulous, arise from near the apex of the pseudobulb and have about 10 to 15 flowers. The flowers are 1.5 to 2.5 cm across, do not open widely and are large for the size of the plant. Flowering is in summer and autumn.

In cultivation, intermediate to cool conditions are required. Watering should be heavy in the growing season, but should be much reduced in winter and early spring, although the plants should not be permitted to dry out for extended periods. Bright filtered light is recommended and the plants should be grown on a slab or in a hanging pot of well-drained medium.

Dendrobium eriaeflorum Griff.

This is a small species from the foothills of the Himalayas, occuring from Nepal and northern India, Myanmar (Burma) and Thailand. It also occurs in Java and perhaps in Peninsular Malaysia, although plants from there are usually considered to be a related species, *D. incurvum*. It grows from 1000 to 2000 m altitudes, usually high up in trees where light levels are high, in areas with a distinct dry season. The pseudobulbs are up to 12 cm long and about 5 mm in diameter, with thin, deciduous leaves up to 12 cm, but more commonly about 6 cm long and 1 cm wide. They are distributed along most of the length of the stem. There are often several inflorescences per stem, arising laterally and near the apex, each with about 8, or occasionally more, flowers 1 to 1.5 cm long and not opening widely. Flowering occurs at the end of the growing season in autumn as the leaves drop.

In cultivation this species does best in intermediate conditions with bright light and a resting period in winter when the plants should be kept rather drier, but not dried out completely for long periods. A pot of well-drained medium that retains a little moisture is recommended.

Dendrobium garrettii Seidenfaden

This miniature epiphytic species has been recorded from an altitude of about 1800 m near the summit of Doi Pa Kao in Thailand. The climate in this area features a distinct dry season and cool nights in winter, with good rainfall and higher summer temperatures. The pseudobulbs grow in small clumps and are less than 2 cm long. There are 2 to 3 leaves at the apex of the pseudobulb. The leaves are about 3.5 cm long and 1.7 cm wide. The inflorescences arise from the apical nodes and are 2 to 5 cm long with 3 to 9 flowers, each about 1.5 cm long. The flowering season is summer.

Temperatures in the habitat are warm in summer with cool to cold winter nights. The plants require a dry resting period in winter when watering is much reduced, but not withheld entirely. A slab or a pot with a well-drained medium is recommended. Bright filtered sunlight is best.

Dendrobium gregulus Seidenfaden

This is a miniature epiphytic species which is restricted to northern and western Thailand, where it occurs at altitudes of about 1000 to 1250 m in deciduous forests. It grows on branches, forming cushions of densely packed pseudobulbs which are leafless for much of the year. The climate in this area is seasonal with a distinct dry season. The pseudobulbs are globose to slightly elongated and about 1 cm in diameter. The leaves are deciduous after quite a brief period and no details have been recorded. The inflorescence is terminal from the leafless pseudobulb and is 3 to 6 cm long with 4 to 6 flowers, each about 1 cm long. Flowering in the habitat is from January to March.

The cultural requirements of this species are not well known. It appears to require intermediate temperatures and a dry resting season in winter when watering is decreased and the plants dry out for long periods between waterings. A slab or a pot of well-drained medium has been used. Bright, filtered sunlight is required.

Dendrobium venustum Teijsm. & Binn.

Synonym : *Dendrobium ciliatum* Parish ex Hook.f., *D. rupicola* Rchb.f.
This miniature epiphytic species occurs in Myanmar (Burma), Thailand, Laos, Cambodia and Vietnam. It grows at low altitudes in areas with a distinct dry season. It is closely related to *D. delacourii*, differing in the longer and narrower pseudobulbs, which are 10 to 50 cm long, more or less cylindrical and becoming pendulous with age. There are about 7 leaves on each pseudobulb, strap-like, persistent and about 12 cm long and 1 cm wide. The inflorescences arise from the apical nodes and are up to 30 cm long, erect or arching, with numerous flowers each about 2.5 cm across. The flowers are very similar to *D. delacourii*, but with a longer fringe on the labellum. Flowering is in summer.

In cultivation, warm temperatures with a slightly cooler winter are required, although the plants will grow in intermediate conditions. A dry resting period in winter, when the watering frequency is reduced and the plants are allowed to dry out for lengthy periods, is required. Bright filtered sunlight is best. A slab or a hanging pot with well-drained medium is recommended, as the plants become pendulous as they grow. Care should be taken when repotting to avoid disturbance of the roots.

Section *Strongyle* Lindl. (Genus *Dendrobium*)

There are about 20 species in this section, distributed from Myanmar (Burma) to New Guinea. The species are evenly spread over this range although the centre could be defined as the South-East Asian mainland and the Indonesian Islands. These are mostly plants of the lowlands below 500 m, growing in rainforest. This section is closely related to *Aporum* and *Rhopalanthe*, possibly forming a link between the two. Some authorities prefer to absorb this section in *Aporum*, but most keep them separate.

The plants grow into small clumps. The stems are erect or pendulous, leafy throughout their length. The leaves are fleshy, not overlapping at the base, mostly terete, but 1 or 2 species have laterally flattened leaves. They are usually well spaced on the stem. There is usually a leafless terminal part to the stem on which the flowers are borne. The flowers are borne singly, or occasionally 2 at a time, from tufts of small bracts. The flowers are small and not long-lasting.

JIM COMBER

Dendrobium acerosum Lindl.

Synonym: *Dendrobium subteres* (Griff.) Lindl.
This small epiphytic or lithophytic species is quite abundant in much of South-East Asia including Myanmar (Burma), Thailand, Peninsular Malaysia, Sumatra, Borneo and Sulawesi. It grows in the hot steamy lowlands, in areas with year-round rainfall and constant high humidity, often in moderately open sites such as cliff faces. The stems are slender and flexible, up to 25 cm long, with the lower two-thirds covered with succulent leaves, which are flattened and 2.5 to 5 cm long. The inflorescences consist of 2 or 3 flowers and are produced on the apical leafless part of the stem. The flowers are about 1.2 to 2 cm long. Flowering can occur at any time of the year.

The pendulous habit makes this species more suited to slab culture or a hanging pot with a well-drained medium. It requires warm temperatures and bright light with good air movement. The plants should be watered throughout the year, but watering should be decreased slightly in winter.

JIM COMBER

Dendrobium kentrophyllum Hook.f.

Synonym: *Dendrobium albicolor* Ridl.
This is a small epiphyte, which occurs in Thailand, Peninsular Malaysia, Sumatra and Borneo. It grows at altitudes of 600 to 1500 m, often in sunny positions, in rainforests where there is year-round rainfall and high humidity. The stems are slender and 10 to 20 cm long, with leaves in 2 ranks along their length. The leaves are 3.5 cm long and 6 mm wide, almost terete, but slightly flattened. The flowers are borne singly from nodes near the apex of the almost leafless stems or in a group, apparently terminally on the leafy stems. They are about 2 cm across and the flowering season is late summer and autumn.

The pendulous habit makes these plants more suited to slab culture, although they may be grown in a hanging pot of well-drained medium. Intermediate to warm conditions are recommended with regular watering year round, although the frequency may be reduced slightly in winter. Bright light is recommended.

Dendrobium litoreum F.M. Bailey

Synonyms: *Dendrobium confusum* Schltr., *D. shipmannii* A.D. Hawkes
This pendulous, epiphytic species occurs on Sulawesi, Ambon and the island of New Guinea at low altitudes usually below 500 m. It grows erect initially, then becomes pendulous, hanging from rainforest trees over streams, forming large, dense, tangled clumps of branched stems. The stems are up to 60 cm long, branched with fleshy, acutely pointed leaves in 2 ranks. The flowers are formed at or near the apex, 2 or 3 at a time. They are about 2 cm across and pure white, with a yellow stripe on the lip. The plants flower gregariously — that is, all plants in an area will be in flower at the same time, probably as a result of rain causing a sudden drop in temperature some time previously. The flowers last about a week and the flowering season is year round.

Warm, moist conditions are required all year and bright, filtered light is best. The plants do well in a small pot of well-drained material, but the pots must be hung to allow for the pendulous habit. A slab is equally suitable. The plants can be propagated by the numerous aerial growths, which should not be removed until there are at least 2 stems and roots are present.

Dendrobium singaporense A.D. Hawkes & A.H. Heller

Synonym: *Dendrobium teres* Lindl.
This is a small to medium sized epiphyte from Thailand, Peninsular Malaysia, Singapore, Sumatra and Borneo. It grows in the hot steamy lowlands in areas with year-round rainfall. The stems are up to 40 cm long, but often shorter, slightly zigzag with leaves well spaced along their length. Almost half of the stem is made up of a slender leafless portion on which the flowers are borne. The leaves are up to 10 cm long, terete, about 3 mm in diameter. The flowers are borne singly on the apical part of the stem from tufts of bracts. They are fragrant, about 2 to 4 cm across, but often do not open fully.

Warm conditions with bright light are recommended. The plants should be watered throughout the year and should not be permitted to dry out for more than a brief period. A pot of well-drained medium or a slab is suitable.

Dendrobium uncatum Lindl.

Synonym: *Dendrobium salicornioides* Teijsm. & Binn.
This small epiphytic species occurs in Java, Krakatau and Borneo, with a report from Vietnam. It grows at about 200 to 300 m altitude in Java, but plants from Borneo have been reported from as high as 1400 m. The habitat is rainforests and rubber plantations in areas where there is year-round rainfall and high humidity. The stems are up to 25 cm long with a distinctive zigzag appearance. They are erect, then pendulous as they lengthen, and have leaves along the entire length. The leaves and stem appear to be continuous. The leaves are terete, slightly curved and 7 mm long and 3 mm wide. The flowers arise singly or in pairs from the stem apex and are about 2 cm long. The flowering season in cultivation is reported as being winter.

The pendulous habit makes these plants more suited to slab culture, although they may be grown in a hanging pot of well-drained medium. Intermediate to warm conditions are recommended with regular watering year round, although the frequency may be reduced slightly in winter. Bright light is recommended.

GEOFF STOCKER

Dendrobium sp. aff. *D. hymenocentrum* Schltr.

The origins of this medium sized species are uncertain. It was observed growing on a stake in the Lae Botanic Garden, Papua New Guinea, and appears to have been established some time ago. The plant was pendulous and about 20 cm in length. The rhizomes are very short, bearing stems less than 1 mm in diameter. The leaves are in 2 ranks, narrowly lanceolate, 40 mm long and 4 mm wide, at about 30° to the stem and curving slightly outwards. The younger leaves are suffused with purple, the older leaves are green. The plant flowers every few months. Flowers are about 1.2 cm across and last about a week. They are pendulous and are borne laterally along the short leafless apical part of the stem. The sectional placement of this species is uncertain, but it lacks the swollen base to the stems which would place it in *Rhopalanthe*.

Seedlings of this species grow easily in a pot filled with peat/perlite medium. They should be grown in a bright, warm, moist environment. Given the habit of this species, a hanging basket or a tree-fern slab may be the most appropriate choice for the culture of mature plants.

Genus *Tetrodon* (Kraenzl.) M.A. Clem. & D.L. Jones

Synonym: Section *Tetrodon* (Kraenzl.) Or merod.
This group was recently raised from sectional to generic status. It consists of 2 species, both restricted to New Caledonia. They occur in rainforest, often on *Araucaria* trees, at moderate altitude, in areas of strong light but year-round humidity. It is closely related to *Inobulbum*.

The pseudobulbs are short and squat and laterally flattened with 2 leaves at the apex. The leaves lack a leaf sheath. The roots are granulose. The flowers are borne on a long raceme or sparsely branched panicle with few to many medium sized flowers. The lip is 3-lobed and there is a prominent mentum.

DAVID BANKS

Tetrodon oppositifolius (Kraenzl.) M.A. Clem. & D.L. Jones

Synonyms: *Eria oppositifolia* Kraenzl., *Dendrobium oppositifolium* (Kraenzl.) N. Hallé
This miniature epiphytic species is restricted to New Caledonia. It often grows on *Araucaria* trees in exposed situations and also on shrubs and trees in rainforest between 300 and 1200 m altitude in areas of year-round rainfall. The pseudobulbs are 2 to 4 cm long and orange in colour. There are 2 leaves, 2 to 5 cm long, at the apex. The inflorescences are branched, erect or arching, produced from the upper nodes of the pseudobulbs, 20 to 40 cm long with up to 12 flowers each 2.5 to 4 cm across. The flowering season is summer and autumn.

Intermediate to warm conditions with year-round rainfall, high humidity and good air movement are recommended. The plants should be kept moist, but not soggy. The plants may be grown on a slab or in a pot with a well-drained medium. Bright filtered light is recommended.

Section *Trachyrhizum* Schltr. (Genus *Dendrobium*)

This is a small section centred in the island of New Guinea, with 1 species extending to New Caledonia and another to north-east Australia. There are about 6 to 9 species in total. Most are species of mountainous habitats around 1000 m, often in areas of year-round moist climates. They are epiphytes or occasionally lithophytes.

G. FULLER

Winika cunninghamii (Lindl.) M.A. Clem., D.L. Jones & Molloy

Synonyms: *Dendrobium cunninghamii* Lindl., *D. lessonii* Colenso
This species is restricted to New Zealand, where it occurs on both the North and South Islands and on the Chatham Islands and Stewart Island, making it the most southern of the Dendrobiinae. It grows epiphytically or on rocks in temperate rainforests, often in at altitudes below 500 m, in relatively well-lit situations. The stems are slender and branched, up to 1.2 m long, pendulous, forming dense clumps. The leaves are 2 to 3 cm long and 3 to 3.5 mm wide, and are borne on the upper half of the final branches of the stems. The inflorescences are lateral and have up to 3 or occasionally 5 or 6 flowers, each about 2.5 cm across.

This species has proved easy to grow if tied firmly to a slab of tree fern or similar material. The large pendulous habit makes it unsuited to pot culture. The plants should be given intermediate to cool temperatures, semi-shade and regular watering.

Glossary

acuminate	having a gradually tapering apex
caudicle	a slender extension of the pollinium
chloroplast	the body within the cell that contains chlorophyll; the place where photosynthesis occurs
cladistics	a theory of classification based on the use of derived characters and based on a strictly monophyletic system of descent
cladogram	a diagram based on cladistic theory that shows the relationship of a group of organisms
column	the central part of the orchid flower made of fused male and female parts
column foot	an extension of the base of the column to which the lip is attached
compots	a pot into which several small seedlings are placed from the flask
connate	joined
conserved name	a well-known name which has been conserved under the Code of Botanical Nomenclature, even though a previous valid name exists
conspecific	belonging to the same species
dipterocarp	trees in the common South-East Asian family *Dipterocarpaceae*
disc	the central part of the lip from which the lobes radiate
DNA	deoxyribonucleic acid, the material in which the genetic code is written
ecotourism	tourism based on nature and natural habitats
elliptic	shaped like an ellipse
epiphyte (epiphytic)	a plant which grows on another plant, but not as a parasite
falcate	sickle-shaped
fusiform	spindle-shaped, i.e. thickest at the middle and tapered towards both ends
glaucous	a surface covered with a bloom that gives a bluish-green appearance
habit	the plant form
habitat	the environment in which a plant grows
herbarium (pl herbaria)	an institution in which dried plant specimens are preserved and where research into plants and their taxonomy and ecology takes place
inflorescence	the portion of the plant devoted to and including the flowers
lanceolate	shaped like a lance, i.e. narrow and tapered at both ends
ligulate	strap-shaped
linear	very narrow with parallel sides
lip (labellum)	the third petal, in orchids usually enlarged and ornate
lithophyte	a plant which grows on rocks or cliffs
mentum	a chin-like projection consisting of the column foot and the bases of the lateral sepals
metabolism (metabolic)	the sum of the processes in an organism by which food is built up into living protoplasm and by which protoplasm is broken down into simpler compounds with the exchange of energy
monocotyledons	one of the major groups of flowering plants, recognised by the single seed leaf or cotyledon
monophyletic	derived from a single ancestral species
morphology	the study of structure or form and its development
mycorrhiza	a symbiotic relationship between fungi and the roots of vascular plants

oblong	longer than broad, with parallel sides
obovate, obovoid	ovate, with the widest part above the middle
ovary	the part of the flower which encloses the ovules and, after fertilisation, develops into the fruit
ovate	shaped like the longitudinal section of an egg with the broadest part below the middle
panicle	a branched inflorescence
pedicel	the stalk of a single flower
peduncle	the basal stalk of an inflorescence
petal	one of the segments which make up the inner whorl of the flower
phenology (phenological)	the study of seasonality, i.e. the relation between growth, flowering, fruiting, etc. and the seasons
photosynthesis	the process by which sunlight converts water to organic substances that can be used by the plant for its maintenance, growth and reproduction
phylogeny	study of the history and development of a group through geological time
phytotoxic	toxic to plants
plate tectonics	the theory that provides the mechanism for continental drift
pollinium (pollinia)	a more or less compact and coherent mass of pollen, usually the contents of an anther cell
proliferation	a tendency for protocorms to grow into a mass of relatively unorganised plant tissue rather than develop into individual plantlets
protocorm	the embryo of a plant which precedes the differentiation into various parts
pseudobulb	a thickened and bulb-like internode or group of internodes in the stem of an orchid
raceme	a simple unbranched inflorescence with stalked flowers
rachis	the main axis of a compound leaf or inflorescence
respiration	the conversion of organic compounds back to carbon dioxide and water vapour, releasing energy for cell growth and maintenance
resupinate	the condition where the labellum is held on the lower part of the flower
rhizome	a horizontal stem under or on the substrate
saccate	deeply concave, sac-like
sepal	one of the segments which make up the outer whorl of the flower
spur	a slender hollow projection from one of the floral segments, usually the labellum
synchronous	occurring at the same time
synonymy	the state when one name is synonymous with another
taxon (pl taxa)	a taxonomic group, e.g. family, genus, species, variety
taxonomist	a person who studies taxonomy
taxonomy	the science of classification
terete	circular in cross-section
type specimen	the specimen designated as typical or representative of the species
typological approach	a view of taxonomy which allows little variation from the type specimen
viscidium (viscidia)	a sticky part of the stigma that serves to attach the pollinia to the pollinator